NAGASAKI

NAGASAKI

THE FORGOTTEN PRISONERS

JOHN WILLIS

MENSCH PUBLISHING

Mensch Publishing

51 Northchurch Road, London N1 4EE, United Kingdom

First published in Great Britain 2022

A catalogue record for this book is available from the British Library

ISBN: HB: 978-1-912914-42-5; eBook: 978-1-912914-43-2

2 4 6 8 10 9 7 5 3 1

Typeset by Newgen KnowledgeWorks Pvt. Ltd., Chennai, India
Printed and bound in Great Britain by CPI Group (UK) Ltd, Croydon CR0 4YY

AUTHOR'S NOTE

In 1984, I was Head of Documentaries and Current Affairs at Yorkshire Television in Leeds and directed documentaries for our award-winning strand, *First Tuesday*. One of the most talented producers in the team was a Yorkshireman called Chris Bryer. One day Chris told me that his father Ron had been a prisoner of war (POW) in Nagasaki when the second atomic bomb was dropped. This was the most powerful bomb known to mankind and struck the industrial heart of the city, wiping thousands of its citizens off the face of the earth in an instant.

Although I had filmed in Hiroshima a few years earlier, this British connection to the atomic bomb was news to me. That August, Ron Bryer and his fellow former POW, Arthur Christie, had been invited back to Nagasaki as a gesture of reconciliation and peace. For us this was a unique opportunity to return to Nagasaki with Ron and Arthur, and to tell this extraordinary story to a wider public for the first time.

Ron Bryer had buried memories of his years as a Japanese POW deep inside. Back in Nagasaki images and sounds from his experiences inevitably resurfaced. Perhaps Ron needed to confront his wartime past so he could finally come to terms with more than three years of brutal imprisonment in the Far East? His return to Nagasaki was also a powerful and unforgettable experience for those of us who travelled with Ron, especially his wife Pat and son Chris.

In summer 2020 I published two books, *Churchill's Few* and *Secret Letters: A Battle of Britain Love Story*, to mark the 80th anniversary of the Battle of Britain. I am full of admiration for the remarkable courage displayed by the men who flew in defence of this country in 1940. Summer 2020 was also the 75th anniversary of the Nagasaki bomb, and those two anniversaries became intertwined in my mind, and sparked thoughts about the nature of heroism. I compared the bravery of Battle of Britain pilots with the resilience of the prisoners who survived the many horrors the Japanese inflicted upon them.

My two 2020 books must have been well enough liked, because my publisher, Richard Charkin at Mensch, quickly asked me to write another book. I thought back to the story of Ron Bryer and the other POWs at Nagasaki; British, Australian, Dutch, and American. It was striking that even now the public knows almost nothing of their experiences. Apart from the building of the Thai-Burma Railway and the Bridge on the River Kwai, which have been portrayed in film, television, and literature many times, the rest of the Japanese POW experience is seriously underrepresented in the cultural mainstream.

The word that comes up regularly in all countries whose citizens were prisoners of the Japanese is 'forgotten' — the 'forgotten army', the 'forgotten squadron', the 'forgotten tragedy', the 'forgotten bomb', the 'forgotten war'. Three years after that conflict ended, news agency APP-Reuters filed a story from Japan with a headline that captured the afterthought status of the second city to be destroyed, *'Hiroshima Famous, But for Nagasaki Oblivion.'*

In America the 25,000 prisoners of the Japanese have, says Australian academic Dr Rosalind Hearder, *'to all intents and purposes been obliterated from American public memory.'* Although they have become significantly more visible in recent years, Dr Hank Nelson noted that for several post-war decades in Australian history books, prisoners of war would just 'be mentioned in a sentence or part of a sentence ... no historian has written a book to cover the range of camps and experiences ... the prisoners have received no permanent place in Australian history. Their story is not immediately recalled on celebratory occasions.'

The same can be said for the official war histories of the United Kingdom. In his excellent book on the River Kwai Railway, Sandhurst military historian Major General Clifford Kinvig pointed out that in the official five-volume *The War Against Japan* just ten pages are devoted to the experiences of thousands of British POWs. The 80th anniversary of the Fall of Singapore on 15 February 2022 was marked in Singapore and Australia but was invisible in the United Kingdom. Yet, for the families of the POWs these men are certainly not forgotten. In recent decades, self-published accounts have mushroomed, often at the instigation of the children of those prisoners, eager to capture their father's experiences before it was too late. Nor should we forget the vast numbers of Japanese civilians who died when bombs were dropped on Nagasaki and Hiroshima.

I have chosen not to start this book with Nagasaki because by the time Ron Bryer, Arthur Christie and hundreds of others were imprisoned in that city, they had already been moulded by eighteen months of Japanese imprisonment. Before the bomb was dropped, they had already endured an extraordinary lottery of life and death which had changed their lives forever. For many, their first taste of war was in the steamy heat of Malaya, Singapore, or Java. Humiliating surrender in those places led to months of imprisonment before thousands were shipped off to build the infamous Thai-Burma Railway. If that was not harsh enough, POWs were then transported to Japan and elsewhere crammed into the holds of what were called hellships. By following their different rocky pathways through the dangers of conflict and capture, I hope that readers can better understand what shaped the behaviour and hopes of Nagasaki's forgotten prisoners by the time the atomic bomb was dropped in August 1945.

Prisoners of Japan were spread throughout the Far East, in Borneo and Taiwan, in Ambon and Sumatra, in Hong Kong and Korea. The events in these countries were extraordinary and merit books dedicated solely to Allied captivity in those territories. I have chosen to focus on the under reported story of the prisoners in Nagasaki, and the experiences these men were subjected to before *Fat Man*, as the atomic bomb was called, was detonated close to their camps.

Contemporary accounts of life as a Japanese POW are rare. It was just too dangerous to keep a diary. Despite the risk, a handful of POWs did write down what happened to them. A diary was not only a way of remembering, but also gave prisoners a sense of purpose which helped them survive. It was a small, very personal, act of resistance. Discovery inevitably resulted in a nasty beating, or worse. It was no wonder that Dr Frank

Murray, from Belfast, wrote riskier sections of his diary in Irish. Or that Australian Dr Rowley Richards buried a summary of his diary in the grave of a fellow POW.

Able Seaman Arthur Bancroft from Western Australia left his meticulous diary in the safe keeping of a mate in Singapore because he was worried that his prison transportation ship to Japan would be sunk, and the diary lost to the ocean. Bancroft was right to be cautious. His hellship—the rusting bucket that carried him to the Japanese homeland—was holed by an American torpedo. On his return to Singapore, Arthur Bancroft found his diary safe but with several months of pages missing. The airmail-style thin paper had proved too tempting to his mates for rolling cigarettes.

Given the lack of contemporary accounts, it is no surprise that the facts are slippery. Even the basic casualty numbers for Hiroshima and Nagasaki are disputed. From the cremation figures, the best estimate is that about 40,000 died instantly at Nagasaki. Radiation expert Colonel Stafford Warren, Chief Medical Officer of the Manhattan Project, calculated, 'there must have been 20,000 or 30,000 more in the ruins or consumed by fire.' Thousands more will have died soon afterwards from their injuries.

The estimated population of Nagasaki in 1945 was 240,000. The death toll claims range from 40,000 dead, up to 100,000. The most frequently cited number is the median figure, between 70,000 and 75,000 dead by the end of 1945, with more dying of radiation-linked cancers and other diseases in subsequent decades. The exact number will remain elusive, but the unavoidable fact is that the number of civilian dead from just a single bomb was enormous.

Memories are often even less reliable than facts. Many personal memoirs were not written until decades after the war, carrying the obvious risk that those memories are incomplete, or over influenced by hindsight. Some ghost-written memoirs have been guilty of embellishment or exaggeration. What incidents were directly witnessed rather than merely being rumours passed between POWs is not always easy to discern. The potent mythology created by *the Bridge on the River Kwai* film has not helped clarity. To some POWs, camps and guards were constantly shifting, so dates and details are not reliable. As Bert Warne from Southampton, still alive at the time of writing in 2021 aged 100, said, *'We didn't know what day it was, what week or month it was, we hardly knew what year it was.'*

Every prisoner endured disease, cruelty, and malnutrition, but the POW camps were not uniform. Some were tolerable, others horrific. Some guards were brutal, but a minority were sympathetic. What is undeniable is that the level of hunger, sickness, and brutality was remarkably high, especially when compared to equivalent POW camps in Germany.

I have done my best to reconcile conflicting numbers and memories, not always successfully, I am sure. More important is that the experiences of the POWs are centre stage. This is their story, much of it in their own words. It is a privilege to curate their voices. Writing this in a pandemic, I realise there is a great deal to be learned from these remarkable men. Their stories, once read, I hope, are forgotten no more. We have, as the French eloquently put it, *le devoir de mémoire*, the duty to remember.

PROLOGUE

Just before 11 a.m. on 9 August 1945, Ron Bryer was mending the damaged roof on a bomb shelter in POW Camp Fukuoka 14b in the Japanese port city of Nagasaki. Bryer hailed from the small village of Follifoot, near Harrogate in Yorkshire, and was serving as a communications engineer in the RAF. He was now twenty-four years old but had been captured by the Japanese in Java aged twenty. His naturally solid frame, as broad as his Yorkshire accent, was skeletal after more than three years as a prisoner of the Japanese.

At the same time, Captain Charles Sweeney, just one year older at twenty-five, was flying a specially adapted American B-29 bomber 30,000 feet above Nagasaki. Sweeney's plane was carrying 'Fat Man', the most powerful bomb man had ever built. The bomber was already so perilously low on fuel that the B-29 was in significant danger of not making it home safely. As a result, the aircraft's bombardier, twenty-five-year-old Texan Kermit Beahan, had just one chance to drop his deadly cargo before the Americans were forced to call the mission off. Below, the bombardier saw the industrial heart of Nagasaki, where steel works and foundries fed the remorseless Japanese war machine. Later he recalled, 'The target was there, pretty as a picture.' The rest of the crew heard Kermit Beahan shout, 'Bombs Away', swiftly corrected to 'Bomb Away'. Cradled like a fat barrel beneath a parachute, the second atomic bomb then headed down towards its detonation point, 1,500 feet above Nagasaki.

There were nearly 200 British, Australian and Dutch POWs held in Camp 14b just 1.15 miles (1800 metres) from the bomb's epicentre. This was dangerously close to a weapon of such destructive power. Ron Bryer heard the recognisable sound of an American bomber and nervously looked out of his shelter through the square entry hole. High in the blue sky he saw the bomb's parachute and idly wondered if a crew member had bailed out. Suddenly, the plane noise reached a crescendo, and he looked away. 'There was a tremendous violet, white, blue flash, almost liquid in intensity. Not a momentary thing. It seemed to last for several seconds right outside the hole above my head...there was a tremendous vibration along with it, not an explosion at all, and then, as the vibrations continued, the wall of the shelter came down.'

Bryer was instantly knocked out by the flying bricks. When he came to the world around him was black. He could see no identifying features, only inky darkness. He thought he was dead.

A fellow POW in the same camp also thought his world had come to an end. 'At once a blinding flash was all around me, it was like the light of a thousand marine-searchlights that had all been switched on at once. A hot wave swept over my body and after that there was a tumult, as if the whole world came down on me. I thought, well, it's done; this is the last you've seen of life.'[1]

[1]Anonymous author, *www.erichooper.org.au*

Sergeant W. F. Heythekker from the Netherlands East Indies Army was also a POW in Camp 14b. 'A yellow light of such intensity that all the shadows disappeared, was over and on us. The world around us seemed without shape and form. I stumbled towards the air raid shelter, a hellish pain sweeping over my shoulders, neck, and arms. Then came explosions as heavy as the human ear can register.'

Close to Camp 14b, a sixteen-year-old postboy called Sumiteru Taniguchi was on his bicycle delivering mail. As usual he was in a cheerful mood. He cycled through tree-lined streets, past the local temple and a women's dormitory for the local Mitsubishi factory. He noticed children playing happily in the road. Then it happened. 'I was thrown off my bicycle by the blast. I thought I was going to die but I told myself I mustn't. As the blast died away, I stood up and noticed that the skin on my arm was hanging down, like an old rag, from the shoulder to the fingertips.'

Ron Bryer and his fellow POWs in Camp 14b had no idea that Nagasaki housed a second and much larger POW camp just 5 miles from the bomb's epicentre. Even at that distance, the 500 prisoners in Fukuoka Camp 2b were not safe from the immense power of the world's most destructive weapon. The senior officer at the camp was an American military dentist, Captain John Willis Farley:

I saw a terrific flash. It was white and glaring, very like a photographer's flare. The light quivered and was prolonged for about thirty seconds. I instantly realised this was something peculiar and hit the ground. The building began to shake and quiver.

Glass shattered around me; most of the windows in the camp broke. After the blast passed, I saw a tall white cumulus cloud, something like a pillar, about four or five thousand feet high. Inside it was brown and churning around.

RAF Flight Engineer John 'Jack' Ford was a Canadian from the tiny community of Port aux Basques on the southwest tip of Newfoundland. From Camp 2b, Ford had a grandstand view:

There were pieces of shrapnel, glass and rock and people running and screaming in all directions. The blast and the intensity struck me, and I hit the ground. Everything that was moveable was flying in the blast and intense heat. We didn't know what had happened to us. The only thing we could think was that the world was coming to an end.

High above Nagasaki, RAF Group Captain Leonard Cheshire was acting as an observer for the British government in one of two aircraft accompanying the American B-29 designated to drop the atom bomb. He was astonished by the bomb's mushroom cloud. 'It seemed to me to be about 2 miles in diameter. It was still bubbling. It was quite a frightening sight...it was completely black. You could actually see particles of dust and soot. And it was impenetrable.'

The industrial centre of Nagasaki, the most European of Japanese cities, had been totally destroyed 'as if someone had taken a giant broom and swept the whole city aside.' The second atomic bomb had done its deadly job. More than 40,000 people had died in an instant, with thousands more doomed to die soon afterwards.

1

MALAYA

© Brian J Green, Prisoners in Java, Southampton, Java FEPOW
1942 Club/Hamwic, 2007

At 7 a.m. on Sunday morning, 7 December 1941, all was quiet on the American Naval Base at Pearl Harbour, Hawaii, where the vast majority of the American Pacific Fleet was asleep at anchor. The dawn peace of Battleship Row, as a section of the Pearl Harbour base was commonly called, was brutally shattered by the sudden crescendo of 183 Japanese fighter planes and torpedo bombers attacking the resting fleet without warning. US aircraft were smashed. Battleships were blown out of the water. The dawn sea was full of men on fire, screaming for their lives. By the time the attacks were over, 2,400 people had been killed, and almost the entire US Pacific Fleet had been sunk. Fortunately, four US aircraft carriers were not in Pearl Harbour that pivotal morning. They were to prove critical to the eventual success of the Pacific War.

A war between European nations now also engulfed America and the rest of the world. Churchill needed America on his side but had not yet persuaded them to enter the conflict. Now Japan had done the job for him, a momentum that was accelerated when Hitler declared war on America. Across the international dateline the Japanese also launched a virtually simultaneous invasion of Malaya, a country rich in vital rubber and iron ore. A major target for Japan was the British strategic naval base in Singapore down at the foot of Malaya, the defensive shield for the entire region, as well as a key distribution port for rubber and oil.

These acts of war were the next step in a policy of expansionism by Japan which had gathered momentum in the two previous decades. In response to Japanese military action in China in 1937, Western nations had placed embargoes on oil and other raw materials. Now

Japan was under significant economic pressure, and these restrictions hit the domestic Japanese economy hard. Japan enviously eyed the rich resources of the Dutch and British colonial empires in the East Indies, Malaya, and Burma; oil, tin and rubber with the potential to drive Japanese industry in both war and peace.

Military leaders, often with extreme political views, increasingly dominated Japanese politics in the pre-war decade. In the 1930s there were several coup d'état attempts by the Imperial Japanese Army and a number of government ministers were assassinated. The army's influence on politics deepened, and much of Japan's national budget was devoted to expenditure on weapons. The war in Europe was shaking up the world order, and Japan's military leaders were determined to take their chance to create a raw-material-rich empire while the military attention of the West was inevitably focused on Europe.

Their grand scheme to grab a giant slice of South East Asia was known as the Greater East Asia Co-Prosperity Sphere. The plan masqueraded as a benefit to the whole region, but undoubtedly Japan would be the primary winner. The ambitious plan was underpinned by an unshakeable Japanese belief that she was superior to other nations in the East. Many Japanese military and political leaders believed that controlling a vast empire was the national destiny of a master race.

Yet, this was more than a war about raw materials. Japan was also convinced she had a duty to shake off centuries-old oppression of Asians by white imperialist nations, and her Co-Prosperity plan was attractive to other counties in the region because it would end Western colonialism. This perspective was underpinned by devotion to their emperor. To the Japanese people, Hirohito was a deity, a god-king. They were fully prepared to die for their spiritual leader, and suicide rather than the dishonour of capture was increasingly lionised in the 1930s.

The samurai honour code *bushido*, the way of the warrior, stretched back many centuries but had been adapted by the Japanese military as a code that guided behaviour in war. The more chivalrous virtues of *bushido* took second place to its military uses. It emphasised the disgrace of surrender not just for the soldier or sailor but for their family. It was believed that fearlessness in the face of death would give Japanese troops a crucial advantage over Allied servicemen who were more afraid to die. By the Second World War, this aspect of *bushido* was hard-wired into both Japanese military and school education.

The Japanese landed early on the morning of 8 December, 1942, on the Malayan north-east coast at Kota Bharu, where a creek led up to the RAF base a mile and a half away. Military defences had recently been strengthened with land mines and barbed wire and gunners from the Indian Army inflicted initial losses on the Japanese as they landed from the sea. This slowed the Japanese advance, but unfortunately vital time was lost consulting with the military commanders in Singapore. As a result, the aerial support essential to stopping the Japanese was called on too slowly.

At the air base, RAF groundcrews were as surprised by the attack as the Americans had been at Pearl Harbour. Some were still in bed. RAF Engineer Sidney Lawrence, whose eventual destination was Fukuoka Camp 14b in Nagasaki, was stationed at Kota Bharu with 36 Torpedo Squadron. Aircraft from No. 1 Squadron, Royal Australian Airforce were hurriedly airborne. They enjoyed some initial success but were outnumbered. 'The success was practically nil. It was such chaos, absolute mayhem. We were not only being strafed we were being shelled as well. And they had very little chance of doing anything, the opposition was so tremendous. I must say, admiration to the Australian squadrons. They were heroic.'[1]

The surprise Japanese invasion was supported by waves of air support from Zero fighters. Built by Mitsubishi, the industrial giants of Nagasaki, the Zero was comparable to a Spitfire; fast, flexible, and well-armed. There were no Spitfires and Hurricanes at the disposal of the Allies. Instead, the Australian pilots at Kota Bharu flew Brewster Buffalo fighters which lacked manoeuvrability and tended to overheat in tropical conditions.

By the afternoon of the invasion, it was clear that the base at Kota Bharu was lost. The brave Australian pilots were then ordered to make a tactical retreat to their better-defended base further south at Sembawang, on the north coast of Singapore itself. Airworthy planes were loaded up with equipment and flown south. Ground troops were hastily evacuated in trucks. Some damaged Allied aircraft capable of repair were hurriedly torched so they did not fall into Japanese hands.

Despite the initial resistance, by the end of the day the superior Japanese forces controlled the RAF station at Kota Bharu, and the dispirited Allies were in retreat. The Imperial Japanese Army, led by Lt Gen Tomoyuki

[1]Imperial War Museum Sound Archive

Yamashita, the Tiger of Malaya, was more than 60,000 strong, many of them elite troops with experience of war in China. Now they had their first foothold on the road to Fortress Singapore.

There were more than twenty air bases in Malaya and Singapore but only Seletar just outside Singapore City was fully equipped with anti-aircraft guns. Canadian Jack Ford had been stationed here with the RAF since before Pearl Harbour. It was a very pleasant peacetime posting for 36 Squadron. Food and duty-free alcohol were plentiful, with pineapple and bananas served every day. In the evenings the servicemen headed into Singapore City fifteen minutes from the base, to drink and dance the night away in the many bars and clubs.

This relaxed lifestyle swiftly came to a halt with the invasion of Malaya. Even well-defended RAF Seletar down in the south was vulnerable to enemy attacks. Ford, who would end his war at Camp 2b in Nagasaki, was still in bed when the Japanese attacked less than an hour after their invasion of Malaya started. 'We didn't feel there was any danger, why would the Japs come down here? [Then] we heard a loud explosion, followed by a second explosion. We could see the cookhouse, which was just 200 feet from us, in flames. It had been bombed. Three of our cooks had been killed instantly.'[2]

These first attacks on Malaya punctured the limited Allied aerial resistance and depleted the number of aircraft available. Even those still airworthy were not up to the job. Two RAF squadrons were equipped with

[2]Jack Fitzgerald, *The Jack Ford Story*, Newfoundland, Canada, Creative Publishers, 2007

torpedo bombers called Vickers Vildebeest, single-engine biplanes developed in 1928 which were hopelessly inadequate for a modern war. Jack Ford worked on the Vildebeest as an RAF engineer at Seletar. A Scottish pilot told Ford before going into combat in his obsolete plane that it was 'a suicide mission'. The pilot never returned.

After being overwhelmed on the first day, Allied forces attempted to regain the initiative by executing a more offensive plan—bombing an advance Japanese base just across the Thai border. But before they were even airborne from RAF Butterworth on Malaya's west coast, virtually every one of 62 Squadron's Blenheim bombers were destroyed or severely damaged in an enemy air attack. Only its Squadron Leader, twenty-eight-year-old Arthur Scarf, escaped with his aircraft. Despite being totally on his own, Scarf was determined to fulfil the squadron's critical mission.

Scarf was soon gravely wounded in the arm and back in intense aerial combat but still managed to attack enemy aircraft parked on the ground. With the help of his navigator, Scarf limped back to Malaya despite being riddled with bullets and managed to crash land close to the hospital at Aloe Star, where his wife was a nurse. Scarf died soon afterwards. For his outstanding example of self-sacrifice, Arthur Scarf was awarded a Victoria Cross. This gave the lie to a comment from one of his schoolmasters who had written about Arthur 'Pongo' Scarf, 'A pleasant boy, maybe not frightfully bracing, but a fine ordinary chap.'

Lieutenant General Arthur Percival, Officer Commanding Malaya, was a fifty-three-year-old with a distinguished service record in World War I behind him. Percival knew that the airpower at his disposal was inadequate. He calculated that he needed over 550 aircraft, but Percival only had 141 planes available. It was not until early January, nearly a month after the initial invasion by the Japanese, that fifty-one Hurricanes arrived at Singapore in crates. Many were hastily assembled, but some of the Hurricanes were never operational. The cream of the RAF's aerial firepower was too occupied fighting the war in Europe.

The Japanese, now with mastery of the air, soon also enjoyed control of the sea. The British rubber merchants and administrators who lived in Singapore were reassured by the frequently used description, Fortress Singapore. The newsreels dubbed it, 'City of the British Lion.' The British government sent the most modern British battleship, HMS *Prince of Wales,* and the battle cruiser, HMS *Repulse*, to defend their fortress. *The Prince of Wales* was fast and heavily armoured, with ten 14-inch guns, an advanced anti-aircraft system, and a crew of 1500 men. In October 1941, Prime Minister Winston Churchill had written in a telegraph to the leaders of Australia, New Zealand, and South Africa. 'In my view, the *Prince of Wales* will be the best possible deterrent.'

Admiral Sir Tom Philips, on the *Prince of Wales*, was an experienced naval commander who was called Tom Thumb because of his diminutive stature. Accompanied by the *Repulse* and four destroyers he slipped secretively out of Singapore to stop the Japanese from further landings on the Malayan coast. The crews prepared for the worst, but Admiral Philips believed that the firepower of the *Prince of Wales* made it virtually invincible against the Japanese. So confident were the British that the *Prince of Wales* also carried two journalists and an Admiralty press officer.

Although Australian fighters were available for aircover, Admiral Philips did not want to risk Japanese discovery and insisted on strict radio silence. Late on the 9 December, the *Prince of Wales* and *Repulse* altered their intended course when they were informed of a Japanese landing at Kuantan, halfway up the Malayan coast. Given its firepower this was a chance for Britain's most modern battleship to seriously disrupt the invasion.

The result was a disaster. The report of the Japanese attack on Kuantan was false. On 10 December, the *Prince of Wales* and the *Repulse* were attacked by waves of torpedo and high-level Mitsubishi bombers. More than eighty aircraft pounded the British ships. Yet even though the Japanese clearly already knew their location, Philips still did not risk breaking radio silence to summon air support. Eleven minutes after being hit by the first torpedo the *Repulse* sank, followed forty-seven minutes later by the *Prince of Wales*.

One of the journalists on board, American Cecil Brown, described her last moments: *Japanese bombers are still winging around like vultures, still attacking the Wales. A few of those shot down are bright orange splotches on the blue South China Sea. Men are tossing overboard rafts, lifebelts, benches, pieces of wood, anything that will float...there are five or six hundred heads in the water...down below is a mess of oil and debris...my mind cannot absorb what my eyes see. It is impossible to believe that these two beautiful, powerful, invulnerable ships are going down. But they are. There is no doubt of that.*

Eventually, Brown jumped 20 feet into the warm, oily water. 'All around me men are swimming, men with blood streaking down their oil-covered faces. The oil burns my eyes as though someone is jabbing hot pokers into the eyes.'[3]

Forty -five minutes after the high-level bombing attack had started, Captain Tennant on the *Repulse* was surprised to discover that his superior, Admiral Philips, had not yet asked for air support. Then Tennant signalled Singapore himself. The eleven Australian aircraft on standby were finally summoned. It was too late. As 453 Squadron of the Royal Australian Air Force arrived, Battle of Britain veteran Flight Lieutenant Tim Vigors just saw the last of the *Prince of Wales* as it slid, nose in air, beneath the waves. Survivors in the sea, including Cecil Brown, were being rescued by the accompanying destroyers. When the pride of the Royal Navy slipped into the ocean depths, 840 men were dead, including Admiral Philips who went down with his ship.

Flight Lieutenant Tim Vigors was full of praise for the courageous sailors struggling in the ocean. He was also certain this had been an avoidable disaster. Vigors was sure that if the Allies had mounted a standing patrol, or had been scrambled earlier, they would have seen off an enemy that lacked fighter support. He later commented sharply: 'I reckon this must have been the last battle in which the Navy reckoned they could get along without the RAF. A pretty damn costly way of learning.'[4]

When Winston Churchill was told the news of the catastrophic sinking, he reflected, 'I was thankful to be alone. In all the war, I never received a more direct shock...As I turned over and twisted in the bed the

[3]Cecil Brown, *Suez to Singapore,* New York, Random House, 1942
[4]Christopher Shores and Brian Cull, *Bloody Shambles*, London, Grub Street, 1992

full horror of the news sank in upon me...over all this vast expanse of waters, Japan was supreme, and we everywhere were weak and naked.'[5]

Nor was Churchill in any doubt about the severe threat Japan posed when he addressed the House of Commons after the sinking. 'No one must understate the gravity of the loss in Malaya and Hawaii, or the power of the new antagonist who has fallen upon us, or the length of time it will take to create, marshal, and mount the great force in the Far East which will be necessary to achieve absolute victory.'

Professor Barry Gough summed up the disaster:

Within three days the Japanese had not only mauled the US Pacific Fleet at Pearl Harbour but had sunk two capital ships some 400 miles from their bases. With the loss of only three aircraft, the Japanese had shattered British sea power in the Far East, isolated Hong Kong, exposed Singapore, imperilled the Pacific Dominions and unravelled an empire... Australia, New Zealand and Burma were threatened. All these results flowed from the catastrophe of 10 December 1941.[6]

With the *Prince of Wales* and *Repulse* at the bottom of the ocean and Japan dominant in the air, the Allies now had to stop the enemy's advance towards Singapore in a land fight. The British expected Fortress Singapore to be attacked from the sea to the south, the direction

---

[5]Winston Churchill, *The Second World War (The Grand Alliance)* London, Cassell, 1952
[6]Prof Barry Gough, International Churchill Conference, Vancouver, 2007

in which its giant defensive guns were pointed. They had not completely ruled out an invasion on the north of the island, but they never imagined that the apparently impenetrable jungle, bush and rivers of Malaya could be crossed by an army so swiftly. But the Japanese troops travelled light, using dirt roads and waterways on their route down through Malaya to Singapore. Their army even rode bicycles for extra speed and flexibility.

The common description of the offensive as the 'Bicycle Blitzkrieg' implies that the British and Australians were outfought by men on bikes. In fact, the Japanese Imperial Army had been in combat with the Chinese for more than four years and were battle-hardened. Their aircraft and weaponry were superior to virtually anything the Allies possessed in Malaya. The 60,000-strong Japanese force was well-equipped with tanks, mortars, and machine guns. Against them ranged a larger Allied force of more than 100,000 men from Britain, Australia, and India, but it was more disparate and less well-equipped than the enemy. They were numerically superior, but the Allies did not have a single tank in all of Malaya.[7] Moreover, the Allies had been trained for war in Europe or the Middle East, rather than a tropical conflict. The soldiers, men from the flat fields of Norfolk or the dusty outback of Western Australia, had no experience of jungle and bush warfare in steaming heat.

---

[7] They did have six cumbersome Lanchester armoured cars, named after Scottish castles FEPOW History Blog, Jon Cooper, Centre for Battlefield Archaeology, University of Glasgow, March 2021

The Japanese were also limited in their experience of jungle warfare, but they adapted to bush fighting more easily than Europeans who were unused to both the climate and the landscape. As they moved swiftly south, Japanese soldiers could live on a diet of rice for several days. European bodies were used to three meals a day, and food was served as if troops were still in England.

From the comfort of their empire might, the British believed in the innate superiority of the white man and universally underestimated the Japanese. On their troopships down to Singapore, British soldiers were lectured about both the inadequacies of the Japanese forces, and the mighty strength of Singapore. Only hours before arriving, Signalman Eric Lomax was reassured by a staff officer that 'The Japanese could not attack through Malaya. There is nothing up there. It's just solid jungle all the way up. They will not come that way.'[8]

The British also had no understanding of the fanatical Japanese warriors who believed their duty was to die for their emperor rather than be captured. RAF Instrument Engineer Sidney Lawrence saw this first-hand. 'The more you shot the Japanese, the more you found them coming in swarms, climbing over their colleagues' dead bodies. There was no stopping them... the whole river turned red with all the blood, but that didn't stop the Japanese coming.'[9]

There were fierce battles with the Japanese all the way down the Malayan peninsula. Gurkhas, Sikhs, Australians, and the Argyll and Sutherland Highlanders,

[8]Eric Lomax, *The Railway Man*, London, Jonathan Cape, 1995
[9]Imperial War Museum Sound Archive

amongst others, fought with conspicuous courage. Yet the Japanese were equipped with superior firepower and sufficient troops to always prevail. Despite fleeting victories, the story of the Malayan conflict is of Allied forces in almost continuous retreat.

Losses of both men and machines were very heavy. Lieutenant General Arthur Percival, overall commander of the Allied troops, concluded that Fortress Singapore would be vulnerable if the embattled Allies persisted in their unequal struggle in Central Malaya. Singapore would soon need every available soldier in its defence, and the Allies could not risk losing many more men and machines defending Malaya. The centre of the country was virtually abandoned, and the exhausted force funnelled south. As a result, the Japanese took the capital city, Kuala Lumpur, on 11 January, almost unopposed.

The civilian elite, including the Governor, had departed in a great hurry. A journalist noted that, 'In the Residency a half-finished whisky and soda stood on the small table by the sofa in the drawing room. Upstairs a woman's dress, half ironed, lay on the ironing table in one of the bedrooms.'[10] Out on the streets, 'Civil authority had broken down...there was looting in progress such as I had never seen before. Most of the big foreign department stores had already been whistled clean.'

On the east coast the scenes of hurried departure from Kuala Lumpur were echoed at the air base at Kuantan, as the Australians based there hurriedly flew

[10]Ian Morrison, *Malayan Postscript*, London, Faber, 1942

their aircraft safely south. Hundreds of ground crews escaped in whatever transport they could find, leaving smashed equipment and personal belongings littered everywhere. Signalman Eric Lomax described the scene:

Out on the runway there were cold mugs of tea half-full by the aircraft on which mechanics had been working. I picked up a blue flimsy envelope with an Australian postmark. It was unopened. The place for which we were supposed to sacrifice our lives had simply been abandoned, without explanation. Our headquarters had told us nothing; the local air force commanders had not consulted us before fleeing. We were left on this awful ground with no air cover.[11]

Churchill himself was aware of the acute strategic difficulty the Allies faced. On one hand, they needed their troops to slow down the rapid Japanese advance so that the vital defences of Singapore had maximum time to be strengthened. On the other, it was the same soldiers fighting in Malaya who would certainly be needed later to bolster troop numbers on Singapore Island itself. It was a delicate balance, and the Allies failed on both fronts.

Prophetic reports Churchill received from V. G. Bowden, the Commonwealth Commissioner in Singapore, in late December made the inevitability of disaster plain:

Present measures for reinforcement of Malayan defences can from a practical viewpoint be little more than gestures. In my belief, only thing that

[11]Eric Lomax, *The Railway Man*, London, Jonathan Cape, 1995

might save Singapore would be the immediate dispatch from the Middle East by air of powerful reinforcements, large numbers of the latest fighter aircraft, with ample operationally trained personnel. Reinforcements should not be in brigades but in divisions, and to be of use, they must arrive urgently. As things stand at present, the fall of Singapore is to my mind only a matter of weeks.[12]

By mid-January, this prophecy looked ever more likely as the remorseless progress of the Japanese reached as far south as the Malayan state of Johore, immediately north of Singapore itself. Fresh troops from the Australian 8th Division killed several hundred Japanese soldiers in an ambush at Gemensah Bridge, with minimal losses themselves. For a moment it looked as if the Allies might finally be stopping the enemy advance. But the Japanese possessed remarkable powers of recovery, and with the aid of their air mastery, eventually outflanked and outnumbered the Allies. Only desperate defence near Muar enabled Indian and Australian soldiers to escape the overwhelming Japanese force.

Australian Tom McInerny fought in the Battle of Muar:

By Christ we had let the Japs know we were there. We had given them a battering and taken one ourselves. The battlefield resembled a butcher shop, the men from both sides cut to pieces. Bayonet fighting was the order of the day...their planes gave

[12]Winston Churchill, *The Second World War (The Hinge of Fate)*, London, Cassell, 1951

16

us hell. We kept watching the sky for Churchill's
promised air support... our stretcher-bearers were
attacked by low flying Jap aircraft as they tried
to pick up the wounded, and some were killed in
doing so.[13]

Having held up the enemy long enough for their fellow Australians to retreat, the 2/19th Battalion then needed to break through the enemy encirclement to escape themselves. They were led by Lieutenant Colonel Charles Anderson, South African-born, but living in New South Wales with his Australian wife. At forty-four, Anderson was old for a battlefield commander, and with his round spectacles, looked more like a country bank manager than a soldier. But Anderson had already won a Military Cross in the Great War and had vital bush fighting experience in Africa.

Anderson bravely led charges on Japanese machine-positions armed with only grenades and his service revolver, and the Australians finally forced their way south to the important crossing at Parit Sulong. After four days of intense fighting with heavy losses, Anderson knew his men would inevitably be wiped out by superior force. He finally ordered every able-bodied soldier to escape through the jungles and swamps to fight another day. Anderson received a Victoria Cross for his inspiring leadership under fire but had no alternative but to leave his wounded men behind.

On 22 January, around 110 Australian and forty Indian wounded soldiers were forced towards a local

[13]Peter Winstanley, POWs of Japan 1942-45, *www.pows-of-japan-net*, Western Australia

building by the Japanese.[14] For several hours the captured prisoners were penned in, desperate for water. Just before sunset the wounded men were linked together in a macabre chain; rope or wire tied their hands which was then threaded round the prisoner's neck before being attached to the next man in line. Stragglers were bayoneted and left for dead. Once these small bands of roped-together prisoners reached the end of the building they were brutally cut down by machine gun fire. The heaps of bodies, some still just alive, were doused with petrol and set alight in funeral pyres of around 150 wounded men. Only two Australians survived the massacre.

Just a week later, an Allied retreat across the Johore Strait to Singapore Island itself was ordered. The Japanese had advanced more than 300 miles through difficult terrain in less than five weeks. The last men across the causeway to Singapore Island were about ninety soldiers from the Argyll and Sutherland Highlanders defiantly playing bagpipes and singing Scottish songs, although no one seems to agree on exactly what tunes they were. Then the northern end of the causeway linking Johore with Singapore was dynamited.

Lieutenant General Arthur Percival announced, 'The Battle of Malaya has come to an end and the Battle of Singapore has started…Today we stand beleaguered in our island fortress. Our task is to hold this fortress until help can come.'

Australian Tom McInerney of the 2/29th Battalion made it across the causeway just in time. He put the

---

[14]Numbers vary from 145 to 163 in different sources.

dire situation more colourfully than Percival. '*Now, here we were, on the island. An island 17 miles by 20, clustered with millions of civilians. What a feast for Jap bombers.*'[15]

It was 31 January, 1942. The Siege of Singapore was about to begin.

[15]Peter Winstanley, POWs of Japan 1942-45, *www.pows-of-japan-net*, Western Australia

2

SINGAPORE

In January 1942, last minute reinforcements finally started to land in Singapore. Among them around 17,000 men of the British 18th (East Anglia) Division, largely based on the Territorial Army. Their original destination had been the Middle East, but the division had been hastily diverted to Singapore in a desperate attempt to plug the huge holes in the Allied defences. Having had left Liverpool in October 1941, thousands of soldiers had spent eleven weeks at sea before finally arriving at Singapore in January 1942, just over two weeks before the Allies surrendered. Before setting off for war, many 18th Division troops had returned to the farms of East Anglia to work on the harvest. They were well fed and healthy, but seriously underprepared for a jungle war, especially after so many weeks on the ocean. The fate of Singapore was so precarious there could be no delay, and the late-arriving soldiers of the 18th Division were propelled directly into the chaos of battle.

Gunner Gus Anckorn of the 118th Field Regiment, Royal Artillery (18th Division), was filled with anxiety as he stepped onto Singapore soil after the long sea journey:

I was so frightened. There was no sign of our planes putting up a fight...this was it. We were finally in this war. It seemed to me that, until now, it had all been a glorious adventure. Right from the start we had been so distant from it all here, now, we had landed in the midst of killing. The sudden realisation that they would kill us, and we should kill them dawned on me, horribly.[1]

South Londoner, twenty-eight-year-old Alfred Allbury, also from 118th Field Regiment, Royal Artillery (18th Division) soon found himself racing to a bomb shelter:

Suddenly the air was filled with screaming. There was a deafening crack, our shelter shook, and a dull echoing rumble reverberated around the island like the mutter of distant thunder. Around us was confusion. A grey mantle of dust, spouting water mains, falling masonry and twisted steel, and death...we helped, numb and silent, to bring out the dead.[2]

Defending the coastline of Singapore was essential, but it stretched for 72 miles. The new arrivals from Britain discovered to their amazement that the north of the island was virtually unprotected. Instead of finding bunkers, trenches and machine gun emplacements ready for immediate use, troops were forced to build their own. The 6th Royal Norfolks, part of the newly arrived 18th Division, only started this task on 25 January, just six days before the causeway directly from the mainland

[1]Peter Fyans, *Conjuror on the Kwai*, Barnsley, Pen and Sword, 2016
[2]AG Allbury, *Bamboo and* Bushido, London, Robert Hale, 1955

into Singapore was dynamited. When he saw a handful of Indian troops putting up a line of wire at the south of the causeway, Major Robert Hamond (5th Norfolks) thought, 'if this is all they have done at the most vital spot, the rest of the coast of the inland must be open. It was a disquieting thought.'[3]

Not only were defences almost non-existent, but reinforcements were extremely poorly equipped. Reg Bulled, Royal Corps of Signals (18th Division), grasped the hopelessness of the situation:

> *It was ridiculous: here we were, an anti-tank regiment with a couple of men from the Royal Corps of Signals, acting as infantry. To make matters worse, we were given rusty old rifles and loose ammunition with no bandoliers or clips to carry them in. What a mess! This was the situation Churchill had sent a whole division into, as lambs to the slaughter. It was so obvious that there was absolutely no hope.*[4]

The 18th Division had been seriously misled about the weaknesses of the enemy. John Stewart Ullman was part of the 15th Field Security Section, an intelligence unit attached to the 18th. A year earlier his rural camp in England had been so relaxed it was supplied with regular parcels from Harrods and Fortnum's. Now he was unexpectedly propelled into the chaos of the Far East. On their ship south the men had been reassured about Japanese capabilities. 'In the air their pilots, we heard, were no match of ours: they all wore glasses...

[3] *Eastern Daily Press* 1995
[4] Reg Bulled, Far Eastern Heroes, *www.far-eastern-heroes.org.uk*

on the ground Japanese riflemen were not to be feared; they had trouble closing one eye when they took aim.'[5]

The 2/4th Machine Gun Battalion from Western Australia also arrived in Singapore just before the causeway was blown up. They too were immediately reassured about the weaknesses of their opponents. 'They sent a Pommy lieutenant and a sergeant down to give us a great talk about the Japanese—they told us they had poor eyesight, they could not see to shoot, their armament was poor and everything.'[6] The new arrivals were not told that these 'poorly-armed, weak-sighted' soldiers had already killed hundreds of Australians as they ripped through Malaya at an astonishing pace.

Eight days after the causeway had been blown up on February 8th 1942, Japanese soldiers landed on Singapore Island using rafts to traverse the narrow stretch of water. The newly arrived Australian 2/4th Machine Gun Battalion were ordered to defend the freshly dynamited causeway:

'The company guarding the causeway fired their Vickers machine guns until the barrels were just about melting, and the water was running red. The Japs kept coming. Apparently, they believed that if they were killed, they would go to paradise to join their ancestors. They had no fear at all.'[7]

Even as the Japanese Army were on their doorstep, thousands of civilian women and children were still

[5]John Stewart, *To the River Kwai*, London, Bloomsbury, 1988
[6]Wally Holding, *www.pows-of-japan.net* Western Australia
[7]Fred Airey, *The Time of the Soldier*, Western Australia, Fremantle Arts Centre Press, 1991

being evacuated. Many had naively stayed on with their husbands, confident that Singapore was indeed a fortress, the Gibraltar of the Far East. Now they were forced to say hasty goodbyes as they struggled onto the crowded ships with what little they could carry.

Around the quay, hundreds of cars belonging to escaping families were abandoned in the streets. On the dockside, civilian administrators and military officers issued travel permits to the thousands of hopeful escapees. RAF Aircraftsman Sid Lawrence was conscious of a racial divide. 'If they were Asiatic they were literally pushed away. If they had a European face...they were usually given a permit...it was heartbreaking really.'[8]

One young girl waiting for evacuation from Singapore Harbour in February 1942 remembered saying goodbye to her father:

> My legs pressed harder around my father's waist, my arms nearly choked him. His horn-rimmed glasses were steamed up from my breath—or was it from his tears. The humming (of Japanese aircraft) in the sky was loud enough for everyone to hear now, and panic spread like ink on a blotter...Japanese planes screeched by, showering bombs. They missed the ship and hit the sea with dull thumps. People shrieked in terror and Mother crossed herself.[9]

As the Japanese bombarded them from the air, Royal Navy officer RG Curry guided civilian escape ships through the minefields in the sea outside Singapore:

[8]Imperial War Museum Sound Archive
[9]Donna Faber, BBC People's War, *www.bbc.co.uk*

I was horrified to see scores of children, and women standing right up to the very edge of Clifford Pier waiting for rescue...I looked at those children, dressed mainly in white with ribbons in their hair, waving to us—no shelter at all—Dear God...I have had the picture of those children in my mind's eye for 34 years.[10]

In the fight for Malaya and Singapore over 2000 Australian soldiers were killed. Aussies had fought courageously upcountry, but in Singapore discipline frayed. Australian deserters were determined to leave and forced their way onto every boat they could. Some new recruits had only been in the army for four weeks, two of those spent at sea. Other nations joined in the attempted exodus, but Australians were most prominent.

Tom McInerney was appalled by the behaviour of his own side. 'Australians were among the looters—Australians were the guards on the warehouse. They not only looted the property of the living; they looted the belongings of soldiers who died in action. Even the army has its scum, and the Australian Army is included.'[11]

Anger was not dimmed when it was revealed that Major General Gordon Bennett, the commander of the 8th Australian Division, had controversially escaped Singapore bound for home in Australia.

Instances of desertion were matched in equal measure by acts of decency. Sergeant Johnny Sherwood, a peacetime footballer with Reading FC, and two colleagues from the Royal Artillery were on duty in

[10]RG Curry, BBC People's War, *www.bbc.co.uk*
[11]Tom McInerney, *www.pows-of-japan.net*, Western Australia

the blazing city. They calmly ushered locals terrified by the relentless Japanese shelling into the relative safety of nearby monsoon-drains. But they were soon too full to accommodate latecomers, including a desperate young girl and her baby. The British soldiers gave the mother food and a blanket and found her the safest shelter possible above ground. The next morning when they returned, 'My heart lurched as I took in the sight. Sometime during those night hours, they had been blasted by a Japanese shell. They were lying dead in a pool of blood, clasped in each other's arms.'[12]

Private Bert Miller from Diss in Norfolk, 196th Field Ambulance Company (18th Division) only arrived in Singapore on 29 January. He was pitched into the middle of complete devastation:

The never-ending flights of bombers blasted everything. Buildings folded like decks of cards on to streets festooned with wire that once fed telephones and power. Thousands of refugees crouched in hollow drainpipes and monsoon ditches, seeking protection from shells, bombs, and the machine-gunning from low flying planes. Meanwhile, demolitions had gone ahead at the naval base with oil tanks well alight. Smoke darkened the sky and midday became dusk. So high and so vast the great columns seemed to go on forever. In the canals and ditches, bloated corpses of air raid victims and their animals floated on oil from the streaming tanks. Among the ruins, stark and stiffening bodies

---

[12]Johnny Sherwood, Michael Doe, *Lucky Johnny*, London, Hodder and Stoughton 2014

lay unburied, while along the throughfares the water from burst mains dowsed new corpses as it rushed to waste. It was devastation of devastation. Casualties were reaching 2000 a day.[13]

Japanese planes attacked without opposition, and fires blazed all over the forlorn wreckage of the pride of the British Empire. The soldiers defending Singapore knew their position was hopeless. No ships would come to the rescue. This was not to be a tropical Dunkirk. Sapper Len Reeve from Norwich wrote in his diary, 'Island now being shelled, mortared and bombed night and day. No RAF planes. We had one single aircraft...Japanese dive-bombed at their hearts content...there was no hope of another Dunkirk.'[14]

Despite this, there was still confidence in the strength of Fortress Singapore. Private Ken Adams, a medical orderly from Harrogate, was based at a dressing station just outside the Tengah Airfield. Although he had tended the victims of heavy fighting in both Malaya and Singapore City, Adams had little sense of the impending doom. 'We had time to sunbathe. We relaxed in a grove of shady trees on a settee and easy chairs removed from one of the houses. We entertained blokes who dropped by with fruit juices and tea...like so many others, I sheltered behind the myths of empire. Singapore was an impregnable bastion.'[15] Both the Cathay Cinema

[13]Bert Miller, BBC People's War, *www.bbc.co.uk*
[14]*Eastern Daily Press*, Norwich, 1995
[15]Ken Adams, edited by Mike Adams, *Healing In Hell,* Barnsley, Pen and Sword 2011

and St Andrew's Cathedral were transformed into makeshift hospitals. When the cathedral was bombed the whole edifice shook violently, so Australian George McNeilly stepped up to the grand organ and played hymns. The assembled company fatalistically thought that if this was the end they might as well go out singing God's tunes.

Not long before, the 4th Royal Norfolks of the 18th Division had been defending the sandy beaches of Great Yarmouth and Gorleston against a possible German invasion. The height of excitement had been blowing a hole in the Britannia Pier, Great Yarmouth to deter invaders. They had been reasonably well trained for conflict in the Middle East, but they were ill-prepared for the desperate fight against the Japanese on the Bukit Timah Road, the main artery into Singapore City.

Among the soldiers in the middle of the fighting was twenty-five-year-old Private Herbert Barker (4th Royal Norfolks) from the village of Bressingham, near Diss. Barker wrote that rare thing, a near-contemporary account of the fighting in Singapore:

> It was a hopeless scene...the Japs must have used
> at least twenty mortars. On the way up to our
> lines that was the start of the hell on earth. We had
> nothing but tommy guns left. Only four of them
> between us...what a hell of a mess it was. Snipers,
> mortars, gunners, and dive bombers razed the area
> for miles. Nothing could hold them back. We lost a
> hell of a lot of men there in a few hours. Everywhere
> we turned men were falling killed and wounded
> by this awful barrage...the stretcher-bearers were

running back and forward. Then I came to my
senses properly, carrying back smashed bodies that
were alive, but could never be made whole again.[16]

General Wavell, Supreme Commander in the region, attempted to stiffen Allied resistance with an order on 10 February:

It will be disgraceful if we yield our boasted fortress
of Singapore to inferior forces. There must be no
thought of sparing our troops or civilian population
and no mercy must be shown to weakness in any
shape or form. Commanders and senior officers
must lead their troops, and if necessary, die with
them. There must be no question or thought of
surrender.

This was his version of the note Churchill sent to Wavell that same day:

The battle must be fought to the bitter end at all
costs. The 18th Division has a chance to make its
name in history. Commanders and senior officers
should die with their troops. The honour of the
British Empire and the British Army is at stake.[17]

The men of the 18th Division were less concerned with making their name in history than surviving the brutal onslaught. By the end of the battle the nearby reservoir was stained crimson with the blood of soldiers killed in the remorseless barrage of Japanese field guns and dive bombers. Len (Snowy) Baynes was a Londoner serving

[16]Robert Bennett, San Francisco Maritime National Park, www.maritime.org
[17]Churchill to General Wavell 10/02/1942

in the 1ˢᵗ Battalion, Cambridgeshire Regiment whose brave defence earned them the nickname of Fen Tigers:

Men fell to the right and left; the huts all caught fire, and some fell burning into our trenches. Many who were not burned to death died later of their terrible burns, including my old friend Sgt Wilson, who in his agony, asked me to shoot him...Dear God, I breathed as I looked into that awful burning face, let it all be a dream. I shouted for the stretcher-bearers, and faithful as ever, they ran over and collected him. I hope they were able to ease the pain of the few days he had left to live.[18]

The Japanese momentum was unstoppable. Allied aerial defences had already been ripped to shreds. When the enemy attacked RAF Seletar on 10 February, a pitifully small handful of remaining aircraft tried to escape, but they were all shot down by the Japanese. The RAF mechanics were left to defend the air base armed only with rifles, before being ordered to retreat south to Singapore City.

The lack of military preparedness was matched by complacency. Officers were as likely to be found in Raffles Hotel as they were in the Combined Operations Room. Three ragged RAF survivors of the assault on Seletar made it safely into Singapore. They were desperately hungry and tried to get a meal at Raffles. That morning Singapore had been bombed and smoke was still curling up from the impact, but the military and civilian elite were merrily eating and drinking as if there was no war

---

[18]Len Baynes, BBC People's War, *www.bbc.co.uk*

just a few miles away. The British officers ignored their men, and it was left to an Australian to make sure the dishevelled bunch were fed.

As the battle raged intensely, Dr Rowley Richards from Sydney was equally appalled when he met an Australian doctor friend in the Goodwood Park Hotel. Richards himself was kitted out in full battle dress but to his horror the friend was dressed in a tuxedo and playing liar dice. Around him lounged women in evening frocks.

The civilian population never fully grasped the danger. Despite the obvious lessons from the bombing of London and other British cities, no blackouts were enforced initially, as lights blazed through the first air attacks. Even as late as the eve of surrender, it was reported that a British officer was told he needed permission from the club committee before he could mount guns on the local golf course.[19]

By 13 February, the causeway across to Singapore Island had been repaired by the enemy, and the Japanese Army moved tanks across in a final assault. Early that morning Gus Anckorn, 118th Royal Artillery, was driving his lorry with a replacement gun picked up at the ordinance dump in Singapore:

> *I saw through my side window an image that has indelibly planted itself on my memory ever since. In a strange mystical slow motion, I was looking at a bomb coming down less than 10 feet away—so close I could have put my hand out and caught it. The rivets on it were plain to see, and Japanese lettering*

[19]The Rise and Fall of Singapore *www.cofepow.org.uk*

*too. I saw the tailfins and a long spike on the front
of the bomb as it went into the ground. I saw the
bomb begin to explode as flames shot out the back
of it. Unbelievably, I saw all this and, in an instant,
I thought, 'I'm dead!'*[20]

Fred Airey, born in Britain's Lake District but now serving with the 2/4th Machine Gun Battalion from Western Australia, was appalled by the unnecessary loss of life. On the final day of the siege, he desperately counselled officers not to order a suicidal assault against the full force of a Japanese machine gun position by soldiers armed only with bayonets.

'You are about to sacrifice all these men's lives and you won't get any return. For God's sake, how the hell do you expect these men to run uphill into machine gun fire. Please reconsider this action. It's murder.' [21]

Despite Airey's protestations the charge went ahead. Few Australians came back, confirming his view that many lives had been sacrificed for no gain.

The Imperial Japanese Army was proving to be a remorseless and brutal opponent. On 14 February, around 100 Japanese soldiers burst into the Alexandra Hospital in Singapore. The Japanese force wore their green uniforms camouflaged with branches and twigs and were armed with rifles, bayonets, and sub-machine guns. When British medical officer Lieutenant Weston raised a sheet as a white flag of surrender, he was bayoneted through his upper chest without hesitation.

[20]Peter Fyans, *Conjuror on the Kwai*, Barnsley, Pen and Sword 2016
[21]Fred Airey, *The Time of the Soldier*, Western Australia, Fremantle Arts Press 1991

The Japanese troops then indiscriminately slaughtered helpless patients with their bayonets, mowing down those who tried to escape with machine guns and rifles. It was a bloodbath. One patient was stabbed to death while under anaesthetic on the operating table.

The killing continued the next day. Staff and patients who had been locked up overnight were marched out into the open air. Those left behind heard fearful cries of anguish and saw a Japanese soldier wiping blood from his bayonet. A large-scale massacre had begun. There are some discrepancies between experts, but most sources claim that 373 people were murdered, including 230 patients, many in their beds. Only a lucky few survived the slaughter.

Twenty-four-year-old Gus Anckorn's arm had been badly hurt when his lorry was bombed the day before. Only half-conscious, he heard the steady thud of the Japanese bayonetting patients. Since the age of fourteen, Anckorn had been a successful conjuror performing under the name Wizardus. He instinctively understood that he would need more than his illusionist skills to survive now. He was reconciled to death but did not want to see it happen and pulled his sheet over his head with his uninjured arm. He survived because, 'when the Japs came to my bed and found blood all over my chest and down on the floor and my face covered—like a corpse—they must have thought me dead already and passed me by.' [22] Wizardus had performed his most successful trick.

Gus Anckorn was not the only lucky survivor. Just before the massacre, Dr Bill Frankland tossed a coin

[22]Peter Fyans, *Conjuror on the Kwai*, Barnsley, Pen and Sword 2016

with a fellow doctor to determine their assignments. 'I called heads and won. The man who lost went to the Alexandra Hospital where he was brutally murdered by Japanese forces in 1942.'[23]

Even before the grim news of the hospital killings emerged, the Governor of the Straits Settlement was deeply concerned about the fate of the growing civilian population sheltering in Singapore. He reported to London on the day of the massacre. 'There are now one million people within radius of three miles. Water supplies very badly damaged and unlikely to last more than twenty-four hours. Many dead lying in the streets and burial impossible.'

The hospital murders were a reminder to Lieutenant General Arthur Percival that losses amongst the large civilian population would be massive at the hands of such a merciless enemy. Percival also feared that in addition to water and food, ammunition would run out. A military fortress was not supposed to also house hundreds of thousands of civilians who needed to be fed, watered, and protected from harm. He wrote to his commanding officer, 'In opinion of commanders troops already committed are too exhausted either to withstand strong attack or launch a counter-attack… there must come a stage when, in the interests of the troops and civilian population, further bloodshed will service no useful purpose.'[24] In fact, the Japanese were also extremely short of ammunition and other supplies, but the Allies did not know that. On 15 February, Percival surrendered.

[23]Obituary, *The Guardian*, 20 April 2020
[24]Lt Gen Percival to Gen Wavell, 13 February, 1942

The impact of surrender on the soldiers, most of whom wanted to fight on, was profound. Corporal George Brown from Lancashire wrote in his diary, 'Have just been ordered to put up white flag on our position, used a towel on two rifles. Can't put it up myself, feel very upset. I think the silence after all the din is very frightening. I am afraid. Broke down and cried as I have never done in my life before.'[25]

Brown was not the only soldier who cried. Private Herbert Barker, from the 4th Royal Norfolks, wrote, 'I remember only too well the first thought that came to my head, it was all over; I was safe; alive…I'll never forget the look upon our Colonel's face when he told us we were beaten. Tears were running down his face.'[26]

Private Frank Percival (no relation to Lt Gen Percival) wrote an eyewitness account of what surrendering troops saw next:

A long line of Japanese were advancing on Fort Canning (British military HQ). Some were pulling handcarts and others wheeling bicycles. Accustomed to the ways of the British Army one could not fail to be surprised by their gait and the general appearance of scruffiness and disorder. Not to be confused with an absence of discipline, as we were to subsequently learn.[27]

It was just not the shabbiness of their uniforms, still camouflaged with twigs and leaves from the jungle, that

[25] George Brown, BBC People's War, *www.bbc.co.uk*
[26] Robert Bennett, San Francisco Maritime Park, *www.maritime.org*
[27] Martin Percival, www.fepowhistory.com, 15 September 2021

astonished the British soldiers. They were also surprised by just how much smaller than Europeans the enemy were. To be beaten by an army not only smaller in number but tiny in stature was humiliating. That this army of 'mites' had travelled by bicycle only added to the shame.

For the captured men, the contrast between the brutal conflict in Singapore and their training on the gentle fields and beaches of Britain was difficult to comprehend, their future uncertain:

> *The air was full of choking dust and during the showers the clouds wept black tears as the rain passed through the oil-laden smoke: there was no escape from the stench of cordite, sewers and rotting flesh...we had been blasted into another world and in this new environment it was a silence that screamed at us. Some wept, some cursed and those too exhausted to curse or weep and unable to fight fatigue any longer, fell where they stood and fitfully slept. Then we waited...we could feel certain only of the past. The present offered nothing but bewilderment and contradiction.*[28]

That anxiety was compounded when the Union Jack flags were lowered in Singapore City, and swiftly replaced by the bright red Japanese sun. As the conqueror's flag fluttered over the greatest trading and military centre in the Far East, it was possible to see the surrender of Singapore as one of the last breaths of the dying British Empire. Japan had ruthlessly conquered Malaya and

---

[28]Bert Miller, BBC People's War, *www.bbc.co.uk*

Singapore within seventy days, an astonishing speed in which to advance down 650 miles of jungle tracks, and then to take Fortress Singapore. Avoiding the logistical headache of managing prisoners by killing them helped the speed of their advance.

Death figures vary between different sources, but best estimates put the Japanese death toll in Malaya and Singapore at around 9,800 and Allied losses at a thousand less than that. Civilian deaths in Singapore were more than six thousand. They might have paid a high price in terms of lost lives, but the enemy now enjoyed military momentum, and further large swathes of Asia, including oil-rich Java, were firmly in their grasp.

Churchill's analysis was unvarnished. He told the British people of 'a heavy and far-reaching military defeat.' In a broadcast on 15 February, he went on to note the efficient Japanese war machine, 'Whether in the air or upon the sea, or man to man on land, they have proved themselves to be formidable, deadly and, I am sorry to say, barbarous antagonists.' The Prime Minister pointed the way forward. 'Let us move steadfastly together into the storm and through the storm.'

On the ground, Churchill's frankness was not universally appreciated, especially by Australians, who blamed him for a fatal error at Gallipoli in the 1914-18 War. Tom McInerney angrily pointed his finger at Churchill himself. 'It was all over in Singapore. Thank you, Winston Churchill for nothing...I detest Churchill and his famous Impenetrable Singapore as he called it. We of the 8th Division call him windbag. There are other names which are unprintable.'[29]

[29]Tom McInerney, *www.pows-of-japan.net*, Western Australia

It was not just Australian POWs who were bitter towards Churchill. Reg Bulled from the 18th Division was angry that a whole division of 17,000 men had been dispatched from their troop ship at Singapore almost directly into a POW camp:

What a mess Churchill had made — sending a whole division, without trucks, guns or ammunition, to defend an island already overrun with too many troops, but desperately in need of guns and supplies. If only Churchill could have heard what the men thought of him and the blunder he had made. He had not only sent us into slavery but had extended the war in the desert by not letting our division go there.[30]

Major General Beckwith-Smith, commanding the 18th Division, left his men in no doubt of the impossible position they had been thrust into. 'The division was sent into a theatre of war for which it was neither trained nor equipped, to fight a clever and cunning enemy who was on the crest of a wave. It was sent to fight a battle already lost...'

Some men, however, had never even seen the enemy. The first Japanese spotted by Dr Bill Frankland was not until after surrender, on his way to imprisonment at Changi. At the ripe old age of 103, Frankland recalled passing the Singapore Cricket Club more than seventy years earlier. 'The first Japanese I ever saw, very near the pitch, was defecating publicly. Why he chose such a public place to carry out this, I have no idea. But that was the first Japanese I ever saw.'[31]

[30]Reg Bulled, *www.fareasternheroes.org.uk*
[31]*www.singaporeevacuation1942.blogspot.com*, 1st September 2016

Their victory had been so swift, so total, that the Japanese had no idea what to do with their prisoners. More than 140,000 Allied POWs was an enormous number of men for the conquering army to house and feed. That figure was matched by a similar number of civilians, including women and children, who were to be imprisoned in different corners of the expanding Japanese empire. More than that, under their code of behaviour the Imperial Japanese Army believed that soldiers should fight to the death. Surrender was dishonourable. Suicide was the noble alternative. So Japanese soldiers told their humiliated prisoners that capitulation was shameful. To make it worse for the POWs, Winston Churchill appeared to blame them, saying 'This is a disaster, the worse disaster and largest capitulation in our history. The retreat from Dunkirk in 1940 was a heavy blow, but the heroes of Dunkirk had not surrendered.'

The world recognises heroism in winners rather than losers, but as prisoners of the Japanese the captured men would prove themselves to be as resilient and brave as the troops at Dunkirk. As they trudged, weary and humiliated, seventeen steamy miles to their camp at Changi, the Allied troops could scarcely imagine the consequences of their loss. They had no idea that they would not see their families or their homes for three and a half more years. During that time, they would face starvation, disease, and both physical and mental torture. Only the strong and the lucky would survive.

3

Prisoners

The seeds of the Singapore disaster were sown long before the ignominy of surrender. The Allies never committed adequate numbers of modern fighting machines to push the Japanese tide back from Malaya and Singapore. As the Japanese stretched Allied defences across the Far East, there were just not enough military resources available to fight against Japan, as well as Germany and Italy. As Churchill himself put it in a message to the Prime Minister of Australia, 'I do not see how anyone could expect Malaya to be defended once the Japanese obtained command of the sea and while we are fighting for our lives against Germany and Italy.'[1]

In effect, Churchill was saying that Malaya was lost when the *Prince of Wales* and *Repulse* were sunk in mid-December. Some observers blamed Lt General Percival, but he was given a very difficult hand to play. Obsolete aircraft, Hurricanes in crates, and ill-equipped troops were never going to enjoy sufficient firepower to beat the well-equipped and fanatical Japanese. As the Commonwealth Commissioner had

[1]Message to Mr Curtin, 14 January 1942

made clear in late December, only an urgent and major increase in military capability could save Singapore. It never came.

POWs on the ground, thinking about the years of captivity ahead, were angry at the lack of support. 2nd Lt Louis Baume of the Royal Artillery, aged twenty-two, expressed what many felt. 'So it is all over. Prisoners: defeated we feel let down rather — no planes, no ships, no tanks except in half-penny numbers: outnumbered, out-manoeuvred and out-bluffed by those little yellow bastards.'[2]

The 100,000 strong British and Australian army outnumbered the enemy, but Churchill reflected that it was already broken before the Battle of Singapore.

'It might be a hundred thousand men; but it was an army no more.' Churchill later doubted the wisdom of fighting all the way down through Malaya. He noted that all the reinforcements, 'were used up in gallant fighting on the peninsula and when these had crossed the causeway to what should have been their supreme battleground their punch was gone.'[3]

Percival and the other military leaders might have been denied adequate resources, but they bore responsibility for both the lack of preparedness and the chaos on the ground. The decision to defend 72 miles of coastline meant that defences were spread too thin. Australian Regimental sergeant major, Fred Airey, 2/4th Machine Gun Battalion, summed it up. 'No

[2]Imperial War Museum Sound Archive
[3]Winston Churchill, *The Second World War (The Hinge of Fate)*, London, Cassell, 1951

42

one seemed to know what was going on. Something had gone amiss at HQ...the whole bloody works was completely confusing.'

In Singapore, there had been huge confidence in the giant 15-inch guns that faced threateningly out to the sea. The widely held view amongst the newly captured troops that the guns could not be switched to fire inland is incorrect. Some could be turned round, but it took many hours. There was also an apparent shortage of high-explosive ammunition. So, the guns only had a limited value when the enemy attacked from the land and not the sea. Whatever the reality, the result was the same, the guns that the British had such confidence in did not do their job.

Singapore Island had desperately needed to be reinforced with gun emplacements and other land defences. This was never seen as a top priority. Twenty-three-year-old Len (Snowie) Baynes from the 1st Cambridgeshire Regiment had a clearer plan than some of his bosses:

A few thousand pounds of concrete pill-boxes, strategically placed, a few mobile guns or tanks and Singapore could well have proved, like Gibraltar, an impregnable fortress. No plans seem to have been worked out for the deployment of troops, however, should the Japanese do the obvious and attack from dry land instead of sailing into the muzzle of our big guns from seaward.[4]

Churchill, who had put so much faith in Singapore as a fortress, was astonished to learn in mid-January 1942

[4]Len Baynes, BBC People's War, *www.bbc.co.uk*

that, 'there were no permanent fortifications covering the landward side of the naval base and the city! Moreover, even more astounding, no measures worth speaking of had been taken by any of the commanders since the war began, and more especially since the Japanese had established themselves in Indochina, to construct field defences. They had not even mentioned the fact they did not exist.' In his book on the Second World War Churchill observed, 'I saw before me the hideous spectacle of the almost naked island and of the wearied, if not exhausted troops retreating upon it. I do not write this in any way to excuse myself. I ought to have known. My advisers ought to have known and I ought to have been told and I ought to have asked.'

Running through every poor decision was a profound underestimation of the technology, determination, and self-sacrifice of the enemy, underpinned by the colonial perception that the Japanese were an inferior race. The ordinary serviceman, now facing many bleak years as a prisoner of the Japanese, had every right to feel let down by the political and military hierarchy. They saw themselves as sacrificial lambs.

Some surrendering troops had never even seen the Japanese, others had been heavily bombarded in what many of them called 'hell'. The day after surrender their next grim chapter started. Padre Eric Cordingly was sent out in a burial party behind enemy lines:

On the bend in the road were two burnt out Bren Carriers, with four or five bodies sprawled across the road-bodies quite naked. Leaning from the carriers were more—parts of men, burnt stumps of men— and this, after two days of tropical sun—the stench of this scene will be with me always. Along in the ditches were others, fifty or more...swollen, sizzling, bursting corpses. We buried each one.[5]

A handful of captured Australian troops from the 2/4th Machine Gun Battalion were also detailed to move bodies and vehicles by the Japanese. After this miserable task the men were locked up for the night. For some reason they could not understand, their Japanese captors were angry. Next day, the fifteen soldiers were marched to a spot overlooking a small creek where water ran down from the jungle hills. The Australians faced away. Seven Japanese soldiers carrying British-made rifles stood behind them. Fred Airey, the senior soldier in the line, knew this was a firing squad. 'I prayed for Gwen and my children, and prayed for my soul. I knew the end was very near.'[6]

Fred Airey played dead in the creek when the Japanese moved round and shot every wounded POW who was still breathing, 'I tried to keep my breaths shallow, and my eyes closed. The shots rang out-thump, thump, I heard them hitting the bodies. I was hit just above the eye, luckily only a superficial graze, and I could feel the blood running into my eye and down my face.' Having survived his execution, Airey made a remarkable escape to Java in a leaky children's canoe, where he was picked up yet again. A second survivor, Les McCann, was saved when the bullet intended for him hit his cigarette case

[5]Eric Cordingly and Louise Reynolds, *Down to Bedrock,* Norwich, Art Angel, 2013
[6]Fred Airey, *The Time of the Soldier,* Western Australia, Fremantle Arts Centre Press, 1991

and paybook. Months later the two lucky Australians were astonished to be reunited in Changi Camp.

It was not just the Australian servicemen now in Japanese hands who faced an uncertain future; the whole nation was anxious. Their fears deepened four days after Singapore's capitulation when Japan launched a massive onslaught on the town of Darwin in the north of Australia. In two separate raids, 242 Japanese aircraft attacked the harbour, airfields, and Darwin itself. Australia lost 236 citizens in the largest-ever single attack on the country. The raid not only damaged a vital Allied base, but highlighted Australia's growing vulnerability.

In Singapore, thousands of newly surrendered prisoners were held for hours crammed onto a tennis court without shelter or water. Finally, the bedraggled band of men were marched by their captors to the British barracks at Changi. It was a sunburnt trek of seventeen miles. The prisoners were already exhausted, thirsty, and anxious for their futures. Like refugees, the snaking line of men carried their few precious possessions including bedding. Some locals lined up to jeer. Others came forward with drinks of water for the desperate marchers. Dead bodies were still on the streets. Some marchers saw the heads of Chinese impaled on the spikes of railings. It was a grim foretaste of what was to come

On that weary trudge through Singapore, Ken Adams, a medical orderly with 198th Field Ambulance, East Anglia, understood for the first time what a catastrophe had taken place in Singapore:

'The place was a shambles. There were smouldering ruins, collapsed buildings, roads blocked with

*masonry, tangled masses of electricity cables, and
smashed vehicles. In some areas, bodies from the
recent fighting still littered the streets; some were
badly burnt; some shapeless, sticky messes covered
with flies; some bloated and rotten and started
to smell badly…the smell of decomposition and
corruption was atrocious.'*[7]

The POWs did not know how long their incarceration
would be. This was a sentence without an end date.
The Japanese language and culture were so alien it was
difficult for the new prisoners to have any clear idea
of how they would be treated by their captors. Among
the 130,000 were men who would later labour for the
Japanese war machine in the factories and dockyards
that sat in the shadow of the Nagasaki bomb. Many
of the prisoners captured in Singapore, or later in Java,
were also destined to build the Thailand – Burma railway,
known more colloquially as the Railway of Death.

In both their conflict with Russia in 1904, and in
World War I, Japan treated their prisoners decently.
In contrast, they slaughtered between 100,000 and
200,000 Chinese in Nanking in 1937. So, the prisoners,
stunned, humiliated, beaten, had no idea what their
eventual fate would be and when, or if, they would ever
see their families again.

[7]Ken Adams and Mike Adams, *Healing in Hell*, Barnsley, Pen and Sword 2011

4

JAVA

In late 1941, twenty-year-old Ron Bryer was dispatched to Singapore by the RAF to work in a new high-speed communications facility. He departed with a sense of adventure, mixed with underlying fear of the unknown that lay ahead. Like so many other young servicemen and women, Bryer knew that Singapore was a vital strategic base for the Allies, but he could scarcely have imagined that Fortress Singapore would be breached so easily. Nor would Ron Bryer have ever guessed that this debacle would propel him onto a precarious path that eventually led to Fukuoka Camp 14b in Nagasaki.

Bryer had a cheeky grin and protruding ears. When his head was shaved as a Japanese POW, he said he looked like 'an egg with wings.' From his accent no one could mistake him for anything other than a Yorkshireman. He was born in the *King's Arms* (now the *Radcliffe Arms*) in the small village of Follifoot, near Harrogate. His father was a painter and decorator, but with little money to show for it. Work on local farms, a bit of poaching on the side, and the sharp elbows needed to prosper in a large rural family, were useful skills for a POW.

Ron Bryer, built like the teenage boxer he was, also possessed a keen intelligence. He passed his exams for

Harrogate Grammar School and, in 1939, like one of his brothers and other young men in his village, he joined up. The RAF clearly spotted an innate ability because he was soon dispatched for high-speed telegraphy training to a semi-secret location near London.

It was these technical communications skills that made Aircraftsman Bryer valuable to the RAF. So, he was one of the servicemen evacuated to Java just as the fortress of Singapore was collapsing. As he slipped hurriedly onto the *City of Canterbury*, he could see Japanese troops trying to repair the shattered causeway that linked Johore to Singapore Island. As the ship slid out of the ruined dockyard she soon passed the blazing skeleton of the troopship, the *Empress of Asia*. Seeing the Japanese forces so close at hand, Ron Bryer sensed that this freedom would not last long.

Not everyone who escaped Singapore was as lucky as Ron Bryer. On the evening of 12 February, three days before Singapore surrendered, the *Vyner Brooke* also escaped hurriedly from the island. The merchant vessel was doing service as a hospital ship and on board were more than 200 hundred civilians and injured service personnel, as well as sixty-five Australian nurses. North of Sumatra, the ship was bombed by the Japanese who scored a direct hit down the funnel. Within fifteen minutes, the ancient ship sank. Nurses and patients clung desperately to the only two serviceable lifeboats, or to wooden debris floating amongst the dead bodies in the water. Some were eventually captured by the enemy.

The women, children, and injured who evaded the Japanese managed to land safely at Radji Beach on the north of Banka Island. Among this group were twenty-two of the Australian nurses. They were soon joined by a band of British soldiers who had survived the sinking of another ship. It was decided that with so many children and injured, and so little food and water, the only course of action was to surrender. An officer from the *Vyner Brooke* was dispatched to report to the Japanese in Muntock to the north. A group of civilian women and children trudged off in the same direction.

The Australian nurses stayed behind to care for the injured. The women immediately set up a makeshift shelter emblazoned by a Red Cross, and they improvised a dozen stretchers. The nurses made sure they were clearly wearing Red Cross armbands. When nearly twenty Japanese troops arrived back with the officer from the ship, the women had no reason to doubt they would be treated as non-combatants. The male survivors were less confident of Japanese intentions. Their pessimism proved to be well-placed when the men were swiftly herded round the headland by the Japanese. The soldiers returned without their captives. Some were wiping blood from their bayonets.

The Red Crosses worn by the women proved no protection. They were forced to form a line and then they were marched into the sea. Once the nurses were up to their waists in water, the Japanese shot the nurses in the back. The Japanese soldiers, laughing according to some accounts, finally bayoneted around ten men and women on stretchers. The estimates of those murdered vary between seventy-two and eighty-three.

Only one nurse survived the massacre. Sister Vivian Bullwinkel was shot in the side of the back and just lay in the water pretending to be dead. When she surfaced the beach was silent and empty. The only other survivor of the massacre was a British private, Patrick Kingsley (called Kinsley in some accounts), who had also played dead after being bayoneted on his makeshift stretcher. They survived for nearly two weeks with the help of local women. Vivian Bullwinkel's bullet wound in the hip began to heal, but it was clear there was no hope of either escape or survival. Reluctantly the two survivors decided to surrender, and soon after Private Kingsley died from his wounds.

Bullwinkel was eventually reunited with the surviving nurses from the *Vyner Brooke* who were already in Japanese captivity. Twelve nurses were drowned and twenty-one massacred on the beach. Sister Bullwinkel and thirty-one other women survived but faced three hard years as prisoners of war. Recent investigations have claimed that before they were massacred the nurses were raped. Sister Bullwinkel maintained that she had been 'gagged' and prevented from speaking about the rapes by the Australian government.[1]

* * *

Even as Singapore was collapsing, military leaders were working out how to stem the remorseless Japanese advance towards the precious oil supplies in the Dutch East Indies. Military commitments elsewhere in the region were always going to make this extremely difficult. General Wavell, the overall Commander in Chief in the region, wrote to Churchill on 16 February, the day after Singapore fell. He pointed out the serious difficulty defending the long northern coastline of Java, 'approximately the distance of London to Inverness'

---

[1] BBC News, *www.bbc.co.uk*, 18 April 2019 and Lynette Silver, *Angels of Mercy*, Australia, Sally Milner, 1 April 2019

and the weakness of the three Dutch divisions left in Java. He also revealed that some of the RAF ground personnel on Java were not even armed. Wavell concluded, 'Landings on Java in near future can only be prevented by local naval and air superiority. Facts given show that it is most unlikely that this superiority can be obtained. Once enemy had effected landing, there is at present little to prevent his rapidly occupying main naval and air bases on island.'

The Japanese swiftly fulfilled Wavell's bleak prediction. In rapid succession, three cruisers—HMAS *Perth* from Australia, the American ship USS *Houston,* and HMS *Exeter* of the Royal Navy—were sunk as they tried to escape larger enemy forces. Over 750 men lost their lives in these three sinkings. Many survivors who were captured by the Japanese were eventually condemned to work as slave-like labour at camps in or near Nagasaki.

With their naval forces at the bottom of the ocean, the Allies desperately needed air strength to defend Java. However, with many aircraft in need of repair, they only had about forty planes available for combat. Although a few Hurricanes were finally ready, the bulk of the air force was a ragbag of ancient or inadequate aircraft, all in tiny numbers. This patchy force had to defend a long coastline with many potential landing sites for Japanese soldiers.

This was an impossible task with such meagre military resources. On the same night the *Exeter* was sunk, Japanese forces landed on Java in three places. In a mirror image of the invasion of Malaya, the Japanese Imperial Army immediately took control of Allied airfields, starting on 1 March with the strategically valuable air base at Kalidjati.

Four British aircraft escaped from Kalidjati just in time, and some soldiers and aircraftsmen made it out on trucks. Those who were captured by the Japanese became POWs, although a large number were killed by the enemy. Around fifty-five men from the 49 Battery, 48th LAA, Royal Artillery disappeared without trace. As they were later found buried in a mass grave in Batavia, it is likely they were massacred by the enemy, although there were no eyewitness. Soon after the invasion, the US flew all their aircraft to Australia. This horrified the Dutch, who called it desertion. As POW Jim Ralphs later put it, 'Java was left to its fate: occupation, degradation, humiliation and death.'[2]

Safely evacuated from Singapore, twenty-year-old Ron Bryer from the RAF was now based in the pleasantly cool city of Bandung (or Bandoeng), built on a plateau in the hills of Central Java. As dance bands played into the night and locals dined happily on the summer terraces of restaurants, he knew this was a fool's paradise. British troops had seen what the Japanese had achieved so ruthlessly in Malaya and Singapore and were astonished by how many locals were enjoying café society, even though the enemy was just a few miles away.

With battleships at the bottom of the sea and air support hopelessly inadequate, once again the Allies were forced to fight a defensive land battle in unknown tropical terrain. The ABDA (American-British-Dutch-Australian) troops were commanded by the Dutch Lieutenant General Hein Ter Poorten, but his 25,000

---

[2]Jim Ralphs and Java FEPOW Club, *Prisoners in Java*, Southampton, Hamwic 2007

soldiers were mainly poorly trained men from the Dutch East Indies. They were supplemented by nearly 10,000 British and Australian troops. To this disparate force was added just over 500 men from an American artillery regiment from Texas.

The British troops were short of adequate weapons. Two British anti-aircraft regiments possessed none of their guns and were forced to act as infantry. Some Australian machine gunners recalled landing on Java armed only with pickaxe handles. Private Jack Thomas from Broken Hill was allocated a Canadian-made Ross rifle which had been designed back in 1903. It was difficult to delay the enemy advance, let alone defeat the Japanese, armed with such pathetic weapons.

Lieutenant Lance Gibson, Australian 2/3 Machine Gun Battalion, was dismayed by the lack of armoury at their disposal. 'Boy, were we well equipped! No guns, no ammunition, no transport. Nothing at all... although we were machine gun specialists, we had to arm ourselves with anything we could lay our hands upon, or what we could gather from Dutch forces on the island.'[3]

Nor could they rely on the Royal Netherlands East Indies Army (KNIL). The average British and Australian soldier had a low opinion of their Allies in the Dutch East Indies force. Australian Milton Fairclough was blunt. 'My old Granny would have beaten the lot of gutless wonders. I have a lot of admiration though for the spirit of the Dutch women who defied the Japs at

---

[3] Lance Gibson, *www.pows-of-japan.net*

every turn. I've seen them belted down, get up and spit in the Jap's face again.'[4]

Up against a well-trained and armed enemy, what Churchill himself called 'this scanty force' had no chance. Only significant reinforcements could save them, and it had already been decided these were more important elsewhere. In his message to Churchill on 16 February, General Wavell summed up that 'Burma and Australia are absolutely vital for war against Japan. Loss of Java, though severe blow from every point of view, would not be fatal. Efforts should not be made to reinforce Java, which might compromise defence of Burma or Australia.' Churchill agreed. If any further Australian divisions were available, they would be diverted away from Java to countries with a greater strategic significance.

The certainty of loss in Java was underlined when Wavell himself was ordered to leave his command. On 23 February he resumed his role of Commander in Chief, India, with responsibility for the defence of Burma. Nonetheless, Churchill emphasised in a direct broadcast to the men on the ground that every day they delayed the enemy advance through Asia was vital. But Churchill's 'scanty force' was now on its own. Nonetheless, they fought tenaciously in a desperate effort to slow down the Japanese.

The 2/3 Machine Gun Battalion, led by Brigadier Arthur Blackburn, an Australian VC from World War One, was supplemented by more Australians and other Allied units in an outfit known as Black Force. In several days of fierce combat, Black Force fought the advancing Japanese Army at Leuwiliang, near Bandung, killing more than 500 of the enemy. Significantly outnumbered and fighting with largely outdated weapons, Black Force was eventually outflanked by additional Japanese companies, but their rear-guard action delayed enemy progress, just as Churchill had demanded. This enabled Allied forces stationed in the capital city of Batavia, to escape south towards the coastal ports, where an escape by sea was possible.

As soon as the news of the invasion reached Bandung, Ron Bryer and other men of the RAF communications unit were ordered out of the city. On their way, they destroyed their fixed equipment and even pulled ripcords on parachutes; anything to make the invasion more difficult for the enemy. In a nearby quarry, they set up a mobile communications centre, transmitting news of Java's invasion throughout the night.

The Allied HQ was in the mountain city of Bandung, but its art deco architecture and elegant pavement cafes were now an irrelevance. Bandung had been transformed into a city of refugees, most of them women and children. Many of the thousands now crammed into the city lived in false hope that the Allies would defend this redoubt long enough for reinforcements to arrive. As the Japanese closed in on all sides, they threatened to bomb the swelling numbers of refugees in Bandung, and to raise the city to the ground. Like General Percival in Singapore, Ter Poorten, the beleaguered Dutch commander of the Allied forces, feared massive loss of civilian life and surrendered.

As the handwritten surrender notice was being typed up, Captain Atholl Duncan of the Argyll and Sutherland

Highlanders had the foresight to have a carbon copy made. He stitched the message into his glengarry (Scottish military cap) and kept the historic document safe for the rest of the war. That was sensible because the original did not survive. The message said, 'Hoist the white flag as a sign of capitulation.'[5] That notice sentenced thousands of Allied troops to nearly four years of imprisonment by the Japanese Empire.

At 9 a.m. on 8 March, Lieutenant General ter Poorten broadcast news of the surrender and instructed Allied troops to lay down their arms. Although he was a lawyer from South Australia by profession, Arthur Blackburn VC was a tough and experienced soldier who had distinguished himself at both Gallipoli and the Somme in World War I. He did not want to surrender and nor did the British commander, General Sitwell. Arthur Blackburn's Black Force dug in and prepared for a last stand in the mountains.

However, it soon became clear to Blackburn and other senior officers that they faced a severe shortage of food, weapons, and medical supplies in the mountains. Brigadier Blackburn knew his men could neither survive nor escape. Blackburn made it clear to his men that it was not his choice to surrender but that they should conform to the decision of the Dutch overall commander. Blackburn and more than 4,500 Allied troops were condemned to become prisoners of war. Many of them would later die in Japanese hands.

The 131st Field Artillery 2nd Battalion, over 500 soldiers drawn from the distant towns of Texas, found

---

[5]Meg Parkes, Liverpool School of Tropical Medicine, *www.fepowhistory.com*, 8 March 2021

surrender a particularly galling experience. Up to this point their losses had been minimal and they wanted to continue the fight, even though their helmets dated back to WWI and they possessed no machine guns. Some sources suggest that even though they were fighting on the same side, the Dutch forced them to capitulate at gunpoint.[6] They became known as the Lost Battalion because for two and a half years they just disappeared. Their families in Texas had no idea if their husbands or sons were dead or alive.

Among the men captured in the mountains was RAF Squadron Leader Aidan MacCarthy, a military doctor from Castletownbere on the lovely Beara peninsula in County Cork. His parents were popular publicans in the town, and Aidan studied medicine at University College, Cork. In 1939, MacCarthy joined the RAF as a young doctor.

By the time he was captured in Java, Squadron Leader Aidan MacCarthy had already almost lost his life twice. At Dunkirk he had spent three desperate days trapped on the beach before finally escaping on a Larne-Stranraer ferry which had been pressed into service with hundreds of small ships. Then in May 1941, at RAF Honington on the Suffolk-Norfolk border, he was on duty in the early hours of the morning when a Wellington bomber clipped the top of the bomb dump as it was coming into land. The plane cartwheeled and burst into flames. Despite the fire and the danger of exploding bombs, MacCarthy and the driver of the fire tender pulled the badly burnt aircrew to safety as the Wellington's fuel tanks blew up

[6]Gavan Daws, *Prisoners of the Japanese*, London, Robson Books 1995

in flames. For courageously risking their own lives, both MacCarthy and the driver were awarded the George Medal. These two near misses were not to be his last close encounters with death. Dr MacCarthy's destiny was to lead him to Camp 14b in Nagasaki, where he became the senior British officer.

MacCarthy and the thousands of other prisoners from Britain, Australia and the Dutch East Indies were transported down from the mountains to the Dutch military airfield at Tasikmalaya in Central Java. The confusion of their captors was immediately apparent. Japanese soldiers were friendly and curious but as soon as prison camp guards replaced the soldiers, the relaxed atmosphere darkened. The new guards demanded that POWs divulge details of their training, and other information the Geneva Convention precluded. When the senior British officer, Wing Commander Edward Steedman, refused to reveal any of this material he was summarily executed by firing squad in front of the rest of the prisoners.

Several small groups in the mountains simply disappeared, melting away rather than surrendering to the Japanese. Some evaded the enemy for several weeks. Others had headed earlier towards the port of Tjilatjap on the south coast. The scenes in the small harbour town were chaotic as thousands struggled to clamber on the last boats to depart. For a few days Tjilatjap looked like a tropical Dunkirk, with buildings burning fiercely, hundreds of vehicles abandoned at the dockside, and desperate troops searching for a boat.

Escape boats were so heavily overcrowded that many soldiers and airmen were left behind. Sergeant Robert Hampson recalled jumping on the very last ship to leave:

I was lucky enough to board the Tung Song ...my abiding memory as the Tung Song drew away from the quayside was the sight of those many hundreds of khaki-clad figures which seemed to cover the grassy banks of the quay, all hoping for another vessel to appear over the horizon.[7]

These unlucky men were later described as 'Stayed Behind in Java.' Ron Bryer, and the rest of the RAF communications unit, were among those left behind. One of this group was Leading Aircraftsman Arthur Christie, from Catford in South London. Christie had left school at fourteen and worked in an engineering works as a machine driller and lathe turner. In 1939 his factory was due to close, so Arthur and a friend decided to join up. After one of their last night shifts, they caught the bus to the recruiting office at the Yorkshire Grey pub in Eltham. Christie was only seventeen but lied about his age so he could join the RAF. He was with No 41 Air Park Stores which was responsible for supplying stores to aircraft. But in Java there were very few aircraft or spare parts. Java could not have been a greater contrast to the streets of South London he knew so well. Arthur Christie and Ron Bryer were to share a barracks in Nagasaki in 1945, but their immediate priority was evading the enemy.

After they were informed of the surrender Ron Bryer, Arthur Christie, and the others packed up and headed in a convoy for the coast. When they arrived at the end of the road a vast expanse of the sea stretched out

[7]Robert *Hampson, Prisoners in Java*, Southampton, Hamwic /Java FEPOW Club, 2007

ahead, but there was no sign of any boats. Their RAF commanding officer was clear about the decision they all had to make; either they returned to join the surrender, or they formed into a guerrilla band. The consequence of being caught as an armed guerrilla was undoubtedly execution.

Bryer, Christie, and their mates decided not to surrender but to tramp about a hundred miles along the coast to Wincoops Bay, where there was a slim possibility of finding a boat. Filled with both reluctance and sadness, they pushed their trucks, full to the brim with specialist communications equipment, over the rocky cliff towards the sea. Machine guns were destroyed, leaving handguns as their only weapons.

It was an anxious but determined band of two officers, eight men and an Alsatian guard dog who marched along the coast in the faint hope that they too could find a boat. They climbed hills, crossed rivers, and tramped through the jungle for a brutally hot 100 miles. For Ron Bryer, this march could not have been more different from his last posting in the UK, a training camp in Blackpool where he ate powdered egg omelettes and enjoyed dances at the Tower Ballroom. Just before the exhausted men reached their destination, they encountered a heavily armed Japanese patrol. There was no chance of escape now. The first act of their captors was to bayonet the Alsatian dog.

Then the Japanese officer raised his revolver and pointed the barrel straight between Ron Bryer's eyes. The soldier asked if Bryer had a gun. Fortunately, the men had all tossed their weapons into the bush minutes before their capture. It was an extremely tense moment:

Down the yawning black tunnel, big enough to crawl into, I seemed to see the shining nose of a bullet waiting to smash into a brain that no longer cared or was afraid. Every small part of me ached with hunger and exhaustion...I lifted my eyes from the gun barrel and looked directly into the almond shaped eyes below the peaked cap. Expressionless eyes, hard and brittle as black marbles in a dead white face. We both knew that at that moment my life lay in the crook of his forefinger.[8]

Ron Bryer was able to truthfully deny he possessed a gun, and so the hard eyes moved on. The soldier lowered his revolver and asked to speak to the commanding officer. When he learned the new captives were British RAF personnel, the Japanese officer simply said, 'Ah, England. All prisoners Nippon now.'

Aircraftsman Ron Bryer and his mates were shipped to a camp at Soekaboemi (Sukabumi). From the first moment of imprisonment, both captives and captors were learning about the other. How far could the Japanese be pushed? What did their mysterious codes of behaviour mean in practice? For their part, the Japanese had to learn to organise thousands of unexpected prisoners, men they regarded as worthless because they had surrendered rather than died. Above all, where were the lines of behaviour clearly understood, and where were they still being drawn?

At Soekaboemi, the camp commandant answered any uncertainties with an immediate and brutal act of deterrence. The whole camp was forced to witness

[8]Ron Bryer, *The White Ghosts of Nagasaki*, Yorkshire, self-published 1997

the public execution of two prisoners. The first was beheaded and the second bayonetted. The prisoners would not forget the gentle stroking of the neck, the sword flashing through the sunlight, then the blood, and the headless corpse slumping forward. It was a reminder, as if the POWs needed one, that the risk of straying out of line was death.

A few months later, Dr Aidan MacCarthy, Ron Bryer and Arthur Christie were lucky to be moved to the cooler climate of Bandung, the attractive mountain town with a reputation as the Paris of Java. Compared to the dangers that lay ahead in Nagasaki and elsewhere life here was tolerable. Work was not back-breaking. Extra food could be bought from willing locals. The buildings were solid and well-ventilated and the benign weather gave the men a chance to build up strength. Gradually, the boundaries of behaviour became clearer, and the British and Australian troops began to organise themselves.

A school for the prisoners was started. Arthur Christie was amazed to find himself taking piano lessons whilst a POW. In the Christmas 1942 edition of the Bandung POW magazine, *Mark Time*, Ron Bryer is thanked for spending evenings diligently typing out the magazine's pages, even after a day's labour. He carried copies of the magazine with him in his knapsack all the way to the end of the war. Precious paper for the magazine was provided by Laurens Van der Post, an intelligence officer—and later a famous author and explorer—whose ability to speak both Dutch and Japanese gave him the reputation of being able to conjure miracles.

A few Japanese soldiers were sympathetic. After helping an elderly serviceman, Bryer and his mates were treated to soft drinks and cakes in his garden. However, Ron Bryer knew that danger was always one tiny miscalculation away, that it never paid to be comfortable or complacent. The executions in Soekaboemi had taught him that. As was the case in many camps, it was a change of command that ushered in a fresh era of danger.

Some Indonesian Dutch prisoners had family in Bandung and occasionally slipped away from the camp for a visit. The guards showed no concern about these unusual domestic arrangements and the prisoners from Java grew relaxed about their incarceration. When the new camp commandant changed the rules so that permission for home visits was required in advance, some Dutch Indonesians failed to sense danger. Three of them made unauthorised family visits and were arrested and executed by the Japanese. Ronald Scholte saw his countrymen fixed on barbed wire at the camp. '*It turned out that they had been killed with bayonet stabs. The Japanese intended to leave the bodies hanging on the barbed wire for 24 hours. It was a terrible sight; the ground was soaked with blood. During the execution I had a pan of pea soup in my hand, but after the execution I was no longer hungry and threw everything away.*'[9]

Australian doctor 'Weary' Dunlop reported in his diary of 22 April 1942 that three men were 'bayoneted to death like pigs, before their comrades.' In contrast, he noted on 13 May 1942 that 'Cpl Clarke gave an excellent lecture on the English Lake District.'[10]

[9]*www.fukuoka 14b.org*
[10]Edward Dunlop, *The War Diaries of Weary Dunlop*, Australia, Thomas Nelson, 1986

In November 1942, hundreds of POWs were moved down from the cool mountains to Bicycle Camp in Batavia (now Jakarta), a former barracks for the 10th Battalion Bicycle Unit of the Netherlands East Indies Army. Hundreds of bicycle racks lined the buildings. As a former Dutch barracks, the facilities were better than in most camps with ample latrines and wash houses.

In the steamy heat of the capital prisoners constructed roads, worked in factories, or laboured on the wharves at Batavia's busy port, Tandjong Priok. The work not only helped the men stay fit but gave them ample chance to explore the essential survival skill of theft. Food, cigarettes, kitchen utensils and paper were all pilfered regularly and smuggled back into the Bicycle Camp, often in the one place the guards did not want to search, beneath the loincloths or shorts of their prisoners.

POWs immediately started to humanise their surroundings. They scrounged disused crates for tables and empty rice sacks for bedding. In those early days before malnutrition and disease made anything beyond basic survival impossible, prisoners in most Java camps organised sport and entertainment to keep their bodies fit and their spirits positive. POWs reported a splendid production of *The Merchant of Venice*. Les Spence recorded in his secret diary, 'Wonderful game last night. Played Aussie rugger and won. A really hard game. A night of musical play, an astounding success.'[11] As Spence had captained Cardiff Rugby Club in 1936, and his prison teammate was Wilf Wooller, who played

[11]Les Spence, edited by Greg Lewis, *From Java to Nagasaki*, Wales, Magic Rat 2012

eighteen times for Wales, victory was not entirely surprising.

The prisoners were not yet resigned to their fate, although many already feared that incarceration would be measured in years not months. Everyone was hungry for news of the war because it offered a glimpse of hope. These were practical men, engineers and sappers, signalmen and gunners. Building handmade radios from scavenged bits and pieces was a challenge they took on enthusiastically. Radios and their constituent parts were hidden in furniture, wall cavities, and even false legs. In the early days, before their only clothing was a G-string or tattered shorts, a kilt was an effective hiding place. Anyone reading the secret diaries of Welshman Les Spence could be forgiven for thinking the POWs were having a good time, as there are references to 'good ice cream'. In fact, this was code for good news. Unfortunately, there was also plenty of 'bad ice cream' from the war, as the Japanese continued their unchecked advance.

Many camp leaders were out of their depth when faced with the challenge of housing, feeding, and employing thousands of servicemen from European cultures. Force was the only way they knew how to manage so many prisoners. Policies towards POWs were framed far away in Japan, creating ideal incubation conditions for brutal behaviour.

So, the treatment of prisoners was unpredictable, justice applied randomly. At Malang, several hundred POWs were building a grass runway. Four RAF escapers were blindfolded and had their hands tied in front of them. They were lined up against the dispersal bay and shot. It took several volleys for them to die. In the end they were finished off from close quarters. They were then bundled into graves that had already been dug. In one of those contradictions that was hard for prisoners to understand, the Japanese also bought flowers for the graves. The commanding officer of the victims, Wing Commander W Walsh recorded, 'The behaviour of the four men was magnificent; no one could have guessed from their demeanour that they were going to their deaths. No sign of fear could be read on their faces.'[12]

In another camp, British telegraphist Jack Hughieson witnessed the random exercise of justice when six eggs were stolen. The Japanese camp commandant stood over a prisoner who had no connection to the crime. He was just nearest to the commandant, who raised his sword above the POWs head and said, '"Tell me who took those eggs, or I'll take this man's head off." Nobody said anything because we just didn't know. He brought his sword down, and he did not really take the man's head off completely. The head just fell forward onto the man's chest, before he fell forward with blood spurting out of the back of the neck. We were in a state of shock.'[13]

In the Lyceum Camp, a POW from Sumatra who had been desperately searching for news of his sick wife was caught talking to a civilian outside the camp. RAF doctor, Aidan MacCarthy wrote, 'the prisoner's head was shaved, and he was buried up to his neck in the centre of the courtyard. He was left there bareheaded, without food or drink, and at the mercy of the tropical sun, flies, and mosquitos. I watched unable to do

[12]*Prisoners of Java* , Southampton, Hamwic/Java FEPOW Club 2007
[13]*Not Forgotten*, BBC Open Space 1984

anything. The Japanese refused to let me offer him any relief at all. At the same time, they insisted that all the POWs walked past him dozens of times a day…insect bites set up immediate infection, his eyes began to close, and his dried lips became set in a permanent snarl. It took two days and a night for him to die.'[14]

At the transit centre of the Bicycle Camp there was a constant flow of prisoners, as new POWs arrived, and others were shipped out. There was one grim warning of what might lie on the road ahead. Charles Whitehead from 42nd Regiment, Royal Artillery saw one group of mostly British arrivals return from building an airfield on the island of Haruku in the Ambon Sea. 'They were skeletons. The men were in a terrible state—just living skeletons with ulcers, sores, and dysentery. Some were in a bad mental state. One had to see these men to imagine that such cruelty could be inflicted on another human being.'[15]

RAF Squadron Leader Aidan MacCarthy saw the same arrivals through his doctor's eyes:

One day the camp gates opened and through them stumbled a procession of scarecrows. They were emaciated, dirty and completely demoralised, and were led by their only sighted member. They presented a macabre sight as each rested a hand on the shoulder of the man in front. Their blindness was due to papillitis, brought on by prolonged vitamin deficiency. They numbered 250.[16]

---

[14]Aidan MacCarthy, *A Doctor's War*, London, Robson Books, 1979
[15]Charles Whitehead, BBC People's War, *www.bbc.co.uk*
[16]Aidan MacCarthy, *A Doctor's War*, London, Robson Books 1979

The 250 skeletal men were the only survivors of the original group of 1000 sent to build the airfield. Although the existing prisoners were not allowed contact with the emaciated survivors, extra food and soap was pilfered by outside working parties to help 'the scarecrows', until some at least recovered their sight.

It was the local women who earned the respect of the POWs. Ron Bryer stayed behind in Bandung when other prisoners were dispatched to the Bicycle Camp in the capital. On the weekly outings for Ron and other POWs to fetch wood back to the camp, local women risked beatings by giving them food and cigarettes. If they were caught, the women's hair was cut off as a punishment. From the windows of the nearby jail, shaven-headed women would wave, and shout encouragement to the prisoners.

Just before he left Java, the RAF's Sidney Lawrence and other POWs were taken to a field near his camp. He knew they were there to witness something bad when 10-15 women of various ages from Holland were led into the field, 'Very lovely, brave Dutch women. They set (dozens of) Japanese soldiers on them there and then and raped them...they just laughingly took turns to violate them. It was horrible to see. How many survived I do not know.' The prisoners were forced to watch, and if they turned away, they were beaten with a rifle butt, 'I wet myself. I am not ashamed of that. And I wept. The helplessness and the pity of having to watch it. I can still weep today when it comes back to me.'[17]

[17]Imperial War Museum Sound Archive

In all Far East prison camps, the treatment of POWs reflected the personality of the camp commandant. Australian POWs found the regime at Bicycle Camp reasonably benign when they arrived, but treatment changed dramatically with the arrival of the new commandant, Lieutenant Kenichi Sonei (also known as Sone), and a fresh group of Japanese and Korean guards. It was soon an open secret that Sonei was an opium addict and a drinker. His behaviour grew ever more erratic and extreme, and he often came back to the camp at night drunk or high on drugs, wildly beating anyone nearby with his stick.

Dr Aidan MacCarthy was one of those welcomed to the Bicycle Camp by Lt Sonei in January 1944. The camp commandant kept them standing in the scorching sun for two hours as he screamed and shouted at the newcomers. He made it clear that treatment would be harsh and that any ill-discipline would be met with beatings. Escape attempts would lead to execution. Then, numbers were pinned to uniforms and heads were shaved. When one POW refused, Lt Sonei himself grabbed the scissors and gouged the hair out until the victim's head was just red pulp and the prisoner was unconscious.

There were also snatched moments of happiness in Java. In one camp, joyful Christmas celebrations were encouraged, and the Japanese commandant gave the men a piano and left the lights on all night. On Boxing Day, church parade was followed by carols from a choir. In the camp at the Batavian port of Tandjong Priok the cooks traded with the locals to provide a Christmas meal including three fried duck eggs, potatoes (whole, boiled), onions, (small, fried) and tomatoes (some, fried).

Catering was credited to Ramsay and Clark, racketeers. The Toast List was led by Pilot Officer Park, toasting the King.[18] When Corporal Grove toasted *Those Across the Sea* thoughts turned to home. Christmas was a short, happy, work-free interlude, but no prisoner could afford to think of home too much.

Christmas celebrations were soon over and, as the war progressed, Japan grew short of manpower to drive the war effort in its mines, factories, and dockyards. The thousands of Allied POWs, a dispensable workforce in the eyes of the Japanese, were usefully on hand to fill the gaps. The next destination for many POWs was the Thai-Burma Railway, for others it was a camp in Japan itself. Battalions and squadrons were broken up and separated, close friendships fractured by different departures.

For some, this was hopeful news. Leading Aircraftsman Arthur Christie, from Catford, was optimistic:

Then came the good news we were being moved to Japan. This raised our spirits. Japan was a civilised country; nothing could really happen to us there. In the savage back-of-beyond of Java, the Japanese troops had very little supervision from their high command. It was the best news we could possibly have received, short of the war ending. We little knew that moment of horror; the glimpse of Dante's Inferno that lay ahead.[19]

[18]*Prisoners in Java, Southampton,* Hamwic/Java FEPOW Club, 2007
[19]Arthur Christie, London, Unpublished notes, September 1981

5

CHANGI

Like Bicycle Camp in Java, Changi in Singapore was primarily a transit camp. Prisoners from all corners of the newly expanded Japanese empire passed through its gates before being shipped off to Thailand, Burma, Japan and elsewhere. Influenced by films and tv series, the name Changi holds a special horror in the public consciousness of Australians. This perception of Changi Camp is more myth than reality. Later in the war, prisoners suffering the extreme deprivations of working on the Thai-Burma Railway would look back fondly at Changi, a camp with light, heat and order.

Relatively speaking, those POWs destined to spend the rest of the war in Changi were the lucky ones. It was a safer camp than the flimsy huts on the Railway of Death, or the forced labour camps serving the dockyards and coalmines of Japan. The former British military garrison was a permanent structure with good facilities. Changi comprised of four three-storey barracks surrounded by officers' bungalows in ten acres of lush green parkland. Facilities included cinemas, swimming pools and squash courts. There was little value in squash courts, however, when Changi was so horribly overcrowded. In the first 48 hours after surrender, more than 52,000 POWs arrived at the camp. The Japanese were utterly astonished by the number of men they had taken prisoner and initially had no idea how to organise, feed and employ them.

As the newly arrived prisoners wandered through the parkland and native villages unhindered by guards, some thought they had landed on their feet. Initially the Japanese held back, and orders were given by British officers. Stores were still full of British Army home comforts like corned beef. But these supplies did not last long with so many thousands of hungry mouths to feed. A less pleasant reality soon dawned on the Changi prisoners when their captors began to provide the food, which consisted mainly of small amounts of rice. The British and Australian cooks associated rice with a sweet dessert and had no idea how to cook it as a savoury main course.

It was not long before it was clear that this initial freedom would have its limits. On 20 February, the Japanese military police were seen forcing a group of half-naked Chinese down to the nearby beach at Changi Point. The men had ropes around their necks and were bound by barbed wire they were forced into the water and shot. About seventy of them were killed and the British and Australian prisoners found another 100 dead bodies on a second beach. This was one of the first massacres in the Japanese purge of the Chinese in Malaya which was called Sook Ching. Many thousands of people were murdered over the following months. The exact numbers are disputed, varying from the 5,000 admitted by the Japanese, to 50,000 claimed by the Chinese. Cary Owtram, who was later to be commandant of the largest POW camp on the railway in Thailand, described sea bathing as 'most enjoyable provided one avoided the dead Chinese who kept floating in on every tide.'[1]

The POWs began to settle in for the long haul. Buildings damaged by Japanese bombs were repaired, power was restored, slit trenches were dug. In March, the Japanese told them to erect barbed wire fences around the camp. The diet of rice often crawling with maggots was supplemented by trading with locals, and by theft. Chickens and ducks were acquired and anything that moved, including snakes, were cooked, and eaten. Vegetables were grown anywhere. Despite that, the food each day was well below the level that POWs used to a European or Australian diet needed. The rice was polished, shorn of the husks that contained vitamins and, in the hands of Allied cooks, grey and flavourless; 'repulsive' was the most common description. As a result, the prisoners rapidly began to lose weight and show signs of malnutrition.

Digging sufficient latrines for such an overcrowded camp was a major job, and initially prisoners did not fully understand the importance of good hygiene. Inevitably, there was a major dysentery epidemic. Sergeant Major Charles Steel composed secret letters to his wife, written but never sent:

> *Dysentery has arrived. The chaotic early conditions, the effects of the tropical sun upon the aftermath of war, the millions of flies, the weakened condition of the men, all have caused or helped to cause the rapid spread of the disease. Men are going down with dysentery in large numbers.*[2]

[1]Cary Owtram, *1000 Days on the Kwai*, Barnsley, Pen and Sword 2017
[2]Charles Steel and Brian Best, *Burma Railway Man*, Barnsley, Pen and Sword 2004

The Allied doctors imprisoned at Changi had brought as much medicine as possible with them, which they carefully hid from their captors. Medical equipment and bedding were scrounged from elsewhere, but around 40 per cent of the Changi population suffered from dysentery at some point. More than 200 men died in the first hundred days after the fall of Singapore. The POWs were angry. Charles Steel wrote to his wife, Louise:

> *I have just seen a gunner die from dysentery and I feel so upset that that I feel I must say how bitter I feel against the Nips, who have caused an epidemic like this by crowding men together like cattle at the end. Once started, a thing like this is hard to stop. Warburton was quite unrecognisable. He could only have weighed six stone — such a skin-covered skeleton. This is worse than dying in action. Forgive my mood.*

Reading FC footballer Johnny Sherwood narrowly survived dysentery in Changi. He said '*I became so weak I could no longer walk and began to pass blood. I sat in the latrines for long intervals throughout the day and night…after about ten to twelve days of absolute agony, and virtually sleeping outside the hospital lavatory door, I began to feel a little better.*' [3]

The doctor put his survival down to the underlying fitness as a professional footballer. In seventy-one games for Reading, Sherwood had scored seventy-two goals.

In addition, there were large numbers of outpatients at Roberts suffering from scrotal dermatitis, universally

---

[3]Johnny Sherwood and Michael Doe, *Lucky Johnny*, London, Hodder 2014

known as 'Changi balls', but also as 'rice balls' or 'strawberry balls.' It was caused by a lack of vitamins. Bombardier Ernest Benford was a victim.

> *'Rice balls to us meant not one of the favourite dishes of the Japanese, but the ripping raw of a man's scrotum and genitals. There was at first a faint discomfort, then the skin spilt and peeled off from the genitals right down the inner thighs. The entire surface became raw, sticky and painful.'*[4]

A few remaining jars of vitamin-rich Marmite left over by the British were used to solve the problem, although some men didn't understand and instead of eating the Marmite rubbed it into their raw scrotal sacks.

As the weeks passed the Japanese captors asserted themselves. Squads of prisoners were sent out to work on the docks in Singapore. Others built roads, cleared debris, or repaired bomb damage. The work details in Singapore meant hard labour in the steamy heat, but they also offered potential for trading with locals, as well as theft. The black market operated by the unscrupulous grew. Dr Jack Ennis noted a kit inspection by the Japanese in his diary where, 'Some fellows had huge wardrobes, Pitt had about 2000 condoms on his bed.'[5]

Back in the camp, the prisoners used their practical skills to create cooking utensils from scraps of waste metal. Kitchen gardens expanded. European cooks, to

[4] E. S. Benford, *The Rising Sun On My Back* — self-published, 1997
[5] Jack Ennis/Jackie Sutherland, *Doctor Behind the Wire,* Barnsley, Pen and Sword, 2021

whom rice was an alien food, learned from the Dutch Indonesians about spices. Living accommodation was improved with improvised shelves or cupboards fashioned from bamboo.

The prisoners soon learned how to catch and eat anything that moved. Frank Fujita, the only Japanese American in Far East combat, was a member of the 'Lost Battalion', the 131st Field Artillery Regiment. He described a natural cycle of life. The open-trench latrine was full of flies laying eggs, *'when they would hatch the maggots would swarm out in all directions from the pit. They were white and made the ground surrounding the pit look as if was covered with snow. Sparrows would come down and feast on the maggots.'* The Americans fashioned homemade catapults from old inner tubes and shot the sparrows before cooking them in a tin helmet. *'Sparrows fried up in red palm oil until they were crisp were really good eating...we would eat the sparrows and in turn pass them back into the trench to begin the whole process again.'*[6] Fujita called this the theory of perpetual motion.

To maintain their spirits, prisoners tried to keep their minds as well as their bodies in the best shape possible. In those early days, before disease and hunger took their full toll, study was energetically pursued. The BBC cricket commentator, E. W. 'Jim' Swanton, was among the POWs active in the informal university started in Changi. Swanton set up a library with books scavenged from Singapore City and thousands of POWs became university students studying everything from

[6]Frank Fujita, *Foo*, Texas, University of North Texas Press, 1993

engineering to Egyptology, science to Spanish. For those not at advanced level, illiterate prisoners were taught to read and write.

Others found comfort in religion. A small mosque was converted into a church, which was renamed St George's. Padre Eric Cordingly helped Jewish prisoners, led by Dr Harry Silman, to use this church on Friday nights as a synagogue. Silman reflected, '*It is strange how men have turned to religion for mental comfort. The Padre has services morning and night and crowded services on Sunday. It gives a certain feeling of relief and satisfaction to lift one's voice in hymns.*'[7]

St George's Chapel, when it wasn't being used as a Friday night synagogue, was so full every Sunday that Padre Eric Cordingly added services in midweek. His positive view of humanity in captivity was marred by thefts from those '*whose selfishness and greed cause unpleasantness*'. During Evensong 'one *of those light-fingered folks removed from my room such spare clothes as I possessed, with oddments of money and toilet articles.*' Such items could not be bought in a prison camp, but friends generously offered replacements '*which has made me feel the privilege of serving among men who are grand and big.*'[8]

For others, sport provided the escape. England played Australia in the Changi Ashes with bats, stumps and a shiny new ball left behind by the previous British occupants. Lancashire county cricketer Geoff Edrich,

[7]Harry Silman and Jacqueline Passman, *Harry's War*, Leeds, Tambar Arts 2020
[8]Eric Cordingly and Louise Reynolds, *Down to Bedrock*, Norwich, Art Angel 2013

brother of the famous Bill, scored centuries in all three matches. The opposition captain, Ben Barnett, had kept wicket for the Australian Test team. Harry Silman never imagined he would watch cricket in Changi, '*It was amazing to see, in a POW camp, spectators sitting around in long cane chairs, some with sunshades, and watching "test cricket".*'

An England v Australia soccer match was less gentle. Such was the Australian desire to beat the Poms at all costs, they showed scant regard for the rules of the game. After twenty minutes the English team walked off in protest, and that was the end of international soccer at Changi.

Changi was as full of theatrical talent as sporting skill. Sapper Ronald Searle, creator of British gag cartoon comic strip series, *St Trinian's*, designed inventive sets and programmes for a range of productions. No doubt his Japanese prison experiences were fertile ground for his post-war series, full of dodgy enterprises and sadistic teachers. Concert parties blossomed. A dozen men liberated a piano in Singapore and smuggled it into camp. Productions ranged from George Bernard Shaw and Noel Coward to female impersonators. Drag artist Arthur Butler, aka Gloria D'Earie, and the Australian Judy (Garland) were so feminine, the Japanese guards questioned if women had been smuggled into the camp. Some shows ended with the impersonator lifting his skirt to reveal his male 'credentials.'

Other POWs sought comfort in secret letters or diaries to their wives or girlfriends back home. Their longing intensified on special occasions. Australian Lt Gillon Griffith, from 2/3 Motor Ambulance, wrote 'We were always hopeful about getting home but time was flying, and my birthday followed quickly on top of our engagement day which, in turn, just as quickly followed by my darling's birthday and our 2nd anniversary. Poor Babe, she has certainly had a rotten married life up to date, two wedding anniversaries, and I have not been home for either.'[9]

Dr Frank Murray, from Belfast, understood the serious consequences of discovery, so he regularly wrote in his secret diary to his wife in Irish. On 16 March he wrote, 'I love you more and more as the days go by and I pray harder that we may be united again soon. I have always loved you my darling and I am very sure that I always shall. There could never be anyone but you.'[10]

The nearby Changi Jail housed sixty children amongst many adults. POWs used their practical skills to fashion homemade Christmas toys for them, everything from rocking horses to dolls. A second jail in Singapore, Outram Road, was an even more brutal environment where POWs who had committed a crime or tried to escape were locked up for years.

Corporal Jack Sharpe, 1st Battalion Leicestershire Regiment, was sentenced to four and a half years of solitary confinement in Outram Road Jail for an escape attempt. Sharpe was 11 stone when he had been captured by the Japanese. At the end of the war, he weighed just four stone. A picture of Sharpe, more skeleton than human, ribs sticking out prominently under parchment skin, became an iconic war photograph in 1945. Skeletal

[9]Gillon Griffith, *www.prisoners-of-japan.net*, Western Australia
[10]Frank Murray and Carl Murray, *The Belfast Doctor, www.belfastdoctor. info*, 2020

though he was, Sharpe was determined to walk out of the jail on his own two feet. His exodus was more of a stumble than a walk but in the famous photograph Sharpe is smiling at the reality of freedom.

Like Jack Sharpe, many POWs felt an obligation to escape but, even if they got out of the camp, where on earth would they go? Japanese were everywhere and escaped prisoners with white faces and with no grip on local language or culture would be quickly spotted. For those who did try, the consequences were even harsher than the punishment endured by Jack Sharpe.

On 30 August 1942, two Australians — Corporal Rodney Breavington, aged thirty-eight, and Private Victor 'Sandy' Gale, twenty-three — were recaptured after escaping. The Australians were in bad shape, having stolen a small boat and rowed nearly 200 miles in the blistering heat in a desperate attempt to reach Ceylon (now Sri Lanka). A fellow prisoner said that Breavington and Gale 'were the finest two blokes one could wish to meet.' Two British Privates, twenty-three-year-old Harold Waters from King's Heath, Birmingham, serving with the 2nd Battalion East Surrey Regiment and Eric Fletcher, twenty-one, from the Royal Army Ordinance Corps, were also recaptured after escaping.

These escapes were a direct challenge to the authority of the new Japanese camp Commandant at Changi, who now demanded that every prisoner sign an agreement not to escape. Virtually every POW refused, because under the terms of the Geneva Conventions on the treatment of prisoners, POWs had a right to try to escape and not be punished for doing so. Japan had signed but never ratified the Geneva Convention. Contradictory views about whether to obey the convention were held by different groups of military and political leaders. Individual camp commandants lacked clear guidance, leaving the rules of behaviour open to a range of interpretations. The refusal to sign the non-escape agreement at Changi was defiance on such a large scale it was intolerable for the new leadership.

As a result, thousands of POWs were marched two miles to the Selarang Barracks and held on a parade ground of just over 200 metres long and 120 metres wide. Accommodation designed for 800 men now had nearly 17,000 POWs crammed into the same space. A Japanese machine-gunner looked down on the prisoners. There was no food, very little water and no toilets in what was, in terms of numbers, now a small town. Soon the stench of human excrement and sweat pervaded the small barracks. Flies outnumbered prisoners. During the first night latrines were dug through the concrete, and cooking facilities were hastily improvised.

The Japanese decided on a stark warning to the rebellious prisoners at Selarang. As thousands of POWs were marched to their overcrowded accommodation, the four escapees were escorted down to the beach to face a firing squad. Rod Breavington had been born in Southend in England but was now a policeman in the Australian state of Victoria. Breavington protested that, as the senior man, he was responsible for the escape, and therefore that Private Gale should not be executed. The Japanese ignored the plea. Senior British and Australian officers were forced to watch as the firing squad shot the four men, all of whom refused to wear blindfolds. The executioners were Indians, many of whom had been persuaded by the Japanese to change sides after the fall of Singapore.

One report suggested that Breavington read from the New Testament, another that he was clutching a photograph of his wife. What is in no doubt is that the executioners botched the job badly. It took at least eight bullets to kill Rod Breavington. His commanding officer, Major General Frederick 'Black Jack' Galleghan, witnessed the executions and tears ran down his face when he described the brutal scene to his men. In a letter to Breavington's wife Margaret, back in Victoria, Galleghan called him 'the bravest man I have ever known.'

Despite the executions, the POWs refused to back down and their spirits remained undimmed. British and Australians were one united force. Doors were ripped off for firewood. An emergency appendicectomy was performed by lamplight. The POWs sang together in a giant choir, starting with *Waltzing Matilda* and followed by *Land of Hope and Glory*. Harry Silman described the night-time atmosphere as 'an amazing sight. The courtyard looked like Hyde Park with its flickering lights, concerts going on in every corner, pianos playing for sing-songs, men feverishly digging latrines by lamplight.'

This defiance could not prevent dysentery breaking out in the unsanitary conditions. The weaker men began to die. The Japanese reduced food further and threatened to move more than 2000 very sick patients from the hospital onto the already brutally overcrowded parade ground. The senior Australian doctor warned that with open latrines and little water a significant rise in deaths was inevitable—400 in the first week alone. After three days, the senior officers finally ordered the men to sign the agreement not to escape, but 'under duress.'

Signatories included Donald Duck, Mickey Mouse, and Ned Kelly.

On the eve of release, the POWs celebrated with a concert including an orchestra and all the stars of the Southern Area Concert Party:

> *A stage was somehow made out of two or three trailers parked together; lights, curtains and props were organised, and when the curtain went up, there must have been nearly 15000 pairs of eyes riveted on the stage. The star turn was Bobby Spong, the best-known female impersonator in Changi, "When Bobby Spong came on magnificently dressed as a woman, the roar that went up from that square must have been heard all over the island."*[11]

Despite the spirit of resistance expressed by the concert, Selarang was a grim foretaste of the future. Soon after, the incident drafts of POWs were shipped out as forced labour for the Japanese war effort. The unluckiest — the men judged to be the strongest — were sent to build the railway from Thailand to Burma, the Railway of Death as it became known. Such were the conditions they were to endure on the railway that, despite the dysentery and brutality, they looked back on Changi with fondness.

[11]Sears Eldredge, *Captive Audiences/Captive Performers*, St Paul, Minnesota, Macalester College, 2004

6

The River Kwai Railway

In 1942 and 1943, thousands of British and Australian POWs in Singapore were told they were being moved out of the camp at Changi. The Japanese promised more food 'up country' and lighter work. Their destination was not revealed, nor was the work the men would be undertaking. Only the fittest were to travel, but even the 'fittest' included undernourished men still suffering from malaria or beriberi. Only the sickest hospital patients were left behind in Singapore.

After long months of hunger and boredom in Changi, the majority were hopeful for the change. The overcrowding and lack of food beyond the daily rice rations meant that surely life had to be better out of the city? It was only with hindsight that the POWs understood that Changi was a relatively safe camp. Australian POW Hugh Clarke summed up the luck involved.

'Being a prisoner of war of the Japanese was to become an involuntary subscriber to an extraordinary lottery. You could remain hungry or bored in Changi but relatively undisturbed by your captors...or you could crack the bad luck jackpot and end up on the railway.'[1]

---

[1]Hugh Clarke, *Last Stop Nagasaki,* Australia, Allen and Unwin, 1984

SIAM TO BURMA RAILWAY

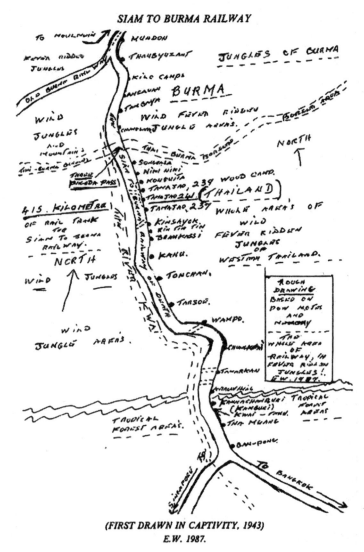

(FIRST DRAWN IN CAPTIVITY, 1943)
E.W. 1987.

Hand drawn in 1943 by Ernest Warwick.

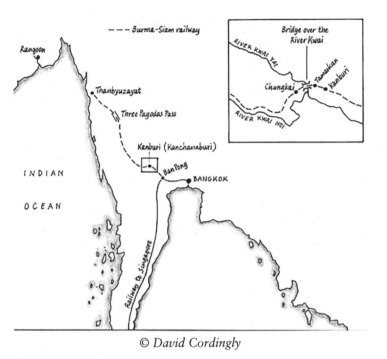

© David Cordingly

The enormously ambitious Thailand (then Siam)-Burma railway project had been considered on several occasions before the war. As far back as 1885, British engineers had surveyed the route but the mountainous terrain, threaded with rivers swollen by the monsoon, had always been full of impossible obstacles and the likely death toll too high. Now the Japanese badly needed a secure supply line from Thailand that could provide its forces in Burma with a regular flow of raw materials, including rice and oil. The alternative sea journey to Rangoon in Burma via Singapore and the Straits of Malacca was long and slow and increasingly vulnerable to Allied attacks. Heavy losses in the Battle of Midway in June 1942 seriously weakened the ability of the Japanese Navy to protect their supply lines. In Tokyo, the case for building a railway became unanswerable.

Luckily for them, the Japanese had a readily available labour force of POWs in Changi Camp and elsewhere. However, their skills as engineers and sappers would be of little value because the prisoners were not given mechanised machinery to construct 258 miles of track, including over 10 miles of bridges. Although some of the railway was to be built across flatter countryside than commonly understood, the majority traversed the most treacherous terrain imaginable. The Thai-Burma Railway was to be built through thick jungles and over swollen rivers, and across mountain passes nearly 5,000 feet high, all with only rudimentary hand tools.

Railway engineers had calculated it would take up to five years to construct such an ambitious line in peacetime, but the Japanese needed the railway to be built in eighteen months or less. Of the 61,000 prisoners shipped out to be railway navvies, half were British. The second largest group consisted of 18,000 Dutch or Dutch-Indonesian prisoners, followed by 13,000 Australians and 650 Americans.

The Australians were mainly transported to the northern end of the line at Thanbyuzayat in Burma, while the British prisoners started in the south at Ban Pong, Thailand. The plan was for the line to link up in the middle near Three Pagodas Pass. This monumental task would involve 4 million cubic metres of earthworks and 300,000 cubic metres of rock clearing in the most hostile environment imaginable. Even before work started, some POWs stood for two hours in the burning sun while a Japanese Lieutenant Colonel made the dispensability of their wretched lives clear, emphasising that the railway would be built over 'the white men's bodies if necessary.'[2] It was no wonder that later it was said that one man died for every sleeper laid on the railway.

Dreams that their new lives in the country would be an improvement on Changi were soon extinguished. At the railway station in Singapore, POWs were crammed into metal trucks at bayonet point, before heading north. Johnny Sherwood, as a professional footballer, was one of the fittest men but said:

It was unbearable. The scorching sun made the steel walls of our truck burning to touch. After travelling for about five hours, men began to pass out and, being packed so tightly together in these trucks, it was almost impossible to fall on the floor, let alone sit down... Some men couldn't help themselves and urinated in the trucks. Others had almost constant diarrhoea. By this time, many of us were in a terrible state and the stench became intolerable.[3]

Alistair Urquhart was also on a draft up to the Thai-Burma Railway from Singapore in Autumn 1942.

'Animals would not be transported like this, I thought...it was like being buried alive. The smell inside the carriage became unbearably foul. Several were very ill with malaria, dysentery, and diarrhoea.

[2]Arthur Bancroft, *www.pows-of-japan.net*
[3]Johnny Sherwood and Michael Doe, *Lucky Johnny*, London, Hodder,2016

People vomited and fainted. Dust swirled around the wagon stinging our eyes and adding to our unquenchable thirst.[4]

In such grim conditions, few prisoners were able to appreciate the natural beauty of the Thai countryside. Gunner Jack Chalker, a brilliant art student, was an exception:

Stop at Kendong, a pretty little station full of flowers. It was brilliantly sunny, and we could see the Malay families in the paddy fields ploughing with water buffalo...a great vista of the blue hills rising from the mist beyond.[5]

Trapped in their stinking metal trucks, the POWs drew an obvious conclusion; their lives meant nothing to the Japanese. After nearly six days the prison train finally ground to a stop at the small Thai town of Ban Pong. Any illusions about the pleasant nature of their new upcountry life that had not been shattered in the cattle trucks were destroyed as soon the men arrived at Ban Pong base camp. Exhausted, they were herded into long bamboo huts. John Wyatt noted 'It stank to high-heaven and was a complete hell-hole...the floor was alive with a sea of mud and maggots, and cockroaches, ants and spiders crawled out from the cess pits used as latrines into the huts.'

Wyatt bedded down next to a man who was shivering with malaria. He wrapped his fellow POW warmly in an

[4]Alistair Urquhart, *The Forgotten Highlander,* London, Little Brown 2010
[5]Quoted in Meg Parkes and Geoff Gill, *Captive Memories,* Lancaster, Palatine Press, 2015

old rice sack and, in that instant, made a friend for life. For clothing, Wyatt had no option but to wear a POW G-string which *'consisted of a piece of cloth about three-feet long brought up between the legs and tied around the waste with a piece of string. It became known as a 'Jap happy' and resembled a large nappy.'*[6]

The lucky had two days' rest in the fetid camp at Ban Pong before they were on the move again. The unlucky did not even stop at Ban Pong but began their long jungle march soon after they arrived on the cattle trains. Different groups of POWs, men from the suburbs of London and the flat fields of Leicestershire, the Highlands of Scotland and the country villages of Norfolk, trudged through the forbidding jungle for six long days and nights. Many marched a distance of a hundred miles. Those prisoners too sick or weak to keep going on their endless trek were carried by their mates, or just had to be left behind.

Most of the planned railway line followed the marker posts planted by British surveyors many years before. A few base camps possessed some infrastructure such as a canteen or a hospital hut, but most camps were simply temporary roofless bamboo huts in the jungle. When a section of railway was completed, the POWs would trudge more jungle miles up to their next temporary home. Working in 100 degree Fahrenheit temperatures, the POWs had only the most basic tools. Earth was cleared, logs carried and boulders moved, all in the blistering sun or sometimes in torrential monsoon rains.

[6]John Wyatt and Cecil Lowry, *No Mercy from the Japanese*, Barnsley, Pen and Sword, 2008

Timber for bridges, cuttings and sleepers was felled from nearby trees and then the huge logs cut and carried by hand. Rock and earth were moved by shovels and picks and then carted away in small bamboo baskets. The POWs quickly understood that they had been reduced, now, to beasts of burden.

Reg Bulled from the Royal Corps of Signals summed up this harsh existence:

Just imagine standing on bare rock with nothing on your feet or head, dressed only in a G-string, with the midday sun often up to 110 degrees, and only a little rice and a little vegetable for meals, swinging a sledgehammer for 12 or 15 hours a day, seven days a week.[7]

The only help was occasional support from an elephant. These creatures were much loved by the prisoners, not just because their strength saved the men from back-breaking work, but for their majesty and gentleness. Raymond Wheeler, a twenty-year-old journalist from Victoria in Australia, spent a few happy weeks driving an elderly elephant, but the animal was as badly treated as the POWs. 'They took me off driving and I came back one night, and there she was dead alongside the track. The next morning the whole carcass was moving from the big maggots that got in. She was a beautiful, real old beast, a dear old soul'.[8]

Neither Japanese nor conscripted Korean guards were educated or experienced. The best Japanese soldiers

[7]Reg Bulled, *www.fareasternheroes.org*
[8]Australian War Film Archive, Canberra, University of NSW, Canberra 15th September 2003

were fighting, and so the role of prison guard in a jungle encampment was reserved for those not capable of serving on the frontline. In addition, the number of guards was limited, and so they were as stretched out as the railway line itself. As a result, a junior soldier could find himself responsible for large numbers of POWs, including officers. They understood as little of Western culture and language as the prisoners did of the Japanese. The potential for misunderstanding was enormous. Under these circumstances, the easiest method of controlling the railway navvies was force. Prisoners reserved a special hatred for the Koreans, who could be especially brutal. This was partly a consequence of the strictly hierarchical organisational structure, with the Koreans at the bottom of the ladder and subject to beatings from the Japanese themselves. Only the POWs were below Koreans in the hierarchy, and when they wanted to hit or kick out the POWs were the inevitable victims.

The railway project was supervised by engineers from the Imperial Japanese Army. They were more brutally unforgiving with the sick and dying than the camp guards, forcing them to work in unbearable conditions even when seriously ill. Whatever the number of labourers demanded each day by the engineers, the Japanese camp authorities had to deliver. Sick prisoners were dragged out of hospital huts by the guards and had to be carried to work on the backs of their mates. Sometimes they were forced to break rocks while still lying on their stretchers.

Doctors often carried the burden of deciding who would work to fulfil the Japanese quotas and who would not. Australian doctor, Kevin Fagan, was forced to choose a hundred men from the malaria-ridden and malnourished to march a hundred miles further up into the jungle to work.

'Some of them were shivering on parade, dressed in a laplap or a pair of shorts, rarely any boots...I found it necessary to walk into the jungle and weep for a while. It was the most terrible thing I've had to do. If I hadn't done it, then the Japanese would have taken the first 100 they found, and they would all have died.'[9]

At the end of their long working days, the exhausted POWs would trudge back to their camps. There was little respite or comfort there. The diet of rice and watery soup was insufficient to sustain the bodies of men toiling for such long hours in back-breaking work. If they were lucky their meagre diet was supplemented with duck eggs or vegetables traded with locals. These extra supplies were often the difference between life and death. Rings, clothes, even gold teeth were less important than food in these miserable conditions. One POW traded his underpants for a block of salt, which made the food taste a little better. Over the coming months, many had reason to be grateful to the Thai trader, Boonpong Sirivejjabhandu, who risked his own life to become an illicit source of money, food, and medicine.

Prisoners were paid a tiny daily wage, usually 10 cents, more for officers. In many camps every man paid money into a central fund to buy extra food or medicine for the sickest. A week's wages might be enough to buy a few duck eggs, which contained a potentially life-saving nutritional value.

[9]Hank Nelson, *Prisoners of War-Australians Under Nippon*, Sydney, ABC Australia, 1985

Thieving skills were also vital. Jack Chalker worked alongside a fellow POW who was a burglar in peacetime. 'He was a cockney, a wonderful cockney…risking his life to bring a few things in, like duck eggs. On one occasion he had seven or eight duck eggs and he went down to the sick and gave half of them to somebody. He thought they could save his life. There was real concern for others.'[10] Even with the extras from theft or local trading the diet was completely inadequate in such harsh working and living conditions.

Every tenth day was a rest or *yasume* day, although these were less frequent later when the Japanese increased working hours. At Konyu camp, the rest day was a rare chance to have a dawn river bath. 'After the bath we stood naked around the log fire we had lit. We stood in the red, glowing cave it burnt in the red grey river mist, like smugglers shivering and baking by turns. Outside the glow was grey, swirling, steamy mist which rose from the river as if it was boiling…the great disc of the sun appears with the fine quality of fire struck from a moist shell by a low sun.'[11]

These flimsy encampments were inevitably seething with jungle wildlife. Huts were shared with cockroaches, scorpions, rats and snakes. The bamboo bed matting was full of ticks and fleas. The latrines were appalling holiday camps for maggots. In these conditions POWs could swiftly sink to a sub-human level.

2nd Lieutenant Louis Baume, from the Royal Artillery, described the relentless misery of it all.

---

[10]Geoff Gill, Liverpool School of Tropical Medicine interview, 27th July 2010
[11]Ray Parkin, *Into the Smother*, London, Hogarth Press 1963

*At the end of the long day's work we stumble back
to the camp in the dark, along a rutted road knee-
deep in thick black jungle mud. And after a poor and
insufficient supper in the pitch dark, or, at most, by
the dim light of a flickering coconut-oil lamp filling
the foul air with its thick black smoke, we lie down to
sleep on the bamboo slats of our filthy hut, crawling
with bed bugs, lice, and maggots…and in the morning
it all starts over again. There is no end to all this-
except one-it just seems to go on and on.*[12]

The POWs shared this grim existence with about 200,000 Asian men, women and children. They were mostly Burmese, Javanese, or Malayan Tamils called *romushas*. Such was the level of rural poverty that many Tamils were recruited with low-level financial promises, but as the shortage of railway labourers grew acute many were pressganged into servitude.

'*The soldiers forced me to get into a lorry. There
were already thirty other people there. I was wearing
only a pair of shorts and sandals. The Japanese
soldiers did not allow me to go home; instead, they
sent me directly to Kuala Lumpur and loaded me
onto a freight train for Siam (now Thailand). Then
we started cutting dense jungle.*'[13]

Their primitive conditions were as intolerable as those inflicted upon the Allied prisoners. But the local labourers did not even benefit from the meagre

[12]Imperial War Museum Sound Archive
[13]Moonaidy Ramasamy in Nakahara Michiko '*Malayan Labour on the Thailand-Burma Railway*'

medical supplies possessed by the POW doctors, or the military leadership and discipline that maintained some sort of order in the jungle chaos. It was no wonder that the death rate for the Asian labourers on the railway was significantly higher than for Allied servicemen.

The Asian labourers, some of whom had wives and children with them, had never been educated in even the most rudimentary principles of hygiene. Arriving at a camp already occupied by native labourers was an unwelcome prospect. British Private Glen Skewes, wrote of the 'Terrible shock: natives who get sick go out a few yards from others and lie in wet and cold until death! I saw it myself, two dying first night we got here. They were dying in the next hut too, moaning all night. Later they were taken into the bush to die, then when they were dead, were hardly covered with soil. They had not the slightest idea of hygiene or sanitation — no lavatory at all — just leave their excreta outside their huts anywhere for flies to carry germs to food. It would be no wonder if a terrible epidemic of disease broke out in this new Camp.'[14]

Sergeant Len Baynes from the Fen Tigers, the Cambridgeshire Regiment, was shocked by the pitiful sight of Tamil workers at their camp further up the line. 'Some were staggering on fleshless legs, most were crawling on hands and knees, too weak to stand. We were soon surrounded by these poor Tamils whose shrunken lips, but still white teeth, gave them appearance

[14]Glen Skewes, *www.britainatwar.org.uk*, Ron Taylor

of walking dead. Belsen could not have looked worse; I shall never forget them.'[15]

As months in the jungle passed, dysentery, beriberi, malaria and tropical ulcers rapidly took their toll. Australian Don Moore was horrified when he saw friends of his being evacuated to hospital. 'I couldn't recognise them because they were skeletons. The whites of their eyes were grey. Their eyes, like broken eggs, were dilated, just a splodge in the middle of the grey. They had no stare, no focus. And I'm afraid that some of them did die.'[16]

Ray Parkin, a survivor of the sinking of the HMAS *Perth* off Java in early 1942, described a scene at the hospital tent at Hintok Road camp:

'A figure of six feet three inches emerges from between the gleaming wet tents. He is so thin that every bone in his body shows...his collars bones jut out, like bent iron bars, over a chest cage that might be that of a dressed fowl in a delicatessen...This is a man. A man who walks naked in the rain to the latrine. Side by side with other wretches, yet alone, he crouches like a dog without a kennel in a bitter wind. He is helpless and racked with violent spasms. Dysentery reduces both body and spirit.'[17]

Gunner Alfred Allbury found his old friend Micky in the dysentery hut at Tarsao Camp. 'Had there ever

[15]Len Baynes, BBC People's War, *www.bbc.co.uk*
[16]Hank Nelson, *Prisoners of War - Australians Under Nippon*, Sydney, ABC Australia, 1985
[17]Ray Parkin, *Into the Smother*, London, Hogarth Press 1963

been, I wondered, a more disgusting, more degrading death than that which came to thousands in the Tarsao dysentery hut? I had hardly recognised Micky. The flesh had melted from his body, his skin was yellow, his eyes were sunk deep into their sockets...he was only twenty-three and would soon be dead.'[18]

Beriberi was as feared as dysentery. The body filled with fluid and blew up like a balloon, soon putting pressure on the heart. Stan Arneil cared for an Australian mate. 'He was lying there like a hippopotamus. His testicles were so large they were just a little bigger than a normal soccer ball...he died; they all died with that sort of thing.'

The famous Australian doctor 'Weary' Dunlop tirelessly worked in the shadowlands between life and death. His experiences made him hate the Japanese, as he wrote in his secret diary on 18 May 1943 at Hintok Camp, 'I see men progressively broken into emaciated, pitiful wrecks, bloated with beriberi, terribly reduced with pellagra, dysentery and malaria, and covered in disgusting sores, a searing hate arises in me whenever I see a Nip. Disgusting, deplorable, hateful men-apes.'[19]

In 1943 the Japanese decided to hurry forward the finishing date of the line by several months as they grew desperately anxious about the conflict in Burma. This was known as the 'speedo period' because the Japanese demand of *speedo, speedo* was regularly shouted at the POWs. Guards drove the men even harder, with

---

[18] A.G Allbury, *Bamboo and Bushido*, London, Robert Hale, 1955
[19] Edward Dunlop, *The War Diaries of Weary Dunlop*, Australia, Thomas Nelson, 1986

work often increased from twelve-hour days to even longer. According to the Thai-Burma Railway Centre, the record working schedule was sixty-two out of seventy-two hours. Jack Chalker remembered 'speedo'. 'The Japanese built bonfires to light the work at night. It looked like something out of hell. They were really working people to death there...'[20]

Alfred Allbury from Lewisham had his own vision of working at night:

Bitten all over from the swarms of whining mosquitos, my muscles aching, my head throbbing dully from the fever that was taking hold of me, I used to crawl back to the camp in a trance of exhaustion. The nights seemed never-ending...it was a weird inhuman scene...bearded, silent, near naked men shuffled along with their litters of stones, their stomachs were ugly swollen bulges bloated from months of eating rice. The blinding fury of the rains would lash their half-naked bodies and from all around would rise the wild mocking cries of the jungle night.[21]

This 'speedo' time was summed up by 2nd Lt Louis Baume:

The tasks on the earth cutting and stone cutting have been doubled to two cubic metres per man. It's well-nigh impossible! The working conditions are almost unbearable—hacking away at the rock in the full glaze of the midday sun or digging up the thick

[20] *Secret History: Miracle on the River Kwai*, London, Channel4/Available Light
[21] A.G. Allbury, *Bamboo and Bushido*, London, Robert Hale, 1955

red clay and mud in teeming rain: bare-footed with
feet cut and bleeding from the broken rock or sharp
bamboo thorns, hatless and naked except for a brief
Jap happy...and all the time the blasted, bloody
Nips screaming and shouting, bellowing, beating,
bashing...forcing and bullying us to work faster,
faster, faster.[22]

The railway engineers planned for hundreds of bridges over the Little Kwai river and tributaries. They included the famous (or infamous) Bridge 277 which became known as the Bridge on the River Kwai, one of the most daunting and ambitious engineering constructions on the railway. In fact, this huge project was to build not one but two bridges. The first was a 100-yard-long wooden bridge, and the second construction was 300 yards long and made of steel and concrete. The bridges were built not over the Kwae Noi (Little Kwai) River, which the railway followed, but over the Maekhlaung River, sometimes known as Kwae Yai (Big Kwai). This engineering feat, almost medieval in its technology (or lack of it), required more than a mile of railway embankment and eleven concrete pillars. Before construction could begin, hundreds of yards of thick jungle needed to be cleared. The whole project was to be built by human muscle, sweat and blood.

The British POWs faced with this enormous task numbered about 1100, and three months later 1000 Dutch prisoners joined them. The men were tightly squashed into bamboo huts at Tamarkan camp. There was huge

[22]Imperial War Museum Sound Archive

pressure to deliver this ambitious project inside a year, and even more rapidly when the 'speedo' period started.

The characters and images from David Lean's Oscar-winning film *Bridge on the River Kwai* cast a long shadow over other portrayals of the Far East POW experience. Inevitably, the powerful mythology shaped by a fictional film elbowed the truth out of public understanding. The film features an American POW but in the real camp at Tamarkan there were none. The film concludes with a commando sabotage attempt, assisted by several attractive young Thai women. No such raid happened.

Cinema audiences assumed that the British Colonel, played by Alec Guinness, was based on Colonel Philip Toosey, the senior British officer on the Kwai. The POWs who built the bridge have made plain over the years that this assumption is deeply unfair. Toosey was a tall, young banker from Merseyside who had been educated at Gresham's School in Norfolk. His smooth looks and smart uniform reflected this privileged upbringing, but also disguised an inner toughness.

What angered Toosey's men most was that the film portrayed their Colonel as a man so obsessed with building the bridge that the welfare of his men took second place. The real Toosey negotiated a fine line between helping the Japanese and not collaborating with them. Accounts written long before David Lean's film was even thought of confirm his courageous leadership. He knew when to compromise with the Japanese and when to stand firm, even it meant a personal punishment. Everything he did was aimed at saving as many of his men's lives as possible.

If the Japanese were reasonably happy, Toosey could negotiate access to extra food and rest days. He traded successfully with locals and built a small hospital and canteen. He was also scrupulous about keeping the camp clean. Every POW was instructed to kill fifty flies a day with homemade fly swats. Even when cholera was ripping through the camps to the north of the bridge, Toosey's determined insistence on good hygiene helped keep the lethal disease out. As a result, the death rate at Tamarkan was lower than in many other camps.

Sergeant Major Charles Steel, who served with Colonel Toosey, wrote to his wife that, *'the Colonel is a great man...his leadership, his optimism, his stubborn defence against the Japs for three and a half years have helped us tremendously. We have had fewer deaths, less trouble with the Nip, less beatings up. Even the Nips admire him.'*[23]

When the prisoners finally left the camp at Tamarkan, with their huge task completed, there was a curious sadness for the captors. At a farewell concert the British were amazed when, for the first time ever, a Japanese guard stood up to sing. It was, recalled Len Baynes, 'a plaintive song on very few notes...his sad expression as he sang told us, without need of a word of understanding, of the nostalgia in his Japanese heart for his homeland.'[24]

If the 'speedo' period meant that building bridges or clearing jungle or gouging cuttings was even more back-breaking, the monsoon season made every aspect of POW life infinitely worse, as 2nd Lieutenant Stephen Alexander described:

'Rain fell, and the darkening jungle seemed to spew out its own entrails. Paths turned to mud.

[23]Charles Steel/Brian Best, *Burma Railway* Man, Barnsley, Pen and Sword, 2004
[24]Len Baynes, BBC People's War, *www.bbc.co.uk*

*Huts leaked. Latrines overflowed. Axes and shovels
became blunt, baskets caked, dynamites damp.
Brew-up fires were harder to light. Work got longer;
rest days shorter. We started to fade out...no one
was excused work; dysentery cases with streaming
legs, and ulcer cases with bandages exuding pus,
tottered about carrying rocks and baskets of
earth.*[25]

In the monsoon, graves in the cemetery filled up with
water and bodies floated to the surface. Maggots from
the flooded latrines were dotted all over the camp like
wriggling white confetti. But none of these problems
were allowed to stop the building of the railway.
Prisoners were caught in a tightening circle of horror.
Slaving all day in the mud and water, they could never
get their feet dry. As a result, red raw, swollen feet were
common, but many POWs did not possess boots. So,
a walk for several miles to work was excruciating. On
arrival they would be beaten by the guards or engineers
for being slow or late before another day's agonising
work in the wet began.

Sometimes a POW was forced into dramatic action
to survive. Tim Hemmings was with the 560th Field
Company Royal Engineers, part of the 18th Division.
His engineering skills were useful to the Japanese
responsible for the Railway of Death, but one day on the
top of an embankment, a guard who was well-known
for his brutality started beating him savagely with his
rifle. His son, also Tim, described the incident, 'Basically,
he wasn't going to survive and my father, I don't know

[25]Stephen Alexander, *Sweet Kwai Run Softly*, Bristol, Merriotts Press, 1995

where he got the strength from, he killed this Japanese soldier.'[26] For such a crime, death was the only possible sentence but, thinking quickly, Hemmings threw the body down the embankment at the same time shouting that the guard was falling. Hemmings managed to get away with this 'accidental death'.

Not all guards were cruel. Padre Eric Cordingly and an Indian doctor were accused of being spies. The two men were handcuffed together and left in a 12-foot-deep pit. In the early hours of the morning, a young Japanese soldier risked execution himself when he jumped in the pit 'with a container of sweetened tea, and two bananas…he indicated that he was a Christian, and he knew I was a Christian priest. Trembling and fearful, he told us to eat and drink quickly.'[27]

To survive, POWs learnt the art of living in the moment, as medical orderly Ken Adams reflected:

'It's amazing how focused your thinking becomes when the margin of subsistence starts to thin. You focus on the moment — you are hot, exceptionally hungry, very tired, your foot is a mass of pain; you are thirsty and can't get boiled water for tea. You don't care about what's around you — the colours of the jungle, the sky if you can see it. You are consumed by getting through the moment and then the day. You endure. You think about food, keeping 'healthy', staying alive. Mates help you. You help

[26]Louise Cordingly, *Echoes of Captivity*, London, High Winds Publishing, 2020
[27]Eric Cordingly/Louise Reynolds, *Down to Bedrock*, Norwich, Art Angel, Norwich, 2013

them. You do your job by instinct. The future barely exists.[28]

Not every prisoner was as focused or resilient. It was hard for minds not to drift onto the past or the future. Mental health suffered as much as the physical. Some POWs became numb and just lost the will to live. Thoughts of home were a comfort, a reason to survive, but they could also be dangerous. Able Seaman Arthur Bancroft from the *Perth* was comforting a fellow POW who was growing delirious. The man showed him a crumpled photograph. 'That's my daughter, I'm going home to see her'...he was losing the will to live because he couldn't see his little daughter. He died a couple of days later, he just gave up hope.'[29]

John Stewart Ullman had similar feelings of hopelessness on the long march to the northern section of the line. He was suffering from malaria and, after thirteen hours on the move, felt he could not go on:

'The rain forest closed in, dank and opaque and we slipped into a leaden lethargy...I slunk away, hid, and when the last column was out of sight, laid myself down on a bed of ferns waiting for death. Lying on my back with my eyes closed, I felt a presence. It was a Thai balancing a bunch of bananas on his head. I opened my pack, offered him a pair of khaki shorts, and mimed putting food in my mouth...I devoured the whole bunch, a dozen

[28]Ken Adams/Mike Adams, *Healing in Hell*, Barnsley, Pen and Sword 2011
[29]Arthur Bancroft, Australian War Film Archive, Canberra, University of NSW, 20 November 2003

*or more bananas. I stood up and a tremendous fart
exploded, breaking the stillness of the forest. The gut
untwisted and I felt life flowing again.'* [30]

The sole priority of the Japanese was to finish the line
within its new, shorter timeframe. The workforce was
expendable, and the Japanese were not concerned about
how many men died. As Australian Brigadier Arthur
Varley put it, 'The Japanese will carry out their schedule
and do not mind if the line is dotted with crosses.'[31] It
was Varley who authorised the selling of the personal
possessions of men who died, using the money to buy
extra food for the sick.

Survival depended enormously on the skill of
doctors and medical orderlies working in the most
primitive conditions. Chungkai was a hospital camp
towards the southern end of the line which at its
peak housed more than 10,000 patients who were
suffering from tropical ulcers, diphtheria, beriberi
and dysentery. Medicines and medical equipment
were almost non-existent, although the hospital for
the Japanese on the railway line was well stocked. As
a result, the Allied prisoners blossomed into master
inventors of medical equipment. Gordon Vaughan,
a British telegraph engineer was in the forefront of
innovation. Tins, rubber bands, wood, string and
glass were all fashioned into homemade medical
equipment, including stretchers and artificial legs.

---

[30]John Stewart, *To the River Kwai,* London, Bloomsbury, 1988
[31]Arthur Varley, Quoted in *The Japanese Thrust,* Lionel Wigmore, Canberra,
Australian War Memorial, 1957

Condoms acquired in native villages or brought up from Singapore were turned into colostomy bags.

Captain Jacob Markowitz, a Canadian doctor who travelled to England in 1941 to join the Royal Army Medical Corps, became an expert in amputations and blood transfusions. Lacking the necessary chemicals, Markowitz and his orderlies stopped blood from coagulating by endless stirring with bamboo sticks. Blood funnels were made from broken bottles. Needles were fashioned out of bamboo. A scrap bicycle was repurposed and powered a homemade machine for separating red blood cells from serum. Forks were turned into retractors to keep incisions open. Markowitz successfully performed about 4000 blood transfusions. The improvised equipment led Markowitz to calling himself *a knife, fork and spoon surgeon.*

After the war, Markowitz noted, 'the Japanese guards fed sick prisoners pig-feed but even pigs could not live on it. It is because of starvation chiefly that to have been a prisoner of war of the Japanese Army in 1942-43 involved, actuarially speaking, a greater risk than a fighter pilot in the Battle of Britain.'[32]

At the Burma end of the line, Melbourne surgeon Lt Col Albert Coates, who had observed Markowitz at work, performed 120 amputations in just one camp without a general anaesthetic. The main problem was gangrenous legs caused by tropical ulcers. These started with cuts from the sharp bamboo spikes which were impossible to avoid when working in the jungle. Reg Bulled described the suffering. 'The tropical ulcers

[32]Jacob Markowitz, *www.roll-of-honour.org.uk*

were covering most of my body, from the top of my feet to the shoulders. They were all oozing puss and bleeding and the flies around them nearly drove me out of my mind. I was no exception, there were hundreds like me.'[33]

Signaller John Trenoweth was horrified by the very basic treatment for tropical leg ulcers:

Scraping the ulcers with a spoon every day was the most painful way of treating them—nerves and sinews would often be completely exposed—a more bloody looking sight could not be imagined. The men would dread the time when their turn approached and often when they were told their leg would be amputated would be glad to have the operation. Amputations were carried out under a mosquito net in the open air. Some of the sights seen in the hospitals were so ghastly that mere description could not in any way paint a true enough picture.[34]

Sharpened kitchen knives, darning needles, and a carpenter's saw were all put to good use in this innovative jungle surgery. The medical equipment available to Albert Coates and the other doctors was probably little better than that used by the surgeons on the First Fleet sailing to Australia in 1787. On one occasion, Coates removed an appendix just using a razor blade. For minor procedures like amputating a gangrenous toe there was no anaesthetic at all. His fastest amputation took only eight minutes.

[33]Reg Bulled, *www.far-eastern-heroes.org.uk*
[34]John Trenoweth, *www.pows-of-japan.net*, Western Australia

Australian Max Venables was sawing bamboo one day to repair a hut when he received a message from Australian surgeon Frank Cahill:

> *The doctor took the handsaw from me and dipped it into boiling water for a while. Several orderlies held the man down by his head, arms, and body, as the doctor cut off his leg just below the knee. He returned the saw to the bucket, gave it to me and I returned to work. I don't know whether any anaesthetic was used but to my knowledge we had none. The doctors did marvellous things with practically nothing, up there in that hell-hole.*[35]

Not that the Australians and British had the monopoly of inventive doctors. Dutch physician Henri Hekking qualified in the Dutch city of Leiden but had mainly spent his working life on Java, where he had wide experience of treating tropical diseases like malaria. Hekking's approach to jungle medicine involved not only fashioning medical instruments from bamboo, food tins or spoons, but using the herbs growing in the jungle as medicine. That way, Hekking avoided amputations and his patients enjoyed a higher-than-average survival rate. The doctor added nutritional understanding to his herbalist skills, supplementing the starvation diet of the POWs with anything he could scrounge, however unpleasant tasting.

His popularity was enhanced by his frequent use of Anglo-Saxon swear words that he learned from the British and Australians building the railway. Overall, he was hugely respected for his holistic approach to

[35]Max *Venables, From Wayville to Changi, www.pows-of-japan.net,* Quoted by Peter Winstanley

death-railway medicine by the Texan soldiers who had been captured on Java and were in his care. Hekking was one of the most effective doctors on the railway.

However inventive the treatment of malaria, tropical leg ulcers, and dysentery, an epidemic of cholera presented a significantly more formidable medical challenge. Open latrines, swollen and overflowing from the monsoon rains, washed through the primitive living quarters in some camps. On 11 June, 1943, Captain Ronald Horner wrote in his diary, 'cholera, or whatever it is, has already claimed something like fifty Tamil coolies and a dozen odd British.' Just two days later, on 13 June, he recorded in his diary, 'Yet another wedding anniversary away from my Flossie—Oh God I hope we celebrate the next one together. My celebration today consisted of carrying on stretchers dead or dying Tamil coolies of whom about 150 have now died...it is the fact that the Japanese have gone ahead with this railway project without regard for human life or the necessities for existence that makes it such a crime against civilisation.'[36]

At Tonchan, Horner's diary noted an invitation to a meal from battalion cook, Sergeant Trowell. Five days later he wrote in his diary, 'Have just heard the news that Sergeant Trowell has died of cholera. Such a kind-hearted fellow, it is hard that he should be singled out to die when there are so many untrustworthy souls that one meets every day.'

The death sentence of cholera was swift. 'One of the symptoms of cholera is a white stool...this fellow looked down and saw a milk-white motion; and he saw

[36]Ronald Horner, *Singapore Diary*, Gloucestershire, Spellmount, 2006

that I saw it. He just gave me a look and it went right through me; it was the look of a condemned man. He knew he had it. He was dead the next morning.'[37]

Gunner Alfred Allbury described the first cholera burial he saw at Tonchan Camp, a popular, young sergeant major called Dixon. 'We piled up a high mound of wet bamboo, saturated it with stolen motor oil and placed on top the pitiably contorted body. Across the silence of the jungle rose the drip of water from the rain-wet leaves and the hiss and cackle of fire spreading through the sodden pyre...we felt like priests who had performed some medieval heathen rite.'[38]

James Smith from Bondi in Australia was also imprisoned at one of the Tonchan camps. He wrote, while the horrors were fresh in his mind, 'We had to go through stinking slime and mud up to our thighs and in very scanty clothing. It was here that the cholera epidemic caught us, and men were dying by the dozens. Still the work carried on with the men starving to death, being beaten to death, and worked to death, but the Japs did not worry as the trains had to get through.'[39]

The prediction that one man would die for every sleeper laid on the railway line was coming true.

[37] Ray Parkin /Hank Nelson, *Prisoners of War: Australians Under Nippon*, Sydney, ABC Australia, 1985
[38] A.G. Allbury, *Bamboo and Bushido*, London, Robert Hale 1955
[39] San Francisco Maritime National Park *www.maritime.org*

7

F Force

In April 1943, around thirteen trainloads of prisoners left the comparative comfort of Changi Camp for the Railway of Death. This was F Force and, of the many men forced to build the Thai-Burma Railway, no group of POWs faced more hostile living and working conditions. The 7000 prisoners comprised 3,334 British and 3,666 Australians, and about 30% were sick and unfit. Rations were noticeably short in Singapore and F Force were reassured by the Japanese that food would be more plentiful in Thailand, and the hill climate beneficial. To many, it sounded like a mountain paradise compared to Changi. To complete the recreation camp picture, the men even took a piano, a church harmonium and stage props.

Like the other POWs destined for the railway they were shunted north in overcrowded, stinking metal trucks for five days, until they reached the base at Ban Pong. Despite all the promises at Changi, the 7000 POWs, including the sick, were then forced to march northwards. Personal possessions, vital supplies of medicine, cooking utensils and even the piano were left behind with promises that they would be sent up country later. They never arrived. F Force endured much more than the 60 or 100-mile exhausting trudge through the jungle other railway prisoners faced. They were forced to march during the night for 185 miles in fifteen stages, a journey that took two and a half weeks.

British Major, Cyril Wild, of the Oxfordshire and Buckinghamshire Light Infantry, had been holding the white flag when Lieutenant General Arthur Percival surrendered in Singapore in February 1942. Now he was the interpreter for F Force. He wrote, 'The march of 300 kilometres would have been arduous for fit troops in normal times. For this force, burdened with its sick and short of food, it proved a trial of unparalleled severity...men toiled through the pitch blackness and torrential rain, sometimes knee-deep in water.'[1]

The appalling conditions on the long march north were compounded by the monsoon. John Stewart Ullman from the 18th Division described its first moments:

The monsoon season opened shortly after midnight with a storm of operatic extravagance. Bolts of lightning illuminated the jungle like magnesium flares...shafts of rain lashed our fragile shelter. The shafts turned into sheets of water and the lean-to collapsed on top of us...we waited for dawn, huddled and shivering at the foot of a tree.[2]

As the men marched on in the driving rain, 'Hour after hour, heading the column, a piper from the Argyll &

[1]Major C.H Wild, Report of Condition of POWs in Thailand, Military Police of Imperial Japanese Army, 1943
[2]John Stewart, *To The River Kwai,* London, Bloomsbury, 1988

Sutherland Highlanders played a dirge, inexplicably tender, infinitely sad.'

F Force finally arrived after their 185-mile trek at seven squalid, muddy camps strung out for more than fifteen miles in the jungle of Northern Thailand. Some accommodation was in roofless bamboo huts, and filth and disease had been left behind by the previous occupants, local labourers. The line was now just a few months from planned completion and, far from being the rest camp they had been promised, the POWs were driven on even harder. Feet swollen, faces gaunt, clothed in rags and often without boots, the POWs now worked longer hours, sometimes as late as 2 a.m.

Padre Noel Duckworth from F Force had coxed the Cambridge Boat Race crew and a British Olympic boat. He was small of stature but resolute of personality. He recalled, 'We were dragged out by the hair to go to work, beaten with bamboo poles and mocked at. We toiled half-naked in the cold unfriendly rain of Upper Thailand...no body of men could have done better. We sank low in spirit, in sickness and in human conduct, but over that dark valley here rose the sun of hope which warmed shrunken frames and wearied souls.'[3]

In a report for the Military Police, Major Cyril Wild summed up the harshness of the work:

As the health of the men grew worse, the demands of the (railway) engineers were more and more difficult to meet and the treatment of our weak men at work became more and more brutal...it became common for our men to be literally driven with wire

[3]Padre J.D. Duckworth, 18 October 1945

whips and bamboo sticks throughout the day...
Hours of work were excessive, 14 hours a day was a
common occurrence and work went on day after day
without a break for months. Many men never saw
their camp in daylight for weeks on end, and never
had a chance to wash themselves or their clothes.

The POWs could not understand how the Japanese, under huge pressure from their masters in Tokyo to complete the railway in record time, could so wilfully neglect the health of the very men they so badly needed to build the line. Ulsterman Colonel Francis Dillon MC of the Royal Indian Army Corps pointed out in an official report that the 'short-sighted policy' of excessive work demands, mixed with lack of food and medicine meant, 'the destruction of their only available labour was just as bad from their point of view as ours.'[4]

Major Bruce Hunt was the senior doctor at F Force's Shimo (Lower) Sonkurai camp which originally housed 1800 Australians. Hunt was an imposing, broad-shouldered figure and a veteran of World War I. In peacetime he was a gynaecologist in Perth, Western Australia. As Bob Kelsey recalled, one evening he addressed the officers, 'Gentlemen, things are grim. I have diagnosed a disease of which I have had no experience. It does not occur in Australia, but I have read of it in textbooks, and I am sure it is cholera.'[5]

Hunt immediately asked the Japanese for cholera vaccines to be sent to the camp. At the same time, Hunt

[4]Col F.J. Dillon, *Condition of POWs in Thailand*, December 1943
[5]Bob Kelsey, *www.bobkelsey.net*

demanded higher hygiene standards from the prisoners to prevent the deadly spread of the disease. An isolation unit for cholera patients was started. Water was boiled for seven minutes. Eating utensils were meticulously sterilised over burning flames. Rice was carefully kept away from any possible contamination by flies. New latrines with wooden lids were built. Any prisoner who transgressed or anyone who stole from a fellow POW was treated robustly by Bruce Hunt. He might have lacked subtlety, but he possessed an unwavering moral certainty. Hunt regularly stood up to the Japanese to ensure that on many occasions the very sickest POWs would not be forced to labour on the railway.

Once cholera arrived, it was a matter of containing rather than escaping the disease. Swift cremation was one way of restricting the spread. Tom McInerney was on cremation duty several times, and said 'Its's the dread of cholera that hangs in the air. It strikes like a rattlesnake and just as deadly…we had to get as close as the heat would allow then throw the body in as near the centre as possible. This method was terrible. In our opinion it's barbaric, but there is no other way to put them into the fire.'

In his diary, Captain Harry Silman, a Jewish doctor from Leeds, described entering a cholera ward:

Over a hundred thin skeleton-like beings, writhing on the long platform, vomiting, and passing motions where they lie. Groans and cries are the only noises to break the silence. Two or three orderlies were giving intravenous injections of saline, using Heath Robinson contraptions. About nine corpses lay outside covered with blankets and ground sheets,

and a little distance away, the smoke of the pyre
where the corpses are burning could be seen.[6]

Australian Stan Arneil recalled one POW being 'carried from the huts, grey of face and limp of body. The ground is becoming covered in slime where these have bogged or vomited...two poor chaps were carted on three poles and wrapped in a blanket or ground sheet were tossed on to a roaring fire five yards from the cemetery. It was a horrible sight and I pray I will not finish that way.'[7]

The Japanese knew that cholera would kill them too, so the vaccine eventually arrived. Together with the much-improved hygiene, the disease was slowed and then stopped, but not before Lower Sonkurai camp lost fifty-one men in just one week. Hunt's tough love was effective because losses here were still lower than in neighbouring camps. Captain Bob Kelsey paid tribute, 'His fearless sheltering of the sick and exhausted from railway slave gangs, and whose medical skill was so energetically applied, hundreds of us must owe our lives to him...there were many good men on the railway, but none better than Bruce Hunt.'[8]

Number 2 Camp Sonkurai originally housed 1600 British POWs who were forced to build another river bridge, which became known as the Bridge of Sighs. This was one of the most inaccessible of camps, dwarfed by mountains, and miles from both transport links and

[6]Harry Silman/Imperial War Museum, quoted in *Keep the Men Alive*, Rosalind Hearder, Sydney, Allen and Unwin, Australia, 2009
[7]Stan Arneil, *One Man's War*, Sydney, Alternative Press, 1980
[8]Bob Kelsey www.bobkelsey.net

local villages. This made Sonkurai 2 a perfect incubator for malnutrition and sickness. When Maj Wild observed the hospital hut there, he realised why the Bridge of Sighs was so named:

> *Their bodies were touching each other down the*
> *whole length of the hut. They were all very thin*
> *and practically naked. In the middle of the hut*
> *were about a hundred and fifty men suffering from*
> *tropical ulcers. This commonly stripped the whole of*
> *a man's flesh from the knee to the ankle. There was*
> *an almost overwhelming smell of putrefaction.*

A cloud of hopelessness shrouded the British camp. Bruce Hunt and his Australians were sent up there to clean the putrid site and improve the poor hygiene standards. Many British officers appeared to have given up. The Lieutenant Colonel in charge was grateful. 'He thanked us for coming up and, as he said, his chaps had got to the stage they had just thrown in the towel, they were dying of starvation, and they just did not have the will to keep going. It was a shocking bloody camp. We got it sorted out a bit.'[9]

In the makeshift camps up the line, sickness and endless work left almost no room for entertainment or sport to lift spirits and keep patients positive. However, in the large hospital camp near the southern end of the line at Chungkai, sick POWs were not working long days. As the railway project neared completion, doctors encouraged plays, concerts, and cabarets. Entertainment blossomed, and productions ranged from *Major Barbara* to *Cinderella*.

[9]Wally Holding, *www.pows-of-japan.net*, Western Australia, Peter Winstanley

In 1944, an outdoor theatre for 2000 sick POWs was carved out of the hillside at Chungkai. Gunner Jack Chalker, whose powerful drawings brilliantly captured the horrors of the railway, worked on some of the productions. 'Some of the costumes, and some of the plays were magnificent...some instruments were made, so we had a very good orchestra, as well as a jazz band.' [10]

On 19 May, 1944, the musical comedy *Wonder Bar* opened the Chungkai Theatre. 'The sets had been constructed from bamboo and palm fronds. Ladies' dresses were made from mosquito netting; high-heeled shoes were carved from wood...the Japanese camp commandant and his staff sat in the front row.'[11]

One of the stars of *Wonder Bar* was Bobby Spong. He was the best-known female impersonator in the Far East prison camps and had topped the bill during the final concert during the Selarang Incident in Singapore. By all accounts, he was so talented and feminine, that occasionally Japanese guards inspected him intimately to make sure he was not really a woman. Fellow performer Hugh de Wardener recalled, 'I remember Bobby Spong because he was so attractive. He really was. He was utterly feminine, utterly.' [12]Spong was later killed when his hell ship was torpedoed on its way to Japan.

[10]Jack Chalker/Geoff Gill, Liverpool, Liverpool School of Tropical Medicine/ Geoff Gill 27 July 2010

[11]Sears Eldredge, *Captive Audiences/Captive Performers*, St Paul, Minnesota, Macalester College, 2014

[12]Sears Eldredge, *Captive Audiences/Captive Performers*, St Paul, Minnesota, Macalester College, 2014

Not all male performers were as feminine as the Incomparable Bobby, as he was called. When a 'woman' was needed for a concert at the hospital camp at Nakom Pathon, the producers were short of volunteers. As Lance Bombardier Len Gibson recalled, 'An Australian tin miner, of all people, stepped forward. He had a great thick moustache and beard, a raucous voice, and huge muscles. A London hairdresser set to work on him. In the end he looked like Marilyn Monroe. It was marvellous.'[13]

When the newly emboldened Gibson and his mates dressed up as chorus girls for the next production the audience response was ecstatic. 'The roar that went up was heard a quarter of a mile away in the hospital.' Their appearance was so successful that the Japanese demanded the show was repeated a few days later, and invited officers from the other Kwai camps. 'They arrived on their river barges, beautifully dressed with their swords. As soon we appeared with our dance there was a terrific roar. We started to sing God save the King, but the Japanese officer banned that. So, we sang There'll Always Be An England. The Japanese didn't complain about that, but the Scots played hell.'

Few guards understood English, which helped the spirit of defiance. As Able Seaman Arthur 'Blood' Bancroft from Western Australia noted, 'It was bizarre to sit there watching some Japanese or Korean thug laughing like a hyena while, up on the platform a kipper (British sailor) in drag was asserting that the bastard's mother copulated with a camel.'[14]

[13]Interview with author, West Herrington, Co Durham, 2021

[14]Arthur Bancroft with John Harman, *Arthur's War*, Sydney, Viking Australia 2010

Concert parties and theatrical productions were survival tools. They kept morale high and hope alive. As Sears Eldredge points out in his definitive study of concert parties in Far East POW camps, *Captive Audiences/Captive Performers*, productions were also an act of resistance — a signal to the Japanese that the prisoners were not giving up, their spirit would not be broken.

Even in the most remote of camps the men found ways of relaxing from the grim reality of their lives. In one camp, dysentery patients amused themselves by holding sweepstakes on the number of bowel movements each day, with a cigarette as the winning prize. On completing the enormous task of building a viaduct at Wampo by hand, it was noted, 'Baker has made a mandolin out of half a biscuit tin, some wood and strands of steel telephone cable. We have one or two men who play it very well and they had quite a concert here tonight.'[15]

Lance Bombardier Len Gibson was a banjo player back home in Sunderland, but his precious musical instrument was lost when his ship, *Empress of Asia,* was sunk just off Singapore. Gibson was lucky that he only lost his banjo. He couldn't swim and 'had never been in the deep end of Sunderland swimming baths.' As a banjo replacement, Gibson stole some mahogany while working in Singapore and carved himself a guitar. The wire inside a length of Japanese telephone cable made up the strings. He carried the guitar with him all the way up to the Railway of Death where he and a gang

[15]Hilary Custance Green(ed), *Surviving the Death Railway*, Barnsley, Pen and Sword, 2016

124

of mates from his hometown cheered everyone up with a song about dreaming of Roast Beef and Yorkshire Pudding.

At the Burma end of the line, the Australians organised a human version of the famous Melbourne Cup horse race. Gordon Nelson, 2/12th Battalion, was one of the 'horses'. Barbed wire bookmakers exclaimed the lineage of 'horses' like *'Hopeful out of Burma by Easter,' 'POW out of Luck by Cripes'*, and *'Out of Camp by Daybreak.'* Some POWs created dresses out of rice bags and transformed themselves into female horseracing fans (or Toorak tarts as one POW wickedly called them) to add to the Melbourne Cup atmosphere. There was great excitement as they set off. 'About halfway down someone in front of me fell, and I fell over him and somebody fell over me. It was a shambles of legs and arms and by the time we had sorted ourselves out, the Melbourne Cup of 1942 was over. And we didn't win it.'[16] The 'race' had cheered everyone up, 'That gave us a bit of spirit. It takes an awful lot to crush Australians.'

Len Gibson felt the same about British spirit. After an exhausting day's work Sunderland's Own, as Len and his mates were called, 'would always build a little fire outside the hut and we'd sit round the fire, and I would get the guitar out. In no time, we would be singing songs, telling jokes, and laughing. The Japs couldn't understand it. We were laughing, knowing the next day we'd be back working hard and suffering the Japs. Yet, at night we used to forget them.'

[16] Australian War Film Archive, Canberra, University of NSW, 18 November 2003

In his officer's camp, Major E. W. 'Jim' Swanton, the post-war cricket journalist who had been instrumental in educational activities at Changi, set men to repair books. This included the 1939 edition of the *Wisden Cricketers' Almanack,* which was so popular that Swanton only allowed it to be borrowed for six hours at a time. Len Gibson recalls Jim Swanton arranging a soccer match against the Japanese. 'They were playing barefoot, but Swanton had big boots on. None of the Japanese ever tackled him.'[17]

The cricket obsession was not appreciated by everyone. When Gunner Gus Anckorn heard Swanton giving his fellow officers an imaginary test match commentary he was appalled. 'This was a bunch of our officers passing the time of day, listening to an account of a cricket match, while their men were being worked, starved or beaten to death on the railway.'[18]

Wisden seems to have been one of the few tomes that escaped use as cigarette paper. In his diary written at Tamarkan, war correspondent Rohan Rivett recorded that it was common to hear a seller shouting, '"Smoke Gone with the Wind-fine quality paper". In spite of certain protests by some of the padres, prayer books and bibles, their sheets being rice paper, have been the most popular smoking material.'

An even more important act of resistance was to build and hide primitive radio sets. As the war turned in favour of the Allies, good news from the front was a welcome boost to the imprisoned servicemen. Even

[17]Interview with author, West Herrington, Co Durham, 2021
[18]Peter Fyans, *Conjuror on the Kwai*, Barnsley, Pen and Sword 2016

in the darkness of jungle life, successful progress of the war in Europe brought hope that the horrors would come to an end. Radios were constructed with stolen materials by skilled engineers, often trained by the RAF or the BBC. They were hidden inside cavities in beds, furniture, even water bottles or false legs or in holes dug in the jungle. The Japanese viewed possession of a radio as an act of espionage. The penalty was often death.

When a radio was found in a coffee can at Kanchanaburi, a succession of brutal beatings with clubs and poles followed over several days, not just the sergeant major who had been caught, but also nine officers. The notorious Japanese secret police, the *Kempeitai*, often likened to the Gestapo, made the offenders stand for five days, kennelled them in tiny cages, and hit the POWs mercilessly.

In his book *The Railway Man*, Eric Lomax from the Royal Signals describes being beaten with pickaxe-shafts after discovery. 'I went down with a blow that shook every bone, and which released a sensation of scorching liquid pain that seared through my entire body. Sudden blows struck me all over...I could identify the periodic stamping of boots on the back of my head, crunching my face into the gravel the crack of bones snapping; my teeth breaking...the worst pain came from the pounding on my pelvic bones and the base of my spine. I think they tried to smash my hips...it went on and on.' The Dutch doctor in the camp counted more than 400 blows on Lomax and his fellow officers.

An eyewitness statement from a British interpreter quoted by war correspondent Rohan Rivett in *Behind Bamboo* confirms the relentlessness of the brutality, the number of blows, and the death of two POWs, whose bodies were dumped into a latrine and not discovered until the end of the war.

Escape was impossible in this jungle terrain, where a European POW would stand out in any tiny village. Nor was it in the interests of locals to risk sheltering or feeding escaped prisoners. Reporting escapees to the Japanese authorities was a much more prudent, and sometimes lucrative, course of action. That did not stop some prisoners from trying. Alistair Urquhart recalled seeing a recaptured escapee one morning who had been beaten so badly he was unrecognisable. He was made to kneel and then, in front of fellow POWs, the Japanese cut the man's head off with a sword. 'I felt a collective gasp of impotent anger and revulsion. It was a scene from another age. I thought of the French revolution when the crowds went mad for the guillotine.'[19]

Almost all POWs were focused on survival, rather than risking escape. They kept their heads down, avoided confrontation, and lived for the moment. But even a prudent man could still be taken away by tropical disease. For all the lack of food and medicine, or the substantial death and sickness toll from cholera, dysentery, beriberi or tropical ulcers, the Japanese pressed on remorselessly. It was what their masters in Tokyo demanded. However many prisoners died, embankments still had to be built, viaducts erected, cuttings gouged, and passes blasted though hillsides.

The Railway of Death was officially opened on 25 October 1943. The opening ceremony was an exercise in

[19]Alistair Urquhart, *The Forgotten Highlander*, London, Little Brown 2010

propaganda; bands played, flags were waved, prisoners had their ragged loin cloths replaced with cheap cotton shorts. Australian Roy Cornford reluctantly held the last symbolic peg in place for a Japanese officer to hammer in the final rail. The railway sleepers had been made by Mitsubishi, who some of the POWs would soon be forced to labour for in Nagasaki. In just sixteen months, more than 250 miles of railway had been built with just primitive hand tools, supplemented by some elephants. Millions of tons of rocks had been shifted, hundreds of bridges built. Thousands of lives had been sacrificed in the process.

The railway never carried as many goods as planned because it became an inevitable magnet for Allied bombings. Bridges that had taken a superhuman effort over months to build could be quickly destroyed in minutes in a bombing raid. The Bridge(s) on the River Kwai and the anti-aircraft battery nearby became an obvious target for Allied bombers. With no POW signs permitted by the Japanese, the camp closest to the bridge was collateral damage. Tamarkan was hit on 29 November 1944, and several times more in the following months. Rohan Rivett was a witness. 'It was not until late on the second day that the last of our seventeen corpses was recovered...from where we lay it was only forty yards to the lip of the (bomb) crater.'

When their heroic labours were completed some of the lucky survivors of the River Kwai Railway were shipped back down the line, mostly to Changi. Many were still suffering from malaria and malnutrition when they returned. Others were shifted to different building projects like the Mergui Road, where conditions were just as bad as on the railway. Estimates of the overall railway death toll vary, because so many died soon after their return. It is most likely that more than 12,000 prisoners, half of them British, died. This was a death rate of about 20 per cent.

F Force laboured in the most savage conditions of all. Out of their 7,000 men, around 3,100 died—a mortality figure of more than 44 per cent—by April 1943. The figures for the British camp at Sonkurai were even more appalling. As Geoff Gill and Meg Parkes note in *Burma Railway Medicine* (Palatine 2017), one F Force report calculated that the death rate in Sonkurai camp 2 was 64 per cent immediately, but with an ultimate death rate close to 100 per cent.

No one knows exactly how many native workers, who worked in similar conditions but without medical support, military organisation, or basic education, lost their lives. Gill and Parkes say that the death figure of 150,000-200,000 in one Australian report is probably 'a little exaggerated' but report that at the camp at Ipoh the Chinese civilian workforce started with 690 men and, eighteen months later only nineteen were still alive, a mortality rate of 91 per cent.

In this grim context, Major Bruce Hunt's determined emphasis on cleanliness and disease prevention kept the deaths at his camp remarkably low. Australian government figures claim that out of 1800 prisoners only 151 died — that is 8 per cent. Even if that is an underestimate, it was still a remarkable achievement. Yet, for the wretched prisoners, it was not just about the numbers of dead, the cold statistics, it was also the appalling circumstances of those deaths.

Signaller John Trenoweth from Sydney summed this up:

Men died not heroically, nor in a clean way, but in filth. There was something clean and noble about the wounds and deaths caused by the war; death often came instantly or in other cases at short intervals. Whereas, on the other hand, men died in Thailand of filthy diseases such as cholera, Dysentery, Typhus, and many others of just plain starvation.[20]

When prisoners lucky enough to defy the terrifying odds arrived back to the relative comfort of Changi, they were delighted. They were also struck by how well the Changi inmates appeared. 'They looked so marvellous themselves. They looked so pink and white; it was like coming home.'[21]

In contrast, those POWs who had stayed behind in Changi were appalled by the terrible apparition of the railway survivors. 'They couldn't believe what they saw. They stood there in silence. They were looking at a bunch of skeletons without boots or shirts. Some of the shorts were in tatters. Men with only one leg now. Some without one arm. One man was without his left arm and right leg. If the bandages were removed from a couple of blokes, they would just about be naked.' They were appalled not just by the ghostly appearance of this ragged, skeletal band, but by how few of their mates had survived. Major Bruce Hunt, whose leadership had been outstanding, was asked about the Australians who had

---

[20]John Trenoweth, *www.pows-of-japan-net*, Western Australia, Peter Winstanley
[21]Rosalind Hearder, *Keeping the Men Alive*, Sydney, Allen and Unwin, Australia 2009

died. 'That tough elderly doctor was crying. He couldn't answer at that moment.'[22]

The grim labour on the Thai-Burma was over, but the risks had not disappeared. What the men did not know was that many of them would soon endure the extreme danger of the hellships transporting them to Japan, and in Nagasaki some would also face the dropping of the most powerful bomb ever created.

[22]Tom McInerney, *No Surrender, www.pows-of-japan.net*, Western Australia, Peter Winstanley

8

Hellship to Japan

Between 1942 and 1945, more than 30,000 Allied POWs were transported to Japan, starting with the *Lisbon Maru* from Hong Kong in September 1942. In the absence of so many Japanese men away at war, the prisoners were desperately needed to labour in the mines, dockyards and factories that fuelled the Japanese war effort. They sailed from Singapore and elsewhere in the Far East on ancient, rusting ships. These vessels carried not only large quantities of bauxite or copper, but also human cargo by the thousands. The living conditions on these grotesquely overcrowded vessels were so appalling that they were universally known as hellships.

Ron Bryer and Arthur Christie departed from their Java prison camp on a hellship with Java Party 17A in September 1943. At this stage in the Pacific War, Japanese convoys were not being consistently threatened by American torpedoes, but the intolerable conditions on the overcrowded hulks still made the journey hell.

Ron Bryer and hundreds of other prisoners were tested for dysentery before sailing. A glass rod about 10 inches long with a small hook at the bottom was roughly pushed into Bryer's rectum and then withdrawn, before being wiped onto a glass slide for blood or mucus, indicating dysentery. POWs who were all clear proceeded on board. On 6 November, 1943, the *Hawaii Maru* sailed from Java to Japan, via Singapore. The rusty ship had been built in Kobe, Japan in 1915, so it was already almost thirty years old.

Bryer, Christie and the ragged band of prisoners were kicked and shoved up the gangway, before looking down into the darkness of the hold. 'I recoiled with disgust at the sight and smell of layers of humanity briefly visible around the access ladders. An endless contortion of sweat-stained humanity pushed and heaved down there. Glistening black limbs and rolling white eyes gazed up from the bowels of the ship...a sight reminiscent of the slaving ships of old.' On another hellship a prisoner noted that the men in the hold were so tightly packed, 'movement occurred only in mass waves, like jelly in slow motion.'

Hatches covered the entrance to the hold, so that prisoners could be shut in the dark whenever the guards wanted. Food was usually lowered down in buckets, and consisted of rice with fish, often just the heads and bones. Down in these fetid holds the POWs slept on wooden shelves and even sitting up was difficult. This is where Arthur Christie from the RAF celebrated his twenty-first birthday.

Ron Bryer, number 634454, was one of the final twenty POWs herded on board and was fortunate to be allocated a place on deck, away from the overcrowded hell holes below. On deck, a handful of young Japanese pilots lived in a railway carriage strapped to the ship. In exchange for practising their English the pilots discreetly donated any leftover scraps of food to the hungry prisoners sharing the deck.

The glass rod test cannot have been foolproof because, when they docked in Singapore, Bryer was already suffering from dysentery and was too sick to sail onto Japan with everyone else. His comrade from their capture in Java, Arthur Christie, was also too ill to travel. They were both moved to Changi in Singapore to recuperate, but this constituted respite rather than escape. In early November, Ron Bryer and Arthur Christie were loaded aboard the 4,026-ton *Macassar Maru,* also bound for Japan.

The hundreds of British POWs on board were amazed to discover the ship had been built on the River Clyde in Scotland in 1917. This time, Bryer was condemned to live in the stench and filth of the holds. His only break from the severe overcrowding was to go to the toilets, which were small wooden cages lashed to the side of the ship, with a single, primitive foot and handrail. 'Previous deposits, from half the Japanese Army and the rest, foul the side of the ship below the cages. As the vessel rolls the foaming water sluices along her sides over the mess and regularly swamps the cages…no one hogged the toilet facilities on that ship.'

Tom Jackson, also in the RAF, could never forget the latrine cages on his hellship. 'When you squatted down in there, the sea was below you and you literally got splashed to the waist…all the excreta that was plastered down the side of the ship got blown back to the never-ending queue of men waiting to go into the lavatories.'[1]

The horrific conditions only served to drive the POWs towards deeper defiance. Java-born Frank Samethini

---

[1]Meg Parkes, Liverpool, Liverpool School of Tropical Medicine, 21 July 2007

recalled a prisoner playing his battered accordion down in the steamy hold. Faltering voices started to sing in the darkness until finally the hold was transformed into 'a massive choir of prisoners singing with heart and soul... this is the one way to fight the fear of the unknown future, to hit back at the enemy. Hundreds of voices sing in praise of the green hills of England and Ireland, the white beaches of Australia, the fair dunes of Holland and the bonnie lads of Scotland. And this choir, this multiplied scream of hope and longing, this prayer rises from the bottom of the cattle ship, soaring upwards, high above the upper deck where the bullet heads gaze down in amazement.'[2]

Ron Bryer and Arthur Christie were relieved to finally land at the drab Kyushu port of Moji in early December 1943, before heading by train to Fukuoka Camp 14b in Nagasaki. The new arrivals, eight British and two American, stood shivering and exhausted in their tattered tropical kit as they instantly encountered their first Japanese winter. They were immediately sprayed with ice-cold disinfectant and given another rectal dysentery test.

Two of Ron and Arthur's mates on the hellship were extremely sick when they landed, but the Japanese soldier responsible for getting the POWs to Nagasaki was surprisingly sympathetic. Jidayu Tajima was a quiet, reserved man and he immediately sent for food. 'He expressed concern about the two sick men, something never met with before in our situation. His

---

[2]Frank Samethini, *The Sky Looked Down*, Sydney, self-published, 20 January 2009

attitude seemed to be one of equality rather than enmity or arrogance and I chose to believe that this was the real Japanese man.'[3] Bryer and Christie were destined to meet Jidayu Tajima again on their return to Nagasaki forty years later.

The encounter with Tajima gave Bryer and Christie hope. Their treatment here on the Japanese mainland, in the heart of a civilised, industrialised nation, must surely be better than on the far away islands of the East Indies? These dreams were soon shattered. When they arrived at Camp 14b after their long journey, no food or drink was offered and their sleeping quarters were just long wooden platforms in double tiers running along the length of their barracks. A machine gun post was perched ominously above the camp. This was to be their home until the atomic bomb was dropped on 9 August1945.

* * *

Six months later, in May 1944, Dr Aidan MacCarthy and a second group of prisoners destined to join Ron Bryer and Arthur Christie at Camp 14b Nagasaki also departed Singapore for Japan in a hellship. When their vessel was badly damaged in a wild storm the POWs were transferred to a larger ship, the 6,700-ton *Tamahoko Maru* at Takao, Formosa (now Taiwan). The suffix *Maru* was attached to Japanese merchant ships and meant 'circle'. Japanese seamen believed that a complete 'circle' round a ship would help them return safely.

[3] R.E. Bryer, *White Ghosts of Nagasaki*, Settle, Yorkshire, self-published, 1997

The ship had been built in 1919 and sailed from Takao to Japan on 20 June, 1944, as part of convoy HO-02 of six ships, escorted by smaller vessels. The *Tamahoko Maru* was transporting a large shipment of copper ore and sugar to Japan. Also on board were 772 British, Australian, Dutch and American POWs, and 500 Japanese soldiers. Lifebelts were not issued and were stored where no prisoner could reach them. Nor did the ship display a Red Cross, or any other sign that POWs were on board. Japan would have argued that as this was not a hospital ship and carried Japanese soldiers, no Red Cross was permissible.

Squadron Leader MacCarthy, who had already survived Dunkirk and capture in Java, was horrified by the conditions:

> *It had previously been used to transport horses and mules to the Philippines and only scant efforts had been made to clear up the mess. The holds were still dirty and smelly and full of rats, which made conditions, even by Japanese standards, quite appalling. The cargo of sugar was soon discovered and systematically raided for the remainder of the voyage, thus improving the flavour of our food and tea. The rats, however, were constant companions.*

This was a significantly more dangerous time to make the Japan run than in 1943, and although the POWs learned to co-exist with the rats, they never escaped the perpetual fear of a torpedo attack. Submarines from their own side were constantly patrolling the route, determined to sink every ship carrying oil or other supplies crucial for the Japanese war effort. Every time there was a torpedo threat the Korean guards would slam the hatch door shut, condemning their terrified human cargo to hours more in the dark. Any peace in the darkness was disturbed by the pulsating sound of depth charges, as the Japanese attempted to ward off the torpedo attacks both prisoners and crew expected any minute.

When the ship finally approached the southern coast of Japan there was an immediate relaxation in the mood on board. The crew were glad to be nearly home and to have escaped American torpedoes. Their prisoners were even more relieved that their nightmare journey was close to the end. At last, the POWs were allowed on deck from the darkness below and drinking and singing started. A Dutch prisoner played the accordion. Australians sang *Waltzing Matilda*. The British belted out wartime numbers made famous by Vera Lynn. With their pockets stuffed with stolen sugar, prisoners wondered how they would smuggle their precious bounty ashore. The men were more cheerful than they had been for weeks, and when the singing was over, they clambered down again to the hard shelves that passed as a bed for the last time. Then the torpedo struck.

It was 11.50 pm on 24 June, 1944, and the *Tamahoku Maru* was only about 40 miles southwest of Nagasaki. Neither the Japanese crew or the POWs knew that a wolfpack of three US submarines—USS *Tang, USS Tinosa, and USS Sealion 2*—were lying in wait for the convoy. Did the submarines know that in the bowels of their intended target, hundreds of desperate POWs were huddled together? The submariners did not, but according to Gregory Michno, US intelligence certainly did. They had tracked the convoy all the way from Singapore. At the bottom of an intelligence intercept were the words,

'The Convoy appears to consist of eleven ships, several of them carrying American prisoners.' Michno is certain that Ultra intelligence pinpointed convoys headed to Japan and 'a number of those Japanese ships were sunk with the full knowledge that there were Allied captives aboard. We not only killed our own, we often knew we were doing it.'[4]

Other sources assert that the intelligence intercepts were too incomplete or garbled to be sure of convoy details, and that the majority emanated from Japanese sources that contained no information on POWs.[5] For the prisoners crammed as sitting ducks on hellships, whether their own side knew about their presence or not was irrelevant to their fate.

Just before midnight, the *Tang*, commanded by Lieutenant Commander Richard O'Kane, fired its weapons. The crew waited in anticipation for the one minute forty-eight seconds it took the torpedoes to reach their target. One exploded directly under the forward hold of the *Tamahoku Maru* and a second hit amidships. Lt Commander O'Kane saw the side of the Japanese ship ripped out by the explosion, killing both prisoners and guards instantly. Two accompanying oil tankers were also set ablaze. Men on the deck of the *Tamahoku Maru* were thrown overboard and immediately swept away in the rushing water. Prisoners plunged to their death down into the cargo hold. The hatch covers were blown off by the torpedo. 'This explosion must have killed many men sleeping on them and numbers of others on deck are

[4]Gregory Michno, *Death on the Hellships*, Barnsley, Pen and Sword 2001
[5]Michael Sturma, *Hellships Down*, North Carolina, McFarland Publishers, 2021

known to have been killed by falling debris...it has been estimated that the ship sank within two minutes.'[6]

Sergeant Peter McGrath-Kerr was one of 105 Australian soldiers from the 2/40th Battalion on the *Tamahoku Maru*. A quiet, thoughtful man from Launceston in Tasmania, McGrath-Kerr was deep in the hold when the torpedo hit. Luckily for him, he was half-awake because he was about to go on deck for his midnight sentry duty. 'There was a big thump and the torpedo hit our ship. It knocked me off my feet... water started pouring in over the hatchway, over the top. The water was also coming up round my feet, and very quickly it got up to my ankles and knees and then up to my hips. And I thought, this looks like the end of the road.'[7]

The iron ladders up from the hold were already crowded with men desperate to escape. As water swept rapidly through the hold McGrath-Kerr saw prisoners drowning right in front of him. He feared the worst because he could not swim. There seemed no point in trying to get out, so McGrath-Kerr just stayed where he was. That decision saved his life. Lights went out leaving the men trying to escape in darkness. He floated automatically upwards to the ceiling where he managed to drag his body along the beams until he felt a hatch cover. Then Peter McGrath-Kerr just popped out into the ocean. 'I shot up to the surface. I had gone down so deep and came up so quickly that my clothing was

[6]Report of Draft sent from Java to Japan and information regarding the *Tamahoku Maru*, Australia, Australian War Museum, 1944
[7]Peter McGrath-Kerr, Australian War Memorial Sound Archive, Canberra

dragged off by the rush of water and when I reached the surface, I was naked.'[8] His only thought was, 'It's taking a long time to drown.'

As a non-swimmer, Peter McGrath-Kerr was relieved to land on a hatch cover in the water. Then he grabbed a Japanese lifejacket as it floated by and pulled it on over his naked body. He spotted a lifebuoy in the water and reached for that too. Within minutes he saw an Indonesian desperately struggling in the water and donated the lifebuoy to him. McGrath-Kerr saw that the sea was full of swirling timber debris. The ocean darkness echoed with the sounds of men shouting and struggling in the water. 'People went drifting past. One of them threw me a pair of trousers. Alan Long that was. Then another Aussie came along, Jack Johnson, and we were sitting on this timber for a while, but it started to break up.'

On the *Tamahoku Maru*, Australian Cedric Mellish, from the engine room of the *Perth*, and British gunner John Brooks (35th Anti-Aircraft Regiment) delayed their own escape to cut small balsa life rafts or floats free from the guardrails. The floats dropped into the middle of all the other timber littering the midnight sea. A raft was exactly what Charles Ericksson, of the Australian Reserve Motor Transport, was looking for. 'I can remember being sucked down as the ship sank. After what seemed like hours, I was propelled upwards and, just when I thought my lungs and chest would explode, I surfaced near a raft or hatch cover.'[9]

[8]Hugh Clarke, *Last Stop Nagasaki,* Sydney, Allen and Unwin, 1985
[9]Hugh Clarke, *Last Stop Nagasaki,* Sydney, Allen and Unwin, 1985

Surviving the initial torpedo impact was largely a matter of luck. Australian soldier, Private Eric Hooper, 2/2nd Pioneer Battalion, had been sleeping in the overcrowded hold but, the night before the sinking, a mate who was sleeping on the deck swapped with him. Hooper was swept into the sea and desperately clung to pieces of wreckage. His only possessions now were his shorts, a medical certificate for malaria, and some photos of his fiancée, Molly.

Claude Belloni, a Dutchman from Java, was equally lucky. 'I was sucked under by the suction of the rapidly sinking ship. This time when I came up my nose was bleeding and my eardrums seemed to burst...but here came God's saving hand, for, as I went down, I reached round and got hold of a rope attached to a raft, which later turned out to be a door.'[10]

Philip Cranefield, a naval officer on *HMS Exeter* when it sank two years earlier, was saved by a call of nature. He had been up on deck to do his business and he was still wide awake when the torpedo hit. Squadron Leader Aidan MacCarthy was sleeping in the section for officers, and because of his duties as a doctor he knew the layout of the ship well. MacCarthy was awake because he was fighting a rat when the torpedo hit. The two officers sleeping next to him were killed instantly. Later he joked that he was saved by a rat not leaving a sinking ship.

MacCarthy battled against the inrushing water and, through the darkness, located the inspection ladder from the hold. He hauled himself up to the deck and plunged

[10]Claude Belloni, *www.fukuoka14b.org*, the Netherlands

into the icy sea. His upbringing on the coast of Ireland meant he was a strong sea swimmer, and he knew to swim as far away from the danger of the sinking ship as he could. That was a wise decision. As he looked back, 'I saw the ship shudder and slide. The propellers had stopped, but some of those who had leapt overboard immediately after the explosion had become entangled in them and their remains were still glued to the blades in a gory mess. The macabre scene was lit up by fires raging in the sole remaining oil tanker.'[11]

Dr MacCarthy found two Aussies clinging to wreckage. One of them recognised him. He spent the next few hours as a swimming medic, struggling through the oily water from one piece of floating debris to the next. He fixed broken collarbones and clamped severed arteries, using bits of wooden debris as makeshift splints. It was the most unusual and wettest surgery that MacCarthy had ever run.

Two Australians showed no mercy to one of the hated Korean guards who was well-known for his sadistic behaviour. They hit the man over the head with a length of wood. With one blow his skull was shattered and he drowned. This guard was not the only one. Years later, MacCarthy revealed that several guards had been killed, with the Aussies taking turns to hit them so that no single prisoner could be blamed. MacCarthy did not know how many died, 'but there was a lot of them.'[12]

The Americans had sunk six ships in less than ten minutes, including two oil tankers and two ships with

[11]Aidan MacCarthy, *A Doctor's War*, London, Robson Books, 1979
[12]*Away to War*, Ireland, RTE Radio, October 1985

passengers on board. The floating human debris in the sea juddered almost uncontrollably every time the Japanese sunk a depth charge in defence against the submarines. Only the most severely injured men rested on top of the small life rafts. In the long darkness of the night, the rest clung grimly onto the sides of the rafts and other pieces of wooden flotsam.

Aidan MacCarthy bobbed precariously in the oily, black water. 'The time passed slowly. We watched the heaving waves which looked like undulating silk sheets, due to the film of oil from the tanker. I can only speak for myself, but I was very afraid. I prayed again, and I hoped, but in the back of my mind was a desperate plea — Please God, don't let me die. Not now. Not after so much.'

As morning dawned, the surviving POWs surveyed the carnage. The ghostly remains of the shattered convoy loomed nearby. Bedraggled survivors were still clinging to pieces of broken wood and upturned life rafts. Bodies floated in the water. A Japanese couple cradled their lifeless child between them. A Dutch survivor kindly encouraged them to let go, and the helpless couple said a prayer and gave their dead child to the sea.

Although the much-hated guards attracted some rough treatment, all the other survivors, including both POWs and Japanese civilians, helped each other. To some British survivors, the Japanese were just fellow human beings in need of help. With the first fingers of light a rescue began, but the hopes of the desperate prisoners were soon crushed when the Japanese only picked up their own survivors. Those POWs who did attempt to board a rescue vessel were pushed roughly back into the water.

Once all the Japanese and Koreans were rescued, it was finally the turn of the Allied prisoners. They had already been floating helplessly in the ocean for more than twelve hours. Some of the men clambered exhaustedly onto a rescue boat only to find their ordeal was not over. Seven survivors were shoved back into the sea and told to swim to a whaler which had been designated to take the survivors ashore. Two of the exhausted prisoners drowned in the transfer because they could not swim.

Dr Aidan MacCarthy was one of a group of about twenty exhausted POWs picked up by a rescue boat around midday. They were given water and rice balls by their captors but just as the men thought they were safe the Japanese started beating them hard. Their confused rescuers spoke only Japanese and had been slow to work out that the survivors were POWs. The men were summarily thrown back into the water. MacCarthy and another prisoner wisely jumped before they could be pushed. 'Several of those who had been beaten unconscious were sucked into the revolving screws of the destroyer and disappeared in a red whirlpool. Helping each other, those of us who had been lucky enough to survive swam back to the wreckage, now some distance away. We reached it exhausted and terrified.'[13]

In his solid lifeboat, Tasmanian Peter McGrath-Kerr was one of the last to be rescued. By then he had been in the water well over twelve hours and was very cold. With modest understatement, he described his condition as 'Not too good.'

[13] Aidan MacCarthy, *A Doctor's War*, London, Robson Books, 1979

Aidan MacCarthy and other men still struggling back in the sea boldly decided to paddle the thirty miles or more to land. Even such a long swim was a safer option than relying on their capricious Japanese rescuers. They all grabbed fragments of wood and headed for the coast of Japan. MacCarthy was a strong swimmer, so perhaps he could make it, however exhausted? He was not optimistic but decided to try. On their long swim towards the shore the battered swimmers were spotted by a separate fleet of Japanese whaling ships. They were returning to Nagasaki following a six-month expedition. Although the crew were desperate to get home after so many months at sea, the lead whaler diligently picked up every survivor they could find.

The rescuers scoured the ocean until they found no one left alive. In a short official report afterwards, Lt Lance Gibson, and the senior Dutch and British officers noted, 'Four Korean guards were also saved including one who had been most helpful...the man proved very useful as interpreter during the rescue.'[14] Gibson believed that the interpreter, Minni San, has been instrumental in persuading the Japanese to rescue the POWs from the water.[15] Gibson was the only Australian officer to survive the torpedo attack.

When the POWs landed in Nagasaki, they were met by the Imperial Japanese Army, who promptly told the captain of the whaling vessel to take the rescued men back to the Sea of Japan. The whaler crew did not want to leave Nagasaki again after so many months away

[14]*Sinking of the Tamahoku Maru,* Canberra, Australian War Memorial, 1944
[15]Gregory Michno, *Death on the Hellships*, Barnsley, Leo Cooper, 2001

from home, so they resolutely refused. The prisoners were then herded together. 'Eighty-two survivors stood naked on the dock, and what a strange looking bunch we were, covered with cuts and abrasions from the nails and sharp edges of the wreckage. Salt encrusted our bodies, and our skins were wrinkled like new-born babies. A few local women gave us water and some makeshift splints and paper bandages before being chased away by the returning army personnel.'[16]

Aidan MacCarthy and the other POWs picked up by the sympathetic men of the Nagasaki whaling fleet were then forced to march through the streets of the city. Battered and bruised, they hobbled for several miles. The most severely injured were carried on makeshift stretchers. Their near nakedness was a temptation to wave penises defiantly at the locals, some of whom were jeering the prisoners. Amongst the survivors there was a strange, almost upbeat mood of resistance. If they could survive a torpedoed hellship, then they could survive anything the war threw at them.

Originally, 772 POWs had sailed on the *Tamahoko Maru* when it left Formosa. Of that number, 560 died in the initial explosion or in the water afterwards. It was impossible for the Allied survivors to understand why hundreds of their colleagues had been killed by their own side. Those prisoners who died included Engine Room Artificer Cedric Mellish, from Coogee, New South Wales, and gunner John Brooks (or Brookes), who helped their mates survive by selflessly cutting the wooden life rafts free when they could have headed

---

[16]Aidan MacCarthy, *A Doctor's War,* London, Robson Books, 1979

for safety themselves. The 211 survivors, including Dr Aidan MacCarthy and Peter McGrath-Kerr, eventually arrived at their new 'home', Camp 14b in Nagasaki, very close to where the second atomic bomb would be dropped. Two days later, a further survivor, Dutchman Marcus Antonio, was brought to the camp.

At war's end in 1945, Squadron Leader Aidan McCarthy had a chance meeting with an American submarine commander. His name was Richard O'Kane. This was the man whose deadly torpedoes had sunk the *Tamahoku Maru* causing the death of more than 560 Allied prisoners. O'Kane had also almost killed his drinking companion, Aidan MacCarthy.

9

BEN'S BUSTERS

The POWs who survived the horrors of the Thai-Burma Railway cannot have imagined that their most dangerous moment in Japanese captivity was yet to come. In September 1944, hundreds of men who had survived cruelty, malnutrition and disease constructing the railway were driven on board a 10,000-ton vessel called the *Kachidoki Maru* by guards brandishing sharp-pointed bamboo sticks. Most of the 900 prisoners were stuffed into two stinking cargo holds. Although they had already been brutalised in jungle camps on the Railway of Death, the men instinctively knew they were now descending into an even darker circle of hell. As one railway survivor put it, 'I had spent over two years of hell and thought that nothing could be worse than this, but how wrong I was — the worst was yet to come.'

Their ancient transportation from Singapore to Japan had been built in Camden, New Jersey in 1921 and was originally named the *Wolverine State,* before being renamed the *President Harrison* in 1923. When she was deliberately beached by the Americans in 1941, the ship was salvaged and re-used by the Japanese. In addition to the anxious prisoners, the *Kachidoki Maru*, as she was now called, carried 6,000 tons of bauxite, which was a vital element in making aluminium for aircraft, and over a thousand Japanese soldiers, more than half of them wounded. Down below the ship contained the ashes of nearly 600 Japanese troops.

Professional footballer, Sergeant Johnny Sherwood, was herded into the hold. 'Herding was the word—treated no better than animals. We were just cattle to our guards...the heat enveloped us like a steaming wet blanket and there was nothing down there but a rudimentary scattering of straw, reinforcing our animal status as far as the Japanese were concerned.'[1]

The smell from the human cargo hung on the narrow steps down to the darkness below. No prisoner wanted to join their colleagues in this floating dungeon, but even when the hold was full the Japanese forced more men down with their bamboo sticks. Some were injured in the crude loading operation, and the stink of sweat was quickly unbearable. Within minutes, men suffering from dysentery could not stop themselves, so now sweat mingled with the stench of excrement.

This was Japan Party Three, the third major draft of forced labourers allocated to Japan's faltering war effort. In the same convoy, HI-72, was a second ship, the *Rakuyo Maru*, also loaded to the gunnels with Allied POWs. There were 716 Australians, 599 British and a handful of Americans — 1317 prisoners all told. The *Rakuyo Maru* was also more than twenty years old. She had been built by Mitsubishi in Nagasaki, at the very

---

[1] Johnny Sherwood and Michael Doe, *Lucky Johnny*, London, Hodder and Stoughton, 2014

shipyard where so many of the POWs now crammed into her hold would later work.

In addition to the wretched prisoners, the ship carried wounded Japanese soldiers. Among the civilians onboard were women and children, including 'comfort women' from Korea and other corners of Asia who were forced to service Japanese troops. The ship also carried further vital supplies of rubber, oil drums, and hemp. Escorting this cargo were another eleven ships, including a destroyer, a frigate and oil tankers. Neither of the POW ships displayed a Red Cross, or any other markings that indicated POWs were on board but there was no obligation, even under the Geneva Convention, to mark prisoner of war transports. This lack of Red Cross markings only added to the fear down in the holds. The prisoners had been told before they left Singapore that they could walk all the way to Japan on periscopes because they were so many predatory Allied submarines in the ocean waiting for them.

On the *Rakuyo Maru*, a sign indicated space designed for just 187 third-class passengers, but now it housed many hundreds of POWs. Their space on the human shelves down below was so small that any movement was difficult. Between so many there were only six latrines, the rudimentary wooden cages slung on the side of the ship in which the prisoners excreted thirty feet above the water in full view of all. After the Australians threatened to revolt at the appalling overcrowding, about 200 lucky prisoners at a time were permitted to sleep on deck. When the human stench became unbearable the captain allowed the POWs to hose themselves down with salt water. The comfort women, or jig-a-jig girls as the British POWs called them, watched the men and laughed at their naked genitalia.

There was a reasonable supply of rice, but the lack of basic cooking facilities for more than a thousand prisoners meant that food was still reduced to just two cups a day, with an occasional supplementary spoonful of watery stew. The overcrowding was so serious that the fresh water supply was severely strained. Arguments and fights were regular accompaniments to the daily struggle for food and water. After a few days the heavens opened with heavy rain. Prisoners crowded on deck with their mouths open.

What, the men thought, if the ship is hit by a torpedo? How on earth would prisoners escape the stinking holds in an emergency, especially the hundred or so men who were already extremely sick? The *Rayoku Maru* men were fortunate to have on board Electrical Artificer 3rd Class Victor Duncan, a survivor of the *HMAS Perth's* sinking off Java. Duncan's experience told him to prepare for the worst. He had been born in Dundee, Scotland before joining the Royal Australian Navy in 1937. Duncan drew up a contingency plan for throwing all wooden items including toilets over the side quickly, and to evacuate the crowded holds as speedily as possible. With other sailors from the *Perth,* he also instructed POWs on basic survival techniques, including swimming quickly away from a sinking ship and not drinking salt water.[2]

In the early hours of 12 September 1944, the convoy was unaware that a trio of American submarines was

---

[2]Joan and Clay Blair Jr, *Return from the River Kwai,* New York, Simon and Schuster, 1979

tracking their movements. The wolfpack was nicknamed Ben's Busters after the commander of the *Growler*, Ben Oakley Jr. His submarine was accompanied by the *Pampanito* and *Sealion 2*. The wolfpack had received intelligence that a large convoy was sailing north from Singapore. *Ben's Busters* believed they could attack the convoy on 12 September if they moved fast.

Ben Oakley had no idea that the convoy carried more than 2,000 Allied prisoners, but it was very probable that American intelligence did. Columbia University historian Sarah Kovner in her recent book is clear that, generally, 'The Americans were aware that POWs were being transported on unmarked ships, but this did not stop them from attacking the convoys.'[3] This vital supply of so much bauxite and oil for Japan's military-industrial machine had to be stopped, whatever the human cost.

At about 2 a.m. on 12 September, *Growler* launched an attack on the convoy. A torpedo hit the frigate accompanying the POW ships. Prisoners on the *Rayoku Maru* cheered from the rails as the Japanese frigate went down, and for a few hours they thought they had escaped. But as dawn ushered in the first light of a fresh day, the wolfpack struck again. *US Sealion 2* torpedoed both a freighter and an oil tanker. The blazing tanker lit up the whole ocean vividly illuminating the obvious next target, the *Rakuyo Maru*. Two torpedoes sliced through the inky water and smashed into the ship, one in the fore and the other in the engine room. Australian Roy Cornford described the horror:

[3]Sarah Kovner, *Prisoners of the Empire*, Cambridge, Massachusetts, Harvard University Press, 2020

The first explosion nearly washed us overboard.
The second torpedo ten seconds later hit the engine
room causing the ship to list and sink ten feet. We
realised that the ship would not sink immediately...
the shock of the water rushing around the deck and
pouring into the hold is something hard to forget.
The torpedo killed a lot of Japanese, mostly in the
engine room.

Gunner Alfred Allbury from the 18th Division had been preparing for the worst for several hours, carefully placing his half-filled water bottle near at hand. 'There was a blinding, shuddering crash, and a sheet of acrid flame, and the ship faltered, and then seemed to leap broken-backed out of the water. I tried to get to my knees, and a wall of green pounded me flat on to the deck. I lay there, flattened, helpless, as the giant seas boiled and hissed about me.'[4]

Australian prisoners sleeping on deck quickly hauled off the hatch covers to liberate their mates in the hold. The relieved POWs calmly climbed the ladders out of their watery dungeon only to find that the Japanese had taken all the lifeboats. The men had no choice but to jump into the boiling sea. The danger was acute, but many POWS reported a strange, almost intoxicating feeling of freedom. They might be struggling for their lives in a hostile ocean, but they had been liberated from the Japanese after nearly three years.

A handful of POWs stayed on deck to seek revenge. 'About ten POWs attacked the shipping artillery men at bow deck gun...in the water, lone Japanese were beaten

[4]A.G. Allbury, *Bamboo and Bushido*, London, Robert Hale, 1955

to death.'[5] Australian Vic Clifford recalled that one of his mates, Frank McGrath, 'went berserk. I shouldn't say berserk. He probably just figured out he was going to take some of them with him...Frank picked up a piece of timber — like a two-by-four — and as the Japs came up he hit them in the head. I stood behind him. He wasn't killing them, just bashing them in the head.'[6] The vast majority of the POWs were too busy trying to survive to contemplate revenge. In desperation, rafts, hatch covers, tables, anything that would float, were thrown by them into the sea. Private Fred 'Curly' Wiles of the Bedfordshire and Hertfordshire Regiment grabbed a toilet and jumped on. This was the strangest and smelliest vessel in the ocean.

Some British POWs drifted fatefully into the huge burning oil slicks from the sunken tanker. Other prisoners died when they were hit by hatch covers or doors thrown into the sea by their comrades. Plaintive voices crying out for their mates echoed across the water in the otherwise silent darkness of the night. In the early hours, some of the prisoners who had stayed on board finally managed to launch a lifeboat that the Japanese had failed to shift. They rescued a frightened jig-a-jig girl who had been left behind to die.[7]

Other prisoners reasoned that they were safer on the sinking ship than in the fiery water and clambered back onto the shattered vessel. Some cut down shallow

[5]POW Research Network, *www.powresearch.jp*
[6]Joan and Clay Blair Jr, *Return from the River Kwai*, New York, Simon and Schuster, 1979
[7]Roy Cornford, *www.pows-of-japan.net*, Western Australia, Peter Winstanley

bamboo rafts or floats that the Japanese had left behind in their panic. Alfred Allbury's tiny float was just six feet by six feet, but already there were more than a dozen desperate men clinging on to it. The floats might be much smaller than the lifeboats the Japanese had commandeered, but they were still an improvement on a floating door or toilet.

As daylight broke fully the sea was carpeted with debris and oil. Dead Japanese and POWs floated lifelessly amongst the survivors. Men without lifejackets liberated them from dead Japanese. Aussie Bill McKittrick had made it up from the hold and jumped in the water. Now he was floating on a refrigerator door. His fellow countryman, Roy Cornford, floated on a large box. Inside were fish but they were too salty for a thirsty man to eat.

As the day progressed, POWs kept returning to the slowly sinking ship. Most men searched for food, water, clothes, anything that would improve survival chances. A few also hunted for cigarettes and alcohol. Some roped together pieces of debris to create homespun rafts. One of the last groups of Australians escaped on their makeshift raft, well stocked with water, rice, dried fish and whisky.

In daylight two Japanese ships arrived and picked up all the Japanese and Korean men and the 'comfort women'. At 6.20 p.m. on 12 September the *Rayoku Maru* finally slid into her watery grave. The Japanese abandoned the search for their own survivors at around 7.00 p.m., and the hopes of the floating prisoners rose. Many were certain it was their turn next. 'We looked at the black silhouette of the merchantman, framed in ebony against the golden sunset. The last of the Japanese had clambered aboard her now...a thousand men lay in the scarcely-moving sea, watching and waiting; our prayers we thought had been answered.'[8]

British and Australian survivors tried to board the rescue boat but were roughly pushed back into the ocean with baseball bats or other weapons. Their job complete, the rescuers turned and steamed away from more than a thousand POWs still clinging onto improvised rafts dotted across the water. Some strugglers saw the Japanese crew waving them goodbye, leaving them to drown. Australian Ray Wheeler was among those strugglers in the ocean wished a fond farewell by a Japanese officer who 'pointed what looked like a Luger pistol at us. He was just saying, "Goodbye you all die".'[9]

As a final horror, the departing Japanese ships sped back through prisoners still alive in the ocean. Many were churned up in the propellors of the frigates, others were severely injured and died. A British survivor, Roy Hudson, recalled, 'I'm sure they deliberately ploughed right through the groups floating around the sea. They made no effort to avoid them. I can remember men being washed high in the air on the bows and then going down again.' Another British serviceman, Wilf Barnett, remembered the same incident killing his colleagues.

At the end of that frightening first day, with the Japanese apparently not interested in rescuing them, some POWs were losing hope. But Vic Duncan, one of the organisers of the evacuation, was not one of them.

[8]A.G. Allbury, *Bamboo and Bushido*, London, Robert Hale, 1955
[9]*The Crossing,* History Channel

The rescue of the Japanese had left space in the large lifeboats they had commandeered. Now survivors who had been clinging onto fragments of wood could be distributed across the empty lifeboats. As darkness descended a few survivors willingly slipped off their fragments of wooden debris and took their own lives. As if in response, defiant sounds drifted across the night sea. A British lifeboat was singing *Rule Britannia*. Soon, the whole sea was alive with voices in song.

The second rusty vessel carrying prisoners of war, the *Kachidoku Maru*, had so far been lucky. As night fell, the men crammed in the holds thought they were safe for another few hours. To avoid a further submarine attack, the Japanese captain twisted and turned on his course as best he could. But neither darkness nor evasive action was enough to escape the submarine *Pampanito*. The American submarine first torpedoed a new oil tanker chartered by the Imperial Japanese Army which was carrying 8000 tons of oil.

Then it was the turn of the *Kachidoku Maru*. She was the largest of the ships left afloat and the easiest target. More than twelve hours had passed since her sister ship, the *Rayoku Maru*, had been torpedoed, and about 11 p.m. on 12 September it was the turn of the *Kachidoku Maru*. Horrified crew members saw a torpedo slicing towards them, a vision that explained the colloquial name of 'electric fish'. The Japanese vessel attempted a last minute hard avoidance turn, but it was too late. The torpedo directly struck a hold. The *Pampanito* crew, captained by thirty-one-year-old Commander Paul Summers from Lexington, Tennessee, had no idea the torpedo had smashed into a ship crammed with 900 trapped Allied POWs.

Men shoved their way towards the ladders leading up to the deck but there was not enough time for everyone to escape from the crowded hold. Just fifteen minutes later the ship was abandoned. She had been smashed by two torpedoes. Despite the speed of the unfolding disaster, the covers of the human dungeon below were somehow released, either by force of water or human hand. As the ship listed heavily the hatches became almost parallel with the sea.

Those already on deck or forced out of the hold by the pressure of water were lucky. Some even grabbed life jackets. Ernest Benford of the Royal Artillery was thrown overboard. 'I could vaguely hear screams and shouts from the holds as the bows began to sink beneath the surface. The breath was knocked out of me, and I had only managed a quick gasp of air before I was sucked under...I could see nothing in the inky blackness, I was being struck by arms and legs which were flailing about all around me.'[10]

The surviving POWs heard the chilling sound of gunfire on the ship as two Japanese soldiers shot all their sick and wounded in a mercy killing. Later, there were rumours that the ship's captain had shot himself. As the ship listed precariously at a sharp angle, Sergeant Johnny Sherwood reflected. 'The next few minutes were the most terrifying of my life. I looked down the hatch and my heart lurched at those thin faces, contorted with anguish and terror as the few most able men, their arms outstretched, desperately tried in vain to scale the ladder, against the pull of gravity, and I could do nothing now

---

[10]E.S. Benford, *The Rising Sun On My Back,* England, Lane Publishers, 1997

to help them. I shall never forget that moment. I see it in my nightmares.'[11]

Ernest Benford was dragged under the water and then thrown to the surface again, hitting his head on a sharp object on the way up, 'My next sensation was a searing pain in my chest, I was on the surface spluttering as I sucked in draughts of air, I vomited a vile mixture of sea water, rice and oil. As I rose and fell with the swell I appeared to be entirely alone, there was no sound not even the breaking of waves.'

Johnny Sherwood knew he must avoid being sucked under the sinking ship, 'I took a deep breath and jumped as far out as I could, landing in the water with a terrible pain in my backside. As I dropped below the surface, I realised I must have landed on someone, and probably killed him, poor soul. At the time I had to focus on survival, but later I felt dreadful about that and wondered who it was.'

The burning tanker lit the scene on the ocean, a floodlight of flame. The sea was a fiery carpet littered with bodies and debris. Those in the water could hear the screams and shouts of their comrades. The men who had jumped, or were propelled into the sea, watched helplessly as the *Kachidoki Maru* disappeared beneath the waves, taking those too sick or too slow to clamber out of the flooded holds into the ocean depths with her. The wounded Japanese soldiers not shot in a 'mercy' killing also went down with the ship. The crew appeared to make little effort to save the

[11]Johnny Sherwood and Michael Doe, *Lucky Johnny*, London, Hodder and Stoughton 2014

women nurses who had been tending the wounded. It was 23.37 p.m.

Once again, the Japanese had grabbed virtually all the large lifeboats. Any attempts to join them by the POWs were repelled with a Japanese sword or fist. The small rafts or floats grabbed by the prisoners were horribly overcrowded with men on top and scores more clinging desperately to the sides. Most of the POWs struggling in the ocean felt lucky to find even the smallest piece of floating debris. Lancastrian James Aspinall from the 5th Searchlight Regiment recalled, 'Some of the survivors swam to lifeboats but the Japanese just hit them, bayonets or anything. Down they went and they were dead, in the water dead.'[12]

Ralph Clifton waited on board the sinking ship until the very last minute. When he surfaced after the *Kachidoki Maru* slipped beneath the waves, he heard a baby crying and saw it floating in the water. He handed the tiny child to her relieved Japanese mother who was clinging onto a raft. When a Japanese officer with a sword tried to slice Clifton's hands to prevent him clambering aboard, it was the baby's mother who stopped the soldier, and said to Clifton 'thank you, English soldier.'[13]

Some survivors floated for more than an hour before they found a fragment of debris to hang on to. Australian Roll Parvin eventually grabbed a small piece of wooden grating with three POWs already attached, 'Talking was

---

[12]James Aspinall, Imperial War Museum sound archive
[13]Aldona Sendzikas, *Lucky 73*, Gainesville, Florida, University of Florida Press, 2010

practically impossible. Every time my mouth opened, oil lapped in with nauseating cloyness, and burned its way down the stomach...For the rest of that year-long night, we sped up shiny black slopes that glistened greasily in the moonlight and slid into dark mysterious valleys that melted into slopes again as soon as we reached them. With salt-clogged, sore and bleary eyes we watched the moon creep very, very slowly across the vast arch of the sky.'[14]

Throughout the night survivors could hear anguished cries for help and watched as dead bodies and broken debris floated by in the moonlight. For a time, Ernest Benford thought he was the sole survivor. Then he drifted towards a raft with both British and Japanese survivors clinging on. 'I lay there helpless, my naked body covered in sticky oil...I hoped that death would come swiftly. Dawn broke and through the mist I could see that there were rafts and wreckage in all directions. Clinging to half-submerged rafts were Jap soldiers, nurses, and civilians and POWs, all shocked, cold and thirsty, covered in black oil.'[15]

British POW Wally Mole described the scene. 'The sea all around was covered with thick oil and, when the ship took its plunge, it left behind a sea of fire...it looked as if, instead of being drowned, we were going to be roasted alive. The fire seemed to be getting closer to us but after a few minutes that seemed like hours, the fire gradually got weaker and petered out.'

For Wally, if he was not drowned or consumed by fire, the risk was being killed by a Japanese soldier. In

[14]Joan Blair and Clay Blair Jr, *Return from the River Kwai*, New York, Simon and Schuster, 1979
[15]E.S. Benford, *The Rising Sun on my Back*, England, Lane Publishers, 1997

the centre of his bamboo raft was a Japanese woman clutching her baby. Two Japanese with knives clambered onto Wally's life raft towards the woman and slashing anyone in their way with their weapons. Wally Mole quietly slipped off the raft

Mole also behaved out of character. 'Suddenly, there was a young Jap swimming alongside me, and he put out his hand for me to help him. I must have gone mad, because I kept hitting him with the piece of timber until he disappeared.'[16]

Others searched for revenge wherever they could find it. Raymond Wheeler witnessed two Australians who 'would swim anywhere to push a Jap under, the two of them in concert. I don't know how many they killed but both of them drowned because they couldn't get back to the main bunch.'[17]

Although some prisoners choked to death on the oil, the thick coating also protected many from both the searing sun and night-time cold. It also acted as a barrier against sharks. Very few shark attacks were recorded but Australian soldier, Raymond Wheeler, saw a Japanese seaman killed. 'He was still alive but horribly burned. Then you could see these fins swimming round him. The next thing, there's a real scurry in the water and the board they had him on turned, and there was a flurry of blood and that was the end of it. Never saw another shark.'[18]

[16]Wally Mole, *www.cofepow.org*, England
[17]*The Crossing*, History Channel
[18]Raymond Wheeler, Australian War Film Archive, Canberra, University of NSW, 15 September 2003

When dawn broke the sea was full of bodies. The lucky were holding on to rafts, the unlucky were clinging on to pieces of wooden debris. In the middle of life there was also death, as the bodies of their comrades drifted past on the silent ocean. Gunner Alfred Allbury welcomed the new day by noticing that there were only nine men left on his raft. Five survivors had simply disappeared in the night. Despite the horror he saw in front of him, one Australian was so pleased to be alive he called it 'the best dawn I have ever seen in my life.'[19]

When a small Japanese warship appeared on the horizon in the late afternoon, the POWs felt a mixture of relief at a possible rescue and fear they would be shot by gunners on the warship. Once more the rescuers only picked up Japanese and Korean survivors from the *Kachidoki Maru*. Suddenly, some floating prisoners heard the distant sound of an argument on deck. Then a Japanese guard shouted that anyone able to reach the ship within fifteen minutes would be rescued and those who did not make it would be left behind.

Johnny Sherwood and his desperate companions struggled to the warship just in time. Ernest Benford was close to death, but there were enough men still alive on his raft to paddle towards their rescuers. Wally Mole was more cautious about the dangers, but when he saw his colleagues helped on board, he swam for his life towards the rescue ship. They were prisoners of war once more, but they were alive.

During the eternal day the sun was brutal. Those men who possessed hats or shirts were fortunate. Everyone

[19] John Huckins, Australian War Memorial, Canberra

was starving and desperate for water. In desperation, some drank from the sea which only made them crazy or suicidal. Sounds of demented men rang out in the darkness. Sergeant Johnny Sherwood and five other survivors took turns to hang onto a small piece of wooden flotsam. Sherwood had wisely tied a water bottle around his waist and shared this out carefully between the six POWs. It may have made the difference between life and death. To keep their spirits up the men sang *Land of Hope and Glory*, or *I Belong to Glasgow*.

Others caught the sound of less earthly singing. After forty-four hours in the water, all Englishman George Wills wanted was to go home to his mother for a cup of tea. As he grew delirious, he heard a choir of beautiful angelic voices in the distance, their heavenly singing ringing out across the ocean. Another survivor hallucinated that his father was just handing him a glass of beer. One man kept slipping off his raft saying he was 'going down to his cabin', only to be dragged back by his mates. So certain were they of death, that some Aussies carved their name and addresses on a plank with the message 'Left to perish by the Japanese on September 12th 1944.'[20]

One of the prisoners with Johnny Sherwood was extremely sick, having swallowed too much oil. Regularly the man drifted away on the heavier waves, but Sherwood and a determined Scottish sergeant always managed to drag him back to safety. Eventually, they knew they could rescue the sick man no more without jeopardising the survival of the rest of the small group.

[20]Michael Sturma, *Hellship Down*, North Carolina, McFarland Publishers, 2021

Reluctantly they took the hard decision to let him slip away next time. 'We felt terrible about it, but what other option did we have? It was survive or die, and this man was beyond saving. But I've been haunted about it ever since, plagued by guilt. How could I have let a man die like that? I don't think I'll ever forgive myself.'[21]

Arthur Bancroft was only twenty-one but he had already survived the sinking of the *HMAS Perth* in the Sunda Straights near Java. His lanky six-foot frame and red hair gave him the obvious nickname of 'Blood'. In civilian life, Blood was a bank clerk in Western Australia, but despite both his youth and desk-bound occupation, he was so resourceful and determined that others listened to him. Adrift with four Australian soldiers he suggested they tied together six solid rafts, 'we can have one each and have a spare, which means we can travel first-class.'

By the third day after the sinkings POWs from both hellships died more frequently. If thirst did not get them desperation did. Gunner James Aspinall from the 5th Searchlight Regiment was by now one of only two men left on his life raft. The other survivor 'kept wanting to go into the water but I kept pulling him back. Not because I was saving his life but as company for me, you see. And we used to tie ourselves onto the raft at night.'[22]

While the survivors of the *Kachidoki Maru* were struggling to stay alive, POWs from the earlier sinking of the *Rayoku Maru* had drifted further away. Vic Duncan, having organised the evacuation of the sinking ship,

[21]John Sherwood and Michael Doe, *Lucky Johnny,* London, Hodder and Stoughton 2015
[22]Imperial War Museum Sound Archive

was leading a clutch of four lifeboats. Although it was 400 miles away, Duncan thought they could make it to China, so what little food and water they possessed was carefully rationed. Also in Vic Duncan's little convoy was the Australian doctor, Captain Rowley Richards, and 135 other POWs. A second group of seven lifeboats were occasionally sighted heading in the same general direction. Leading them were Australian Brigadier Arthur Varley, and American Colonel, Harry Melton from Kentucky. Varley had been hugely respected by thousands of Australian POWs under his charge on the Railway of Death.

A single man was spotted adrift on a hatch cover by the men in Duncan's boat. It was the Australian doctor, Major John Chalmers. He was slowly pulled onto the raft:

He was delirious. He had dysentery and I could see that he was dying...as darkness came, he lay quiet, unmoving...at dawn we found he was dead. And as I looked at him, his mouth agape, his face a thousand years old, his eyes still fixed with pain and delirium. I remembered all he had done for me and for so many others. And for a few moments I became a human being again and was filled with sorrow and compassion. He was one of the finest men I had ever known...we rolled his body off the edge of the raft.

On 14 September, two days after their ship had been torpedoed, Vic Duncan and Rowley Richards' group spotted three small Japanese warships. The vessel heading towards them was heavily armed. The men in the lifeboats assumed that this was the end. They fatalistically shook hands with each other. The Japanese shouted at them and asked questions. They must have been satisfied with the answers because the surprised survivors were eventually hauled aboard. Some were hit by the Japanese as they struggled to safety, but they were finally rewarded with a drink and biscuits. Rowley Richards recognised better than anyone that this unexpected rescue required a measure of courage from the Japanese. Both their ships and their lives were at risk from further submarine attacks.

The other seven lifeboats led by Arthur Varley were too far away to be spotted by any of the newly rescued prisoners. They were not as lucky. The seven Varley lifeboats were never seen again. Surviving POWs like Roy Cornford heard the story later. 'They had set out to row to land. We later learned that they had been sighted by a Japanese naval vessel which opened fire on them, killing all 350 POWs in the lifeboats. We did not know of this until after the war.'[23]

It is just possible that the prisoners died in a storm. However, earlier the men in the Duncan and Richards lifeboats heard gunfire across the water from the north, and so it is probable, if unproven, that the prisoners in the Varley group of lifeboats were all murdered. That is what Rowley Richards believed. The lifeboats and all the men in them simply disappeared. No record has ever been found of them. Cornford's number of 350 killed might not be accurate, but whatever the exact figure, a very large number of helpless prisoners had been killed. It appears that within a few minutes one Japanese captain and his crew had been *'tender-hearted'*, as one survivor described them, but another Japanese captain had committed hundreds of brutal murders.

[23]Roy Cornford, *www.pows-of-japan.net*, Western Australia, Peter Winstanley

10

Rescue

The survivors of the *Kachidoki Maru* were relieved to be finally out of the water and in the relative safety of a Japanese vessel. Their happiness soon turned to anguish when an alarm blared out and the Japanese ship suddenly stopped her rescue effort. As their vessel sped away, Johnny Sherwood, Ernest Benford and the others saw that the ocean was still littered with friends and comrades clinging desperately on to doors and toilets, tables and hatch covers.

For those men agonisingly left behind, a third day drifted into the fourth. Jim Campbell started that day with twenty men alive on his raft. 'Horror filled the day. Six died before nightfall after what had seemed years of suffering. Most had gone mad.' Harry Wiegand saw the same delirium. 'Men were begging for water… our mouths were burnt with oil, and my tongue was swollen. I had great difficulty talking. I must have been going delirious. I saw ships wherever I looked.' Others hallucinated about palm trees, or their families, even flashing signs advertising fish and chips.[1]

[1]Joan Blair and Clay Blair Jr, *Return From the River Kwai*, New York, Simon and Schuster, 1979

Thirst overwhelmed them. Despite warnings that drinking sea water would only worsen thirst and make men delirious, some drank from the ocean. Others urinated into each other's mouths to quench the unquenchable. Desperate men even tried drinking the blood of the dead, or their own blood. Wilf Barnett from Blackpool drank blood from a dead Japanese and concluded, 'It's not very nice but it wets your lips.' [2]

On Arthur Bancroft's roped-together collection of six floats, Bancroft came up with an ingenious solution to their desperate thirst. As a sailor he knew that it was dangerous to drink salt water, but he remembered reading something in *Mutiny on the Bounty*. The survivors began to swill sea water round their mouths, spitting it out, but never swallowing more than a dribble. It was enough.

Raymond Wheeler from Melbourne was with two mates on a float, but in the night, 'Both of them died without a whimper or a sigh or anything, and in the morning, they were just stiff. And I closed their eyes and shoved them off.' Wheeler did not want to stay on this float without his dead mates, but he was very weak. As he floated past the small gang of Aussies led by Arthur Bancroft, he raised a weary arm. Bancroft and another survivor swam over to Wheeler and hauled him up onto their rafts.

On the afternoon of that fourth day, 15 September, the two American submarines, *Pampanito* and *Sealion 2*, that had been responsible for the horror were patrolling the area once again, hunting for more Japanese vessels

[2]*The Crossing*, History Channel

to sink. Instead of an enemy convoy, this time *Pampanito* spotted wreckage bobbing in the ocean. The submarine moved closer to investigate. Ahead they identified men clinging to pieces of wood or sitting lifelessly on rafts.

Their first assumption was that these wretched survivors were Japanese. Accordingly, guns were prepared. Perhaps Commander Paul Summers planned to take the Japanese prisoners, or maybe he planned to shoot them? According to several sources, submariners arrived on deck with an array of weapons including machine guns. Several were sure the intention was to shoot the men who were afloat, like sitting ducks in the water. Some liked the idea, others were troubled. Commander Summers claimed that the arms were readied to take prisoners.

Fortunately, no one on the *Pampanito* was put to that test. One of the crew spotted a curly haired man standing up and waving a hat. This was Western Australian David 'Curly' Martin. With him was Frank Farmer, an Australian schoolteacher, and neither looked Japanese. Other crew members spotted about fifteen men on two bamboo rafts, several wearing Australian digger hats. The exhausted survivors shouted that they were British and Australian POWs. The skipper cautiously shouted back, 'Get the one who speaks English.' The reply was angry, 'You bloody bastards, we all speak English.'

Frank Farmer was the first man to be hauled aboard, and he explained who the prisoners adrift in the oily sea were. The submariners of the *Pampanito* were horrified. Their torpedoes had killed hundreds of POWs from their own side. Now they rushed to help. Despite the risk to their own lives, submariners immediately dived into the water to rescue men who were too weak to climb aboard. A photograph taken at the time shows two prisoners covered head to toe in oil being helped from their makeshift survival raft. The patrol report from Commander Summers called it 'a pitiful sight none of us will ever forget.'

Pampanito spent the rest of the afternoon diligently looking for further survivors and called *Sealion 2* to join the search. Frederick Wiles, from the Bedfordshire and Hertfordshire Regiment, remembered that moment. 'The fifth day arrived, and there was still no sign of help...the party that I was in, originally numbered ten when we left the ship, was now down to three, consisting of two Australians and myself. About noon one of the Australians passed away, leaving the two of us.' Then Wiles heard engine noise. 'It was rather difficult to see as our eyes were full of oil, then out of the blue appeared a ship. Our hearts lifted, and as it drew near, we could see it was a submarine, and American at that.'[3]

Many of the POWs had given up hope. One of the larger rafts had once held forty-eight men. Now just nine were alive. When Michael Deguarra was finally picked up he recalled, ' "I knew I was among friends. I broke down and cried like a kid." There were eight men left on one raft. As the giant submarine drew close, submariners shouted instructions to stay with their rafts. One over eager survivor could not wait and dived into the sea. He was churned up in the propellor of the submarine.'[4]

[3]Fred Wiles, *www.far-eastern-heroes.org.uk*
[4]Aldona Sendzikas, *Lucky 73*, Gainesville, Florida, University of Florida Press, 2010

The final group of seven survivors were the only men left alive from an original band of eighteen who had tied two rafts together. They included Roy Cornford, from New South Wales. One of the submariners swam to him with a rescue rope. It had been Cornford who held the last peg down for the Japanese to ceremonially hammer the final rail into the Railway of Death. Now he had survived a torpedo and several brutal days adrift at sea as well. Only one more man was picked up. At 7.57 p.m., the *Pampanito* picked up a last survivor, British prisoner William Mandley, who had been floating alone on his raft.

Lt Commander Landon Davis was on the *Pampanito* as it rescued POWs:

> *They were just as happy as could be—I remember the first one up, he actually kissed the man as he pulled him up on deck he was so happy to get on there...I remember they said, 'You bloody Yanks, you sink us one night and pick us up the next...we gave then water right away, that was their biggest need, they hadn't had any water. Some of them couldn't even drink the water, we had to give them a wet rag to chew on.'*

The only man on board the submarine with any medical experience was a lowly pharmacist's mate, Maurice Demers from Manchester, New Hampshire. Demers possessed extremely limited medical supplies to tend to the wounded. Crew members sluiced the oil and dirt from the POWs and what little remained of their clothing was cut off. Down in what was a now very crowded torpedo room, the survivors were given fresh American clothes to wear, followed by tea and soup.

The highlight that evening was the first white bread they had eaten in three years.

Demers remembered, 'they were half-dead creatures. Few of them could speak. They were just looking at you like they were ready to pass out or die any minute. They were in shock. I had to give fifteen of them morphine shots…their eyes were real bad. Full of oil and dirt.'[5]

It was night-time now and the *Pampanito* had picked up seventy-three men from the sea. That almost doubled the size of the crew and seriously overloaded the sub. There were no other survivors they could see in the gathering darkness, and so Commander Summers decided to head for shore. As Landon Davis reported formally at Pearl Harbour in 1944, 'It was a good thing for us that we were able to pick every single man that we sighted…it was very lucky — I would have had to make the decision when to leave some of those poor souls back in the water.'[6]

That was exactly the decision that Eli Reich, commanding *Sealion,* was forced to make. They rescued fifty-four survivors. About half of them could not see because of the thick oil, and crew member Bill Hornkohl recalled the terrible state they were in. 'Some of their flesh would actually start peeling off. I never expected half of them to survive anyway.'[7] As darkness fell, Reich issued orders to leave. Perhaps he felt vulnerable laying still on the surface or maybe he thought he had no room

[5]Joan Blair and Clay Blair Jr, *Return From the River Kwai*, New York, Simon and Schuster, 1979
[6]San Francisco Maritime Park, *www.maritime.org*
[7]*The Crossing*, History Channel/ITV Granada,2009

on board for more men, even if he could find them in the deepening gloom. In any event, around 9 p.m., *Sealion* headed the 1800 miles to the nearest base at Saipan.

Some crew members were very unhappy with their commander's call, others understood what a difficult decision it was. As the *Sealion* departed there were still survivors in the sea and their cries for help could he heard across the still waters. Submariner Joe Bates recalled a man yelling at the *Sealion*, desperate to be picked up. 'We left the poor guy and I am sure he died.' Bill Hornkohl was convinced there was more room below, and was distressed by the decision. 'It hurt me very much. I never really knew why we left.' Reich's patrol report recognised there were men still alive. He wrote that 'It was heartbreaking to leave so many dying men behind.'

Of course, the heartbreak was much greater for the men still in the ocean. For Arthur Bancroft and the five men with him it was horrifying to spot the submarine and then not be rescued. They stood up, waving and yelling frantically, but *Sealion* suddenly stopped half a mile from the rafts, turned away and slipped out of sight. 'With hearts sinking and tears at the back of our eyes we watched unbelievingly as it turned away and sailed into the gathering gloom, listening to the diesel engines fading until there was nothing but the slap of waves on the raft.' [8] The men were at a low ebb, and wondered if this was the end, but Bancroft and the five men with him were not giving up. In the morning light they figured out that if there had been one submarine in the area there could be a second.

[8] Arthur Bancroft with John Harman, *Arthur's War*, Sydney, Viking Australia, 2010

They had successfully hydrated themselves with their technique of swilling sea water round their mouths. They scavenged for any flotsam in the wide-open sea and were amazed to see a single melon floating past. It was oily and full of salt water, but the men cleaned it up and drank the juice. On their fifth day, the wind came up and nature gave them a helping hand. 'Rain. It was beautiful, you just lay there with your mouths open and you had this rain pouring down your gullet. We'd already picked a little rice bucket that had floated past... and that gave us rainwater for the rest of the day.'[9] For the men drifting on the endless ocean, it was the most beautiful drink of their lives.

In the sea, Bancroft and his mates were eerily alone. There was nothing ahead or behind them; no ships, no submarines, no other rafts, 'just water, water, and more water.' As a distraction, they lay back on the rafts and 'talked about the food we hadn't eaten...we went through menus.'[10] The rescued men safely on the submarines no longer had to fantasise about food. They were tasting the real thing. Not only were they alive but, by a miracle, they were also free from Japanese imprisonment.

Their ordeal went on until the sixth day. By then, two other submarines, *Barb* and *Queenfish,* had been ordered by the US Navy to join the search but, unfortunately, they encountered a Japanese convoy on the way. Their decision to attack the convoy delayed their arrival in the rescue zone.

[9] Australian War Film Archive, Canberra, University of NSW, 20 November, 2003
[10] Tim Bowden interview, Australian War Memorial, ABC Australia, 11 November, 1982

Able Seaman Arthur Bancroft and his five comrades were still afloat. On their sixth day in the ocean, a storm blew up. A typhoon was on the way. Raymond Wheeler reckoned the waves reached as high as forty feet. The water was so rough the six men tied themselves to their rafts. As they were swept relentlessly up and down on the waves, they heard a diesel engine. At 5 p.m. on that day, 17 September, a submarine appeared out of the never-ending horizon. They knew it was a submarine and glimpsed it briefly as it zigzagged in the sea looking for survivors, only for it to disappear again in the rolling waves. It was enough to give them hope. The Australians waved and yelled. The submarine vanished again. Then it surfaced just a hundred yards away. As it grew closer, they saw that not only was it a submarine, but it was an Allied sub. 'We didn't know whether to laugh or cry-so most of us did both.'[11]

Bancroft and his mates were the last men to be rescued by the *Queenfish*, but their resourcefulness had also made them the strongest. Even after almost six full days in the sea, four of them still climbed up the steps onto the submarine. Raymond Wheeler was so weak he had to be tied to a line and hauled aboard. Finally, as 'captain' of his little raft, Able Seaman Arthur Bancroft clambered on board. In a reflex action, he saluted the captain of the *Queenfish* and said, 'Able Seaman Bancroft, permission to come aboard, sir.' Then, less formally he shouted, 'I knew you bloody Yanks would rescue me.'

The oil was scrubbed off the men, and they rested on clean sheets. They were immediately struck by how

[11]Arthur Bancroft with John Harman, *Arthur's War*, Sydney, Viking Australia 2010

clean, big and strong the Americans were compared to their Japanese guards on the Thai-Burma Railway. Then they were given a sip of brandy which felt like a fire in their parched throats, before the rescued men settled down to broth and freshly baked bread. Queenslander Bill Smith was amazed. 'Although we were smothered in black oil, they wrapped us in snow white blankets. Then they washed our faces a bit, and gave us a small drink of water, the first for 144 hours, and let us have a little warm soup...it was too much to think that not only were we saved from the sea but were no longer prisoners of the Japs.'[12]

Full of the confidence of youth, Blood Bancroft and his fellow survivors on the rafts had always been positive about their chances. 'I felt I was indestructible...I never thought for a minute that I wasn't going to get out of it...most of us felt we were going to survive.'[13] Blood Bancroft had also survived the sinking of HMAS *Perth* near Java, more than two years before. Of the forty-one survivors of the *Perth* on the *Rayoku Maru*, only eight made it back to Australia. Those who were not killed on the hellship died later in Japanese camps.

After six days, Londoner Alfred Allbury, a gunner in the British 18th Division, was alone in the ocean, out of sight of the *Queenfish*. 'The raft slid up and down steep-sided waves. It had been my home for nearly a week now. I could see nothing, and tiny speck that

---

[12]Aldona Sendzikas, *Lucky 73*, Gainesville, Florida, University of Florida Press, 2010
[13]Tim Bowden interview, Australian War Memorial, ABC Australia, 11 November 1982

I was upon the endless water, I knew that nothing could see me.'

Allbury drifted in and out of consciousness. One minute he imagined being back in his garden at home in Lewisham planting beans with his wife, and the next he dreamt of his brutal experiences building the Thai-Burma Railway. 'I woke from the dream, and I knew it could not be very long now. This was the end...I felt nothing, no emotion. I was past feeling anything at all. Mine I knew was the calmness from which I could slip only into unconsciousness and death.'[14]

However, the USS *Barb*, which was commanded by Eugene Fluckey, was still hunting the seas in the faint hope of finding more survivors. With the typhoon now imminent, *Barb* was preparing to submerge and give up her search. Then a final speck was spotted, a body splayed out on a wooden float. It was Alfred Allbury. He was scarcely conscious as he was hauled aboard, barely alive. All he could whisper was, 'Yanks', before he slipped into unconsciousness. The submariners searched for a further half an hour until 7 p.m. but they could see no other survivors, and so Fluckey finally turned away.

Barb had to be content with saving fourteen lives—ten Australians and four British. *Queenfish* rescued eighteen more POWs. Eugene Fluckey was a tough warrior, but he was deeply affected by the experience. He wrote in his patrol report:

> *The expression on their faces is something that is hard to describe. They were so thankful for being picked up. Most of them couldn't talk but would*

[14]A.G. Allbury, *Bamboo and Bushido*, London, Robert Hale, 1955

just cry; even in their condition they had a few
tears left. In their glazed, oil-soaked eyes you could
see the expression of gratitude. As an afterthought
inserted here, having seen the piteous plight of
the fourteen survivors we rescued, I can say that
I would forgo the pleasure of an attack on a Jap
Task Force to rescue any one of them. There is little
room for sentiment in submarine warfare, but the
measure of saving one Allied life against sinking a
Japanese ship is one that leaves no question, once
experienced.[15]

As *Barb* and *Queenfish* were picking up the final survivors, the *Pampanito*, overflowing with its seventy-three extra passengers, was heading for the base at Saipan. On the way, Gordon Highlander John Campbell, who had been close to death lying on top of a bamboo raft, passed away. He was solemnly buried at sea. Maurice Demers, the *Pampanito's* pharmacist's mate but now a makeshift emergency doctor, treated the survivors suffering from malaria, exposure and starvation. They were all partially blind from the oil, and their eyes needed careful cleaning and irrigation. Demers recalled that 'Their eyes were like dead men's eyes, dim, lifeless, as though they had lost everything but their souls.'[16]

On the *Sealion 2*, pharmacist's mate Roy Williams was also transformed into an emergency doctor. He recalled one man who had been in the sea so long that

---

[15]Aldona Sendzikas, *Lucky 73*, Gainesville, Florida, University of Florida Press, 2010
[16]Maurice Demers, Letter to Admiral Tommy Dykers, 1958

he could not stop treading water in his bunk. He was one of four survivors who died on the journey back to Saipan and were buried at sea. The navy in Saipan sent a doctor aboard a destroyer to care for the survivors. The submariners had behaved with compassion to all the men they had rescued but, recalled Joe Bates, the doctor was different. He did nothing for the men and left caring to the pharmacist's mate. 'I have never been more disappointed by a man in my life.' Later he added, 'The guy was drunk...that was an unworthy moment. I felt ashamed that the navy could send out such a man.'[17]

Before they left the *Pampanito,* some of the prisoners wrote down their stories. It was the first draft of a remarkable history. One Australian from Melbourne wrote, 'Water, tomato soup and crackers...something that we never had in two and a half years. I don't know how to put my feelings into words, but may God bless the captain and the crew for the wonderful job they did in saving our lives. There is not a man that will forget it.'

Private Herbert Barker from the 4th Norfolks echoed those sentiments, 'Thanks to the crew and officers of the USS Pampanito, we are free again after two and a half years of misery and slavery...I will take this opportunity of thanking all members of this wonderful submarine from that terrible experience of being sunk in the sea and being left in the sea for three and a half days.' Jack Cocking from Western Australia knew he was heading for 'happiest time of my life...my wife will be very

---

[17]*The Crossing*, History Channel, ITV Granada, 2009

surprised to hear from me having received no mail since late 1942.'[18]

In Saipan, the lucky British and Australian POWs picked up by the four US submarines enjoyed their first taste of freedom. Four days at sea with food and care had transformed them from half-blinded, oil-covered skeletons who were 'skinny little buggers who were picked up and carried around like dolls', to something resembling human beings again in their US Navy uniforms. The American nurses caring for them were the first white women they had seen in years, 'It was just as if you were in God's hands. It was beautiful. There were some lovely girls amongst them.'[19]

Men from the first sinking, the *Rayoku Maru*, were shocked by the condition of their fellow survivors when they were joined ashore by prisoners from the *Kachidoki Maru*. Many could not see because their eyes were awash with oil. Dr Rowley Richards recalled, 'they were covered in oil and in a dreadful state. They were burned. They were moaning and groaning. They were in excruciating pain from fractured limbs, sunburn, and the oil. It was horrible — equalled only by the worst death huts on the railway.'[20]

Even among those ragged survivors, some nearer death than life, there was a defiant spirit, a resistance. They may be captives again, but they were alive. They broke into a spontaneous version of *Singing In the Rain*,

[18]San Francisco Maritime Park, *www.maritime.org*
[19]Ray Wheeler, *The Crossing*, History Channel ITV Granada, 2009
[20]Joan Blair and Clay Blair Jr, *Return From the River Kwai*, New York, Simon and Schuster,1979

which was very rude about their captors. Despite the horrors they had endured, the sinking by American submarines was also a hopeful sign. The war had turned back towards the Allies.

Hellship survival was random. Some POWs suffered horrific journeys but were spared the lethal torpedo attacks. Others had the misfortune to be travelling on torpedo targets. Men sleeping on deck had a better chance of surviving the initial explosion than those crammed into the holds. Resourcefulness and swimming ability helped once POWs were in the water, but chance also played a hand. So, prisoners on the Duncan and Richards life rafts were rescued by the Japanese but their mates in the accompanying Varley rafts all disappeared, almost certainly shot dead. Prisoners who were picked up by the Japanese were alive but still POWs, headed onto forced labour camps in Japan. On the other hand, the lucky men rescued by American submarines were free to eat meat and white bread and go home to their families.

Of the 1318 prisoners on the *Rayoku Maru*, 1159 died, leaving just 159 survivors. On the *Kachidoki Maru,* of the 900 POWs, 400 were killed. Many of the survivors believed that not painting Red Crosses on the POW ships was a war crime, although the hellships were also carrying Japanese troops and could not justify a Red Cross.

What is clear is that sailing to Japan on a hellship was the most dangerous undertaking for any POW. The hellships sunk by the *Pampanito* and *Tang* were not unique or exceptional. On the day the rescued men steamed towards the safety of Saipan, thousands of miles away a British submarine, HMS *Tradewind,* torpedoed a hellship off the west coast of Sumatra. The *Junyo Maru*, originally British-built, was carrying around 2,300 Allied POWs and 4,200 native labourers, or *romushas*. Only 700 Allied POWs and a couple of hundred *romushas* survived, a massive death toll of more than 5,500 lives.

In November 1943, the Americans torpedoed the *Suez Maru* and more than 250 British and Dutch servicemen who had escaped the impact of the torpedo were afloat in the water. Rather than rescue them, the Japanese proceeded to shoot every single survivor. It took over two hours to murder them all. A total of 414 British POWs were killed that day, more from Japanese guns than friendly fire.

According to Gregory Michno, there were 126,064 POWs journeys on hellships to Japan. On those journeys 21,039 prisoners died. Other sources put the numbers lower. Whatever the exact number, travelling in these rusty targets for torpedoes was as life-threatening as building the Thai-Burma Railway. Yet, some remarkably resilient POWs survived both those terrifying experiences.

11

CAMP 14B, NAGASAKI

Over 140,000 Allied troops were captured by the Japanese in World War II — British, Americans, Australians and Dutch. There was scarcely a coal mine, munitions factory or shipyard in Japan that did not function without the forced labour of POWs. Nagasaki itself housed Fukuoka Camp 2b and Fukuoka Camp 14b, named after the administrative district of Fukuoka on the southern island of Kyushu. The Nagasaki camps were just two of more than twenty prison labour camps in the region.

Camp 14b was the smaller of the two Nagasaki camps and was situated in the industrial district of Saiwamachi, sandwiched between the railway station and the Urakami River which flowed through Nagasaki. Given the terrible experiences they had already endured, its inmates were either the strong or the lucky, but mainly a combination of both. The camp serviced the Mitsubishi Dockyard and the company's foundries nearby. In Nagasaki, Mitsubishi manufactured ships, torpedoes, ammunition and heavy weapons. At its peak the camp held 545 prisoners of the war, including more than 200 survivors of the *Tamahoku Maru* sinking. The majority of those incarcerated were from the Dutch

East Indies, and the rest were Australian, American and British.

When they bombed Nagasaki, the Allies obliterated the most European and Christian of all Japanese cities. Western contact dated as far back as 1568 and the first church was built soon after. Three hundred years later a British merchant, Thomas Glover, laid Japan's first railway track. His elegant 1863 Nagasaki mansion was the likely inspiration for Puccini's *Madame Butterfly*. Nagasaki housed 22,000 Catholics and Japan's only Catholic Cathedral.

On their trudge from the quayside to the camp, the ragged band of prisoners from the hellships were too tired to notice that Nagasaki was an attractive city, complete with Western churches and elegant residences. It nestled in a bowl surrounded by green hills crisscrossed by paddy fields. The ocean was the gateway to the city and the key to the trade that was its lifeblood.

Mitsubishi had created an enormous industrial and military zone in Nagasaki, and so the area where Camp 14b was situated was a functional rather than an attractive section of the city. To the POWs, much of it looked neglected and littered with debris. Camp 14b had been a pre-war cotton factory. Sleeping accommodation was on wooden platforms in double tiers like bunks, with each room holding about thirty-two prisoners. It was primitive, but preferable to the squalid holds of the hellships.

Every day the POWs rose at 5.00 a.m. and ate rice and seaweed soup for breakfast, before filling little bamboo lunch boxes with more rice for lunch. Under the watchful eyes of their guards, they would then march four miles to their work in the Mitsubishi shipyard. In

1940 the world's largest battleship, the *Musashi*, had been launched here and its array of military vessels and oil tankers made this one of the largest shipyards in East Asia, responsible for 15% of the Japanese Navy's warships.

At dawn, Nagasaki was already alive. On their long march to work the prisoners passed small dwellings with families gathered round a charcoal fire eating breakfast, or just keeping warm from the winter cold. Some had a single hen tied to a stake. Along the road, carts, sometimes pulled by spindly dogs, trundled about on their daily business. Arthur Christie, from the RAF, who had been so optimistic when they left Java, soon changed his mind on the trek to and from the shipyard. 'At times some of the people would throw stones and spit at us. The Japanese guards would beat any man who lagged behind, this was particularly hard on the older men.'[1]

The original 300 prisoners in Camp 14b were mainly from the Dutch East Indies. Arthur Christie and Ron Bryer were among eight British POWs who arrived at the camp five months later, before the 212 survivors of the *Tamahoku Maru* almost doubled the population in June 1944. In the shipyard, the British were amazed to see a crane built in Scotland in 1911, and two light engines manufactured in Hunslet in Leeds, only a few miles from Ron's family home near Harrogate. These engines made Bryer think of his parents. His family back in Yorkshire still had no idea their son was a prisoner of the Japanese.

---

[1] Arthur Christie, Unpublished notes, September 1981

© *Rene Schafer, Terug Naar Fukuoka 14, Amsterdam, Jan Mets, 1985*

The POWs had no experience of shipbuilding, so taller prisoners like Ron Bryer and Arthur Christie were allocated work as shipyard riveters, and smaller men became rivet heaters. Skills that might have been learnt during a five-year apprenticeship at home now had to be mastered in a few days. For men weakened by years of hunger and illness, the daily four-mile march to the Mitsubishi shipyards was an ordeal, even before they started their day as shipbuilders. It was tough work. 'You were riveting there in temperatures of 90 degrees, riveting plates on the oil tankers, plates about an inch thick. You came off at night with just a khaki jacket and shorts and your clothing was white with salt from perspiration.'[2] The labour was so hard that Bryer 'personally carried dead and dying men back to camp from the dockyard at the end of a working day.'

In a letter written in 1979, Bryer wrote about the conditions the POWs had to endure:

Free time after supper was a time for cleaning
clothes soiled with excreta on the long walks to and
from camp, for no one was allowed to break ranks
on the journey. If it rained, wet clothing must remain
wet for the following morning, even in winter. There
was no hot water for washing and no heat for drying
and we had one working jacket and trousers only.

Rivets were gunned into ships at significant heights by inexperienced workers wielding heavy equipment. This made the Mitsubishi shipyard a dangerous workplace. Added to the physical danger was the force used by the shipyard guards to keep control. 'The Mitsubishi police strolled through the dockyard all day long, and never gave us any quarter.' They wielded large staves designed, 'to inflict the maximum amount of pain. They were used

[2] *First Tuesday: Return to Nagasaki*, Leeds, Yorkshire Television, 4 November 1984

like a club on any part of the body, or using the sharp end, striking from the front on each side of the head.'[3]

In his first months at Camp 14b, Bryer noted that the only medical staff was a Japanese orderly. 'I cannot recall a single instance when this man provided medical treatment of any kind. If a man claimed to be sick, he was often beaten and sent to work. Two Englishmen from our party of eight died during the worst period of malnutrition, pneumonia and neglect.'[4]

On returning from work around 7 p.m. the men were counted and shared a communal bath, sometimes with warm water. There would often be a whack with a rifle-butt for some misdemeanour, real or imagined, during the day's work. This was followed by their third rice meal of the day, accompanied once again by watery soup. As the war progressed, supplies for the Japanese themselves diminished, and the already inadequate camp rations were reduced. In this tiring, undernourished world there were none of the classes or clubs, theatres or cabarets some POWs had known in Changi and elsewhere. After the rice, the men flopped exhausted onto the flea-infested bamboo mat they called bed. The next day the whole wretched business would start again.

Dutch, British, and Australian prisoners were kept apart. The Australian prisoners worked closer to hand in a Mitsubishi foundry three hundred yards away. They made pipe joints and castings for use in the shipyards. One peacetime railway employee was appalled to be sorting scrap metal marked *New South Wales Government*

[3]Ron Bryer, Unpublished notes
[4]Ron Bryer Letter, 16 May 1979

© *Rene Schafer, Terug Naar Fukuoka 14, Amsterdam, Jan Mets, 1985*

Railways. Corporal Richard Downie of the Royal Australian Air Force summed up camp life. 'That was our miserable existence, up each day before daybreak, usual small amount of rice (while it lasted — we finished

193

eating millet for the last six months). Then off to work in the foundry. In the winter months it would be bloody near dark when we arrived back.'[5]

The straw mats they slept on were infested not only with fleas but with other creatures:

'They got into your clothes. On a very cold morning it took a lot of effort to take your clothes off and to begin to go through them and clean them. Some people just didn't bother to do this. One of them became infested with vermin and he wouldn't take his clothes off at all...you could see that he was in a very bad way. He was scratching himself and developed sores under his clothes. He just gave up trying. It wasn't long after this that he was dead.'[6]

2/40 Battalion Sergeant Peter McGrath-Kerr from Launceston, Tasmania, wandered up the corridor in his barracks and 'observed his pale work trousers accumulating dark specks. By the time he got to the other end he was black to the knees with fleas.'[7]

Ron Bryer soon learned the necessity of starting his day before the official early get up to go on a lice and flea killing spree. Bryer was meticulous, rising early to kill, and thereby to clean. 'A midget tortoiseshell variety easily taking the first prize for the most vicious. I counted over two hundred killed in minutes on a bare leg one evening...each night their nocturnal activities coloured skin a bright pink from head to toe.'[8]

[5] Hugh V Clarke, *Last Stop Nagasaki*, Sydney, Allen and Unwin, 1985
[6] *First Tuesday: Return to Nagasaki*, Leeds, Yorkshire Television, 4 November 1984
[7] Craig Collie, *Nagasaki*, London, Portobello Books, 2011
[8] R E Bryer, *White Ghosts of Nagasaki*, Settle, Yorkshire, self-published, 1997

Bryer was lucky to survive the dangers of the dockyard. Small pieces from the rivets regularly burnt his skin. A finger was cut open to the bone in an accident, and he stitched the wound himself. His head was badly hurt when a very heavy spanner was deliberately dropped from on-high by a Japanese. Ron Bryer was not going to risk having his skull crushed. With the help of a Javanese rivet heater, he stole enough felt to fully pad his Japanese hat. Now there was some protection against missiles dropped from above, deliberately or otherwise.

To Ron and the dockyard's other forced labourers, these shipyard injuries were minor compared to the steady stream of men suffering with pneumonia or beriberi, many of whom died. When that happened, their bodies were carried in simple whitewood boxes to the crematorium across the Urakami River. Often the boxes were too small for tall European bodies, and legs had to be broken to fit inside the box. After cremation, their ashes were placed in a separate box, carefully labelled, and taken to the graveyard at Sakamoto where foreigners were buried. The whitewood box was then brought back to Camp 14b for the next body.

In June 1944, Bryer and the other POWs already settled in Nagasaki were joined by 212 extra prisoners still recovering from their ordeal on the torpedoed hellship *Tamahoku Maru*. Among the new arrivals was Dr Aidan MacCarthy, the RAF physician from Castletownbere, County Cork. Two years before, MacCarthy had been imprisoned in the same camp in Bandung, Java as Ron Bryer and his mates from the RAF. Now they were reunited in the industrial heart of Nagasaki.

For the first five weeks, the new arrivals from the *Tamakoku Maru* were isolated in one very cramped room.

The long wait was probably because the extra POWs had been destined for another city in Japan rather than Nagasaki, or perhaps because the Japanese believed that there were spies amongst the survivors. The room was hot and humid with only a couple of buckets for toilet facilities. The uncertainty and the lack of privacy was extremely stressful. According to Dr MacCarthy, 'The claustrophobic conditions became so unbearable that, in desperation, two of the Dutch-Indonesian prisoners committed suicide by biting through their wrist veins. With no medical supplies, the rest of the prisoners could only watch as they bled to death.'[9]

The arrival of the newcomers coincided with the better news for Ron Bryer and Arthur Christie that their work in the dockyard was finished. The original British contingent was transferred to the foundry near the camp. Their endless days of riveting continued, but the long daily trudge to and from the dockyard was over.

The arrival of 212 additional POWs almost doubled the total number in Camp 14b. This put extra pressure on the already inadequate facilities. The communal latrine was just a pit about 10 feet deep with slats above it and was totally inadequate for so many extra men. Prisoners too weak to work in the foundry were rewarded by being sent down into the latrine once a week to clear it out. Knee-deep in faeces they shovelled away, hauling the waste up in buckets until the pit was empty for another week. The stinking prisoners emerged with maggots crawling over their face and hair.

[9]Bob Jackson, *A Doctor's Sword*, Dublin, The Collins Press, 2016

Many of the new arrivals were still suffering from the aftermath of the torpedo attack but Dr Aidan MacCarthy was expected to perform miracles without either medicine or equipment. The only medical kit given to him by the Japanese were some inadequate bandages, red eye disinfectant, and scores of safety pins. MacCarthy was helped by the practical skill of prisoners, just as the doctors on the Railway of Death had been. Men stole metal scraps from the foundry to make a few crude homemade medical instruments for the doctor. MacCarthy operated on two prisoners suffering with life-threatening lung abscesses by cutting them open with a razor blade. Then the fluid was drained off using instruments secretly made from stolen metal. A homemade syringe was used to suck out the pus. The two patients survived this primitive barbed wire surgery.

From early on sex had stopped being a subject of interest. Food became the overwhelming topic of conversation. Menus were devised and favourite foods discussed. In this world of acute hunger and widespread sickness, Ron Bryer found it hard to understand the unending trade of food for cigarettes. Every night, Dutch Indonesians would come round to the British quarters offering to exchange food for the British ration of Japanese cigarettes. Bryer was astonished those men who were literally dying of hunger would sacrifice their meagre food ration for a smoke.

Even the desperate imploring of Dr Aidan MacCarthy had little effect on the men who were dying of malnutrition but still exchanged food for smokes. 'The staring defiant eyes of a man who had sold all his rations for cigarettes haunt my memory. He had turned his back to avoid watching the others eat, puffing away at his all too expensive cigarette.'[10]

A mate of Ron Bryer was already extremely sick when he arrived in Nagasaki, but still craved cigarettes more than food. Bryer visited him in the sick bay. 'He died in my arms last night as I raised him to puff a long-denied cigarette...the haggard face through its ginger stubble smiled through lips dry and broken by the sores of pneumonia...it was past midnight under the pale-yellow light in the sick room that smelled of urine and death.'[11]

It was not just Ron Bryer's large hands and wide frame that made him formidable. He also possessed a strength of character, a personality that marked him out as a survivor. He was the second eldest in a rural family of twelve children, one sister and eleven brothers. No doubt life in such a large working family with not much money helped equip him for Japanese imprisonment. A beating from a guard was just a more extreme version of the clouts dished out by their father to Ron and his ten brothers. Bryer knew that supplementing the meagre rice-based diet was essential. He stole from the Japanese and pilfered in the shipyard or foundry. He caught a cat, wrung its neck, and then cooked it. On his trudges through Nagasaki to work he picked up orange peel which he later burnt and charred. Then he ate the charcoal because he knew it would improve his ability to digest.

In total, 105 POWs died in Camp 14b, a rate of roughly one a week. On arrival at their camp after work the first

[10]RTE Radio, October 1995
[11]R.E. Bryer, *White Ghosts of Nagasaki*, Settle, Yorkshire, self-published, 1997

thing the men asked was 'How many died today?' The list of those who died, drawn up by the POW Research Network of Japan, paints a vivid picture. The eleven dead Australian servicemen, from Leo Bailey at one end of the alphabet to Phillip Williams at the other, all had *croup pneumonia* recorded as the cause of death. The Dutch, who were significantly the largest group in the camp, lost ninety men in 1943 and 1944. Prisoners had come from the steaming heat of the tropics and their malnourished bodies now had to cope with a brutal Nagasaki winter. Alternating work between the heat inside the foundry and the bitter cold outside was extremely dangerous.

In an affidavit at the end of the war, Eric Hooper, from Victoria, reported that the problem for the underfed Australian POWs was the deliberate mixing of hot and cold extremes by the guard in charge. '(He) sent Smith, Tickle, Bailey, Connor, Prior and Williams to work on the furnace in extreme heat and, after a period, would send them out in the snow to get scrap iron...they all died of pneumonia.'[12]

Frederick (or Frits) de Ruuk was one of the Dutch Javanese pneumonia victims. De Ruuk's mother and sister, his wife Anna, and their son were all held in a Japanese camp in Java while Frits was imprisoned in Nagasaki. After Frits died on 26 August, 1944, a Dutch POW nurse wrote to Anna de Ruuk:

> '(Frits) showed me his photos which he kept as his
> main possession. A memory of you and his child.
> In him, I saw ideals in the middle of the deepest

[12]Eric Hooper, War Crime Affidavit, Melbourne, 20 June 1947

*misery. It's been hell. At the beginning of August
1944, he began to suffer seriously. Suffering from
beriberi. Walking was very difficult. In addition, he
contracted bronchitis that would not go away. Our
doctors were powerless...as a nurse, I knew, and
prepared him gently. And calmly he accepted the
hard truth. But he did not surrender. He would fight
to the very end.'*[13]

His brother Bart had died a year earlier as a POW in
another camp, Fukuoka Camp 13.

For Leading Aircraftsman Arthur Christie, working 50
feet up on the side of a ship carrying his heavy rivet-gun
and rivets was frightening. Although he was eventually
confident enough to run across the thin girders, he
was always fearful of falling. Several prisoners were
injured or killed in shipyard accidents. They were the
exceptions to the long list of pneumonia deaths. Gerard
Goldman died of a 'fractured cranium' in September
1944 and Tjapko Pik of 'fracture of the cranium and
both forearms' in November of the same year. Pik was a
cook who had been ordered to exchange his stove for a
shipyard drill when he became ill. Despite his weakness,
Pik was forced to work by the Japanese and fell from a
high scaffold down onto the ship the men were building.
Other prisoners could hear his screams as he plunged to
his death.

The foundry was also a dangerous workplace.
Australian Sergeant, Peter McGrath-Kerr of the 2/40
Battalion, recalled an accidental death. 'One chap was
sitting down alongside a big ladle that was carried along

[13]*www.fukuoka14b.org*, The Netherlands.

on the crane, and the handle fell down and smashed his head. A Dutchman.'[14] Fellow Australian, Eric Hooper from Victoria, calculated that of the twenty-five men who started work with him in the foundry only six survived the war.

There were two ways for the POWs to win small victories. The thin rations, which grew more meagre as the war went on, could occasionally be supplemented by theft. light-fingered prisoners would steal a single carrot or beetroot from the waste bin outside the Japanese cookhouse. At their luckiest, POWs might find a fish head. A Dutch prisoner removed the sole of his shoe so he could pick up discarded orange peelings on the road to work with his feet.

When the cookhouse was moved, prisoners took even greater risks. Ron Bryer and his friend Brummy Harrison regularly broke into the Japanese quartermaster's store and stole small items like a tin of milk powder. Unfortunately, some Indonesian prisoners took the same risk, and the Japanese soon realised that food was being stolen. They searched the camp thoroughly, but the British had hidden their prizes in a water drain. The Indonesians were not as smart and were beaten for their crime. The quartermaster's store became a fortress after that.

The other cause for quiet satisfaction was sabotage. Rivets were overheated so they crumbled; wrong-sized bolts were used; work was slowed down whenever possible. In the minds of the weary POWs, every moment of defiance was a small but joyful act of war. Sometimes

---

[14]Peter McGrath-Kerr, Canberra, Australian War Memorial Sound Archive

sabotage took an uglier turn. According to Dr Aidan MacCarthy, there were a few 'accidents' on the high scaffolding of the shipyard when hated guards plunged mysteriously to their death.

In all camps, guards were given nicknames like Gorilla, Pigface, or Napoleon. To veterans of the River Kwai Railway there was less brutality in Nagasaki than in Thailand and Burma, but guards still imposed discipline by force. Sometimes ill-treatment was for genuine offences, but POWs were also beaten because it gave guards pleasure. Officers did not escape punishment. In Autumn 1944, when the senior officers were moved out of Nagasaki, Squadron Leader MacCarthy became the commanding officer in Camp 14b. In Japanese eyes that meant he shared responsibility for his men's crimes. 'I was beaten each time offences were committed and thus ensured a daily beating. I was given a blow on the head with a bamboo cane or a blow on the face for each offender. Then the offenders themselves received several blows.'[15]

At the end of one day, Arthur Christie was smacked hard in the face by three Japanese guards in turn. His offence was failing to empty his water bottle. When one of his fellow POWs struck a Japanese civilian, the man was put on half rations and made to stand in front of his comrades with a heavy plank of wood over his head every dinner time. That punishment lasted for a month.

The POWs were not the only workers who suffered. Thousands of Japanese men, women and children 'slaved' alongside them. Despite both the risk and their own profound poverty, civilian labourers sometimes tried to help the POWs. One woman gave a prisoner

[15]Aidan MacCarthy, *A Doctor's War*, London, Robson Books, 1979

a handful of dried beans. For the crime of accepting the woman's offering, the feared Mitsubishi police smashed the Allied prisoner about the head with a large stick. In many ways, the lives of civilian workers were as desperate as those of the Allied prisoners, as Peter McGrath-Kerr observed. 'There were young girls and young fellows working in the machine shop next door. They were schoolchildren these kiddies. They were short of manpower. There were two women mixing concrete with shards. One with a baby on her back. They were doing the labouring, unloading coal from barges, using two baskets on a pole, working just as hard as the men.'[16]

Fellow Australian, Driver Charles Ericksson, was working in the foundry when, 'a woman carrying scrap iron to the furnace collapsed and in 30 minutes gave birth to a child. The guard cut the cord with his bayonet, and the baby was washed in cold water, wrapped, and put into a basket near the furnace we were loading. Two hours after the birth the woman was forced to commence work. This nearly caused a riot with the Australians.'[17]

When the war turned against Japan, food supplies for the civilian population fell. Inevitably, that also meant a reduction in the already pathetic amount of food given to the POWs. Red Cross parcels did not improve the diet because they were stolen by the guards, apart from one delivery at Christmas. The precious tinned food, chocolate, tea and condensed milk were never seen. The Dutch stole back some tins which they hid by lowering them on a rope into the latrines where no guard would want to look.

[16]Peter McGrath-Kerr, Canberra, Australian War Memorial Sound Archive
[17]Hugh Clarke, *Last Stop Nagasaki,* Sydney, Allen and Unwin, Australia, 1984

As the food supply worsened, beatings increased. Perhaps it was anger at their own starvation rations, or the growing sense that the war was slipping away from Japan. As another bitter winter began in 1944, the 'bash merchants' amongst the guards beat the sick and injured more often and filled the isolation cage more frequently.

By Spring 1945, there was a hopeful indication that the war was in its final stages because work in the foundry largely dried up. Many Camp 14b POWs were moved to an open cast coal mine about two miles out of the city. Every morning they marched two miles to the mine, and then made a weary trudge back in the evening. The only consolation for spending so long in darkness was that the mine was full of snakes. The POWs became adept at catching and killing them. Back in the camp they were stewed for hours to supplement their increasingly meagre diet. The mines made them almost nostalgic for the shipyard and foundry back in the 'lost haven' of Nagasaki.

Despite increased sickness in one of the coldest winters on record, POWs began to feel an inner hope. News from the outside world was elusive because there were no homemade radios in Camp14b. But the POWs picked up vital snippets of war news, a brief word with a local worker here, a torn scrap of newspaper there. Tajima, the guard who had treated the survivors of the hellships with humanity when they arrived at Moji, was also a secret source of information. They knew that the war was going in the right direction but, at the same time were fearful of what a vengeful Japan would do if the Allies invaded. They would be lucky, the POWs thought, to get out of Nagasaki alive.

12

CAMP 2B, NAGASAKI

A second and much larger camp in Nagasaki sat about five miles from Camp 14b on a small island called Koyagi. Fukuoka Camp 2b had been carved out of a hillside and built on reclaimed land in the bay. The small compound was surrounded by a ten-foot high bamboo fence. Inside were about twenty-three barracks, 20 by 40 feet, with double decker bunks covered in straw matting. Each barrack could accommodate sixty men.

In April 1945, Camp 2b was a prison to 1422 POWs, roughly divided between British, Australians and Dutch inmates. The camp also housed about 100 Americans, mainly crew from the USS *Houston* which had also been sunk near Java with a terrible death toll of about 350 crew members. Among the prisoners was a small group of much older American civilians who had been captured building a runway on Wake Island. The British POWs included sixty-eight survivors of the HMS *Exeter*, which had sunk on 1 March 1941 off Java.

They were the first arrivals at Camp 2b in 1942. There were no doors or windows and the concrete floors had not even set. As it was late October, their flimsy clothes and coarse blankets offered little protection against the bitter Nagasaki winter. They were subjected to lengthy speeches from the camp authorities, making it clear that the men were in Nagasaki to work and that any shirking would result in heavy punishment. Later arrivals in 1943 had already survived building the Railway of Death and their first impressions were more favourable. For these newly arrived veterans of those railway jungle camps the contrast was stark. Dry barracks, electric light, and shoes were instant luxuries.

The POWs all laboured in the nearby shipyard for the Kawanami Shipbuilding Company. It was hot and heavy work, whether it was riveting, caulking, welding, slaving at the furnaces or smashing red-hot ship plates with huge sledgehammers. Canadian Jack Ford from the RAF recalled his first shipyard job making masts:

We put large plates into the fires of a very hot furnace. It was so hot it was hard to work near it, but the Japanese forced us to stay at the station. When these plates came out, they were red-hot and we had to swing a sledgehammer to make the plate round. There were a lot of us all doing the same thing, swinging the hammer, hitting the metal, sparks flying in all directions, and suffering the intense heat.[1]

The POWs would leave for the shipyard around 6.00 a.m. and not return until about 6.45 p.m. The long, snaking column of a thousand men trudging to work looked like a line of ants on the move. Each man was given a little wooden badge sewn on their jacket with

[1] Jack Fitzgerald, *The Jack Ford Story*, Newfoundland, Canada, Creative Publishers, Newfoundland, 2007

their prisoner number stamped on it. The lunch break was half an hour to eat what rice was left in the small bamboo container they had been given to cover both breakfast and lunch, a tiny amount of food for such heavy and demanding work.

Like their fellow prisoners in the industrial zone, resistance was confined to minor acts of sabotage. The riveters made a pact that each of them would throw one bolt over the side every day, which added up to hundreds over time. They just needed to avoid the scrutiny of the Japanese Navy guards who supervised the dockyard. They were unforgiving, as the camp's senior American officer reported. 'With a few rare exceptions, the navy were very brutal; inflicted severe punishments, often without cause; were guilty of gross maltreatment...the use of sledgehammer handles, iron pipes or 2x4 boards was quite common.'[2]

After a day's hard labour, the POWs enjoyed an occasional communal bath, forty men at a time, but most days the grime of a hard day's work was washed off by a thin trickle of water from a pipe. Soap was a rarity for prisoners and local Japanese alike. Then they collected their meagre rice supper from the cookhouse. Occasionally, this was supplemented by watery soup with a few scraps of vegetable added. By 9.30 pm, having killed as many lice and fleas in their bedding as possible, the exhausted men flopped to sleep. Every ten days was a rest day when there was a chance to wash clothes, play cards, read a book, and kill more fleas and lice.

[2]Lt Col William Horrigan, Affidavit, San Francisco, 26 September 1945

In the dockyard, burns from red-hot rivets and other injuries were commonplace. On 3 May 1943 Harold Jeffs, a survivor of the sinking of HMS *Exeter*, was crushed to death when a cauldron of molten steel fell on him. Others were luckier. Aircraftsman Benjamin da Cunha from the RAF was working in a dry dock at the yard when a crack in the sea wall appeared. The prisoners scrambled out hurriedly, and when their Japanese guards ordered them back, they refused. Instead, a Japanese officer instructed twenty soldiers to go down into the dock and pick up the tools that the POWs had left behind. 'The poor fellows, the 60-foot wall gave way. The sea water came gushing in at a terrific speed...they did not stand a chance. The lot of them were drowned.'[3]

Alongside the 1500 POWs worked 60,000 young, civilian Japanese workers who were billeted in a 'boys' town and 'girls' town within the shipbuilding complex. Their conditions were scarcely better than those of Allied prisoners. Other ranks in Camp 2b were paid 10 cents per day for their dockyard work, officers more. The Japanese authorities sometimes kept these 'wages' and with it bought the prisoners mandarins, cigarettes and occasional small packets of dried seaweed. Occasionally, kindly civilians gave the POWs scraps of waste food.

The first wave of POWs to arrive at 2b in 1942 had been lucky to find a sympathetic camp commander, Chui Shirabe. According to a file note written by the senior American prisoner, Major William Horrigan, Shirabe was liked and respected, 'a Christian in both

---

[3]Radio Weekly, 3 February 1957

name and practice...He fed the POWs the best of any C.O.; listened to all requests and complaints, tried to comply with them.'

When Shirabe attempted to improve working conditions he was blocked by both navy and civilian officials at the dockyard. Shirabe understood the significance of Christmas to his prisoners. In 1942 'he did far more than we requested to make the holiday a pleasant one for POWs. He did all he could to stop the beatings.'[4]

In April 1943, Shirabe sanctioned a rare evening of music and comedy in honour of the emperor's birthday:

It was surprising the talent that these walking skeletons had. Some had fashioned musical instruments out of odds and ends and they played them fairly well. Now most of the participants were Limeys and when you heard them talk you would have thought that the King's English or at least half of the King's English consisted of some form or tense of the slang word for sexual intercourse. They could speak a sentence that contained fifteen words and ten of them would be some form of this word.[5]

It would be wrong to generalise about the conditions and regimes in Japan's camps. Some were brutally run; others were more humane. Some POWs received extra food and clothing, including Red Cross parcels. Others starved and then froze in the tough Japanese winter.

[4] Lt Col William Horrigan, Affidavit, San Francisco, California, 28 September 1945
[5] Frank Fujita, *Foo*, Texas, University of North Texas Press, 1993

Allied leadership also varied in the skill of managing their Japanese masters. Some senior officers negotiated better conditions for their prisoners with a mixture of robust and agile leadership. Others were weak and unable to protect the POWs under their command.

A significant number of POWs recalled kindnesses from individual guards. In Camp 2b, Don Hibbert, another survivor from the sinking of the *Exeter*, was sometimes given a mandarin or a potato by a sympathetic shipyard supervisor. In the same camp, Clyde Shelton of the 131st Field Artillery in Texas was grateful to a Japanese interpreter who risked his own neck by bringing him food after Shelton had been severely beaten. In Singapore, Bill Norways, a talented artist, was supplied with paper and pencils, as well as food, by a humanitarian guard. After the war, the two men exchanged letters for more than thirty years.

Unfortunately for the POWs, Shirabe was moved from Camp 2b in the summer of 1943, and in the final two years of the war the leadership was much harsher. His replacement as camp commander was invisible to the POWs, and power resided with a brutal, solidly built sergeant major called Bokogo (or Bokugo), rumoured to have been a Tokyo policeman before the war. He was rarely separated from the samurai sword he carried with him. Now, discipline was imposed almost exclusively with the help of sticks, clubs, and other weapons. A simple offence like a failure to bow represented a loss of face to the guards and would result in a punch or a whack with a bamboo stick. Geoffrey Holt, who had joined the Royal Navy as a fifteen-year-old in 1939, remembered being slow to move before bedtime 'and four of us were taken outside and given a taste of a baseball bat.'[6]

Alex Smith, an RAF Wireless Operator, and a friend, were punished for having an illicit match to smoke with. 'We were beaten up by two guards and a sergeant major, we were all black and blue because they were using sticks similar to baseball bats.' Smith was then locked up for eight days in the bamboo punishment cage in the bitter winter cold. His fellow smoker died soon after their punishment.

Canadian RAF Flight Engineer Jack Ford witnessed regular examples of the Japanese guards trying to break the spirit of the prisoners. 'There were many tortures. Fellows kneeled on a broom handle with a brick in each hand and as the brick would fall down, they would beat you and beat you...I saw someone beat up pretty badly, to the extent that he died in the night.'[7]

Edward Anderson was a survivor of the HMS *Exeter* sinking. Every day a group of about fifty POWs were paraded in front of the Japanese Navy hut and, without reason, some were selected for a beating. On one occasion, Anderson was hit by five or six guards with baseball bats. When they were finished with Anderson, they set on a Dutchman breaking several ribs. 'I've always said they were beasts, absolute beasts, the civilisation is a mere thin veneer and once that's scratched you find a beast underneath.'[8]

[6]Geoffrey Holt, London, Imperial War Museum Sound Archive
[7]CBC News Canada, 1985
[8]Edward Anderson, London, Imperial War Museum Sound Archive

Captain Millet Straughan, from San Antonio, Texas, told the United States War Crimes Department in 1947 that Sergeant Major Bukiogo (or Bokogo), 'seemed to enjoy assaulting prisoners. He was constantly looking for a reason to beat the prisoners, as if he went into a trance while beating a person. He seemed to be seeing a sadistic, perverted sexual satisfaction in the torture he inflicted on the prisoners.'

The worst punishment was reserved for Americans, probably in revenge for their growing success in the war. The Japanese were furious when they discovered that POWs had been using bottles to urinate in during the night, rather than risk the hazard of a night-time trip to the latrines. Queenslander Hugh Clarke had a ringside seat looking into room 24 and saw the guards smash the Americans with baseball bats. 'I could no longer bear to watch the brutal clubbing and turned away from the window. I could still hear the sickening thud of the baseball bats on bone and limb.'[9]

Jack Ford witnessed the sergeant major beating a young American who was a civilian clerk in the US forces. 'Blood came from everywhere. His eyes, nose and ears bled. His face and arms were cut. When he was tired of beating the American, he ordered that he be placed in an underground prison cell. No medical attention whatsoever was offered. The next morning the man was found dead.'[10]

In an affidavit signed after the war, American Staff Sergeant O. B. Williams from Ratan, Texas, confirmed

[9]Hugh Clarke, *Last Stop Nagasaki*, Sydney, Allen and Unwin Australia, 1985
[10]Jack Fitzgerald, *The Jack Ford Story*, Newfoundland, Canada, Creative Publishers, 2007

the torture of thirteen Dutch prisoners who were suspected of stealing food from the cafeteria. 'These thirteen people were beaten and kicked while on the ground. Boiling water was poured down their throats and they were beaten for the reason of making them admit their crimes.' Williams himself was hit 'with a bat the size of a baseball bat for owning a pen.'[11]

American 1st Lieutenant Millet Straughan of the Lost Battalion (131st Field Artillery), added, 'they beat the prisoners for 1 to 1 and a half hours and after a short break the abuse continued. The guards acted like maniacs, cheering, shouting...they seemed to have a lot of fun doing it.'[12]

No one was more fearful than Sergeant Frank 'Foo' Fujita also from the 'Lost Battalion' of Texans captured on Java. Not only was Fujita an American, the most hated of the Allies, but his father was a Japanese man who had been born in Nagasaki in 1914 and still had relatives living in the city. In Japanese eyes, fighting against the homeland and their emperor would have been the ultimate treachery by Fujita, so his life was at risk if he failed to keep his ancestry secret.

When an assault with a club finally came, it was brutal:

Wham! Wham! Wham! Oh how that did hurt. I did not know that pain could attain such a high degree of intensity. My entire head seemed to explode, my

[11]O.B. Williams, Affidavit to US War Crimes Dept, Fisher County, Texas ,19 August 1948
[12]Millet Straughan, Affidavit to USA War Crimes Dept, San Antonio, Texas, 27 January 1947

senses spun round and seemed to pulsate in and
out, bordering on unconsciousness, and then came
the frontal attack. This time the guard kicked me in
the chest with his heavy army shoes and at the same
time his shin crashed into my already battered face...
Blood was gushing out of my face at all points,
but I was still standing proud and erect, or at least
I thought I was.[13]

A more serious offence than stealing food was smuggling information into the camp. To the Japanese guards this was an act of espionage. One British prisoner smuggled newspaper clippings under his false teeth. He was wise to be careful. An American prisoner was caught with a Japanese newspaper. He was shoved into solitary confinement in a wooden cage which was too small to stand up in. When the American was finally released, Hugh Clarke described him as 'an emaciated shadow of his former fine physique, and with his head battered into the shape of an ironbark pumpkin. He had not informed on his Japanese accomplices in the dockyard, and his tormentors had finally given up.'[14]

Next door to this small wooden cage was another hut, surrounded by a stockade. Its solitary, melancholy inmate was a Dutch East Indies POW suffering from leprosy. The doctor was the only person allowed to bring him sustenance and this was supplemented by scraps of food and cigarettes thrown over his fence by fellow prisoners. Leading Stoker Alf King, a Welshman from Aberdare, recalled, 'The loneliness he suffered must have

[13]Frank Fujita, *Foo*, Texas, University of North Texas Press, 1993
[14]Hugh Clarke, *Last Stop Nagasaki*, Sydney, Allen and Unwin Australia 1984

been heartbreaking. He asked for a piece of bamboo to make a flute and in a few weeks, he had completed it and was practising with it...on quiet evenings it could be heard all over the camp. There was something haunting and beautiful about it.'[15]

Christmas was almost the only respite for the POWs. In a bow to the Christian traditions of Nagasaki, the guards gave their prisoners time off work and provided additional food, or at least allowed the prisoners access to some Red Cross parcels, split between five or six men. Even Sergeant Major Bokogo mellowed a little. Dutch POW, Jouwert Postma, described Christmas in Camp 2b, with buns filled with Red Cross corned beef, carrot and onions, plus coffee. 'In the afternoon cabaret and in the evening Christmas carols were sung in the courtyard. This was the best day in captivity.'[16]

Christmas might have offered a short window of jollity, but locals claimed that winter 1944 was the worst for seventy years. Snow was thick on the ground and even a blanket or an old greatcoat was not enough to keep warm. The extreme switch between hot, sweaty labour and the bitterly cold winter was lethal and deaths occurred as regularly from pneumonia as they did in Camp 14b. Frank Fujita's simple handwritten diary recorded deaths in a few sad lines, 'Victor Syrett, a Canadian Pvt of my room died of pneumonia. Fleas, lice, bedbugs, rats, land crabs.'[17]

Sometimes deaths were the direct result of cruelty as well as neglect. Harry Eldron Reed was an American

[15]Alf King, *www.far-eastern-heroes.org*
[16]Jouwert Postma, *www.mansell.com*
[17]Frank Fujita, *Foo*, Texas, University of North Texas Press 1993

civilian aged about fifty who had been captured on Wake Island. Unlike the imprisoned serviceman, he had neither the training nor physique to survive. According to an affidavit by First Lieutenant Millet Straughan, Reed was a hunchback and on 3 April, 1945, when he could no longer run to his workplace, 'the prisoner was beaten and kicked...beaten with belts and rifle butts...he died at approximately 11 a.m. the same morning.'[18]

A month later, war in Europe came to an end but the war with Japan was not yet over. Like many prisoners, Australian Hugh Clarke was certain that an American invasion would bring both freedom and death. 'The life of a prisoner of war in Japan continued to be hopeless. A succession of days; from meagre news we gathered there could be no happy ending. We had no illusions about what our fate would be if Japan was invaded and, as we saw it, invasion was inevitable.'[19]

POWs often thought about escape from this pitiful existence, but this was fantasy rather than a realistic option. Making a successful run for it in an enemy and alien land was impossible. For some, there was only one other possibility. Leading Stoker John Black, another survivor of HMS *Exeter*, came to feel that life was just not worth living. The Scot, from Airdrie, was thin, exhausted and desperate. One day in the dockyard he quietly slipped away to die. He was woken by a Japanese woman forcing a precious orange into his mouth. The

[18]Millet Straughan, Affidavit to USA War Crimes Dept, San Antonio, Texas, 27 January 1947
[19]Hugh Clarke, *Last Stop Nagasaki*, Sydney, Allen and Unwin Australia 1984

sympathetic local would have faced severe punishment if she had been caught. Her selflessness made John Black resolve to live, not die.

Twenty-two-year-old Australian, Lang Fraser, displayed the same willpower when suffering badly from pneumonia. Fraser had written a will leaving all he possessed, which was just a spoon and a packet of cigarettes, to his mate Hugh Clarke. He recalled, 'I really thought I was going to die. First it was fear, then I began to think bugger it, I'm going to beat these bastards. I won't die...then I realised I had never had a woman really and I began to think I'd like to live and have a kid of my own.'

Apart from food and friendship, the only other comfort was the possibility of letters to and from home. The POWs themselves were restricted to a few bland lines to their loved ones. This correspondence, usually on pro forma postcards, was limited to one or two a year and sometimes took six or even twelve months or more to arrive in Birmingham or Brisbane. These cards might have contained minimal content, but at least families at home finally knew their son was alive, or at least had been six months earlier.

The Japanese ensured that messages home never reflected the grim reality of Camp 2b life. Don Hibbert's mother kept a card reading,

Dear All, I am imprisoned in Japan. The weather is warm. I am very well. I hope you are well too. The food is fine, and I can buy small luxury items with the money I earn by working. Regards to you all. Your loving son, Donald. Decades later Hibbert reflected, 'In fact, we had very bad food, and with

the money I earned by working for four months,
I could buy one cigarette'.[20]

Some prisoners had been married or engaged before their troop ships left for war. Welshman Les Spence had kept a secret diary since his capture on Java. Now imprisoned in a camp forty miles from Nagasaki, his thrill at receiving news from home was typical:

I received letters from my dear Mother and Dad,
Ken and Babs (his fiancée). I could hardly read them
because my eyes were dimmed by the tears that
came and I'm not ashamed to say it, I have already
read them over a dozen times...how those I loved
must have suffered in these 17 months of anxiety,
not knowing if I was alive or not...Bab's letter
was a gem and I hope that if I am spared to return
home, Babs will be my wife. Oh, I do feel happy.[21]

In his Japanese prison camp, Captain Atholl Duncan drew up lists of what food and other home comforts he longed for. *Dishes I have craved for as a POW,* started:

1. *Steak and Kidney Pie*
2. *Lemon Curd*
3. *Mother's Ginger Cake.*

His list of *Longings* included: *To sit down at a neatly laid table and eat a civilised meal with civilised utensils,* and *To go to a dance with Elizabeth* (his fiancée).[22]

---

[20]Don Hibbert, Unpublished interview, Jill Turton, 1984
[21]Les Spence, edited by Greg Lewis, *From Java to Nagasaki,* Wales, Magic Rat, 2012
[22]Meg Parkes, *A.A. Duncan is OK,* Merseyside, Kranji Publications, 2003

Dr Frank Murray from Belfast, wrote in his diary of one simple desire.

Freedom is a very wonderful goal. Freedom of thought, of word, of action. Freedom brings a happiness that one cannot appreciate until one has seen what lack of freedom can do to people…Oh! to stretch out my arms to the heavens and look into unbounded space from an Irish hillside and breathe one word, Freedom.[23]

Murray was a devout Catholic. He was emotionally supported by his faith and by letters from his fiancée, Eileen, even if they had taken more a than a year to arrive. He wrote in his secret letters to her, 'I am under my mosquito net again to tell you how much I love you, your letters and everything about you. If you could but know the solace, the happiness that one of your letters brings to me, what a difference it makes to my captivity.' Clearly thinking forward to marriage, Murray added, 'Our bottom drawer seems to be almost full up. I am dying to hear about our new dinner set.'

Letters from home also carried the potential for crushing disappointment. If there was nothing for him when a bundle of letters finally arrived at a camp a prisoner was even more lonely and isolated. There was also the risk that a letter could carry bad news. A parent dead, a sibling killed in the war, or a girlfriend marrying another man, was devastating news to read when locked up in a Japanese camp. One POW in Camp 2b was so depressed when he did not receive any cards or

---

[23]Frank Murray/Carl Murray, *The Belfast Doctor*, Belfast, 2020

letters from home, he threw himself from the top of a crane down into the dry dock. The following day a card arrived for him.

As the senior officer in Camp 14b, Aidan MacCarthy was particularly concerned about the effects of letters from home. 'Even the most out of date news from home was far too great an emotional experience for us all. We had had two and a half years of captivity; our morale was almost non-existent. We were considerably debilitated and found each day a battle for survival. A further drop in morale resulted...they had lost the will to live.'

MacCarthy and the senior Dutch and Australian officers made a controversial and unanimous decision. They burned two deliveries of mail unopened. The officers were fearful that, if discovered, the POWs would be mutinous, but the men never found out that their precious mail had been incinerated. Morale was so desperately low at that stage of the war that, even decades later, MacCarthy had no regrets. He believed that in the special circumstances of that time and place, burning the letters was still the right decision.

The best doctors knew they needed to treat the whole man, mental as well as physical wellbeing. The senior doctor at Camp 2b, Captain Waisfiz, colloquially known as 'Dr Ricefish' or 'Dr Fish Paste,' did not even manage the sick bodies in his care. One POW called the Dutch Army doctor a butcher. Jack Ford agreed. 'He was very, very cruel. He cooperated with the Japanese in order to get favours for himself. He put us to work when we were too sick to work.'[24]

---

[24]Jack Fitzgerald, *The Jack Ford Story*, Newfoundland, Canada, Creative Publishing, Newfoundland 2007. Ford spells the doctor's name incorrectly as Vich Weitch

These criticisms were confirmed by an American nurse, John Tracy from Carthage, South Dakota. At Fort Lewis, Washington in October 1945 Tracy signed an affidavit which said, 'Captain Waisfisz also refused to hospitalise people who were seriously ill... Dr Waisfisz refusal of treatment was common, but to my knowledge three patients have died due to insufficient medical attention.' Frank Fujita witnessed him eating the rations of a man who was dying but still alive.

Even the more responsible doctors and medical orderlies were handicapped by the lack of basic materials. Sufficient medicines and equipment were available, but the Japanese refused to give them to the Allied doctors. Bandages were washed up to sixty times, and prisoners cut up their own mosquito nets to make more. Even when the shipyard owner offered a factory doctor to help in the camp, the camp commandant refused. In an official affidavit at the end of the war, Major JC Rinaman, from the US Army Medical Corps stated, 'In general, it was extremely difficult to get medicines in a normal way. This, despite the fact that the medicines were available...on September 2nd, 1945, I took these supplies under management. Caves full of medicines and bandages were then surrendered to me. The stock was sufficient for years.'

In a three-year period, more than seventy POWs died in Camp 2b. Apart from a handful of Americans, the dead were all British or Dutch. In a post-war affidavit, British Navy surgeon Lt Deryck Syred reported that around 2/3 of the British deaths were the result of illness, the rest were due to shipyard accidents. Syred concluded that the majority 'would not have died if their good medical care had been allowed. Many shipyard accidents would not have happened if the civilian in charge had taken the normal safety precautions.'[25]

[25]Deryck Syred, *War Crimes Affidavit*, Westminster, London, 16th April 1947

13

BEFORE THE BOMB

In the early summer of 1945, the prisoners in Nagasaki's two camps gathered enough snippets of news to know that the war in Europe was over. This gave them hope, but at the same time friends and family in Europe were joyfully celebrating VE day, the POWs still faced a bleak and uncertain future.

In his announcement of German surrender in early May, Churchill emphasised that the war was not at an end:

> *We may allow ourselves a brief period of rejoicing; but let us not forget for a moment the toil and efforts that lie ahead. Japan, with all her treachery and greed, remains unsubdued. The injury she has inflicted on Great Britain, the United States and other countries, and her detestable cruelties, call for justice and retribution. We must now devote all our strength and resources to the completion of our task, both at home and abroad. Advance Britannia! Long live the cause of freedom! God save the King!*

When the snows of the Nagasaki winter finally melted there were 1422 POWs in Camp 2b. In a clear sign that the conflict had shifted decisively away from Japan, work in the shipyards dried up. In June 1945, all RAF and Australian prisoners, apart from two men who were seriously ill, were moved out to Camp 21 in Nakama, northern Kyushu to work in a coalmine. Labouring in dark and dangerous conditions underground reminded them of their earlier transportation in the holds of hellships.

The coal seam ran beneath a lake and access was by a mile-long tunnel sloping sharply down from the surface. Australian Bombardier Hugh Clarke described the grim experience of the night shift:

> *Each night was the same. Climb into a coal skip*
> *and roll down miniature rails while the glistening*
> *wet sides of the tunnel reflected the glare of our*
> *headlamps...then we alighted and walked the rest of*
> *the way down along a long, winding, slippery tunnel*
> *until the coalface, about four feet thick, reflected*
> *our lights like a silvery black ribbon. Water from the*
> *lake seeped into the tunnels and the shafts where we*
> *worked were walled with green timber prop which*
> *bulged and cracked alarmingly.*[1]

When the mine creaked and groaned everyone was thankful for the presence of experienced coalminers from Wales. 'They saved our lives on more than one occasion...we were terrified...it appeared as if any minute we were going to be entombed...as soon as the Welshmen said move, we moved.'[2]

At Fukuoka Camp 17, Americans were so fearful of labour down a coal mine they deliberately had their

[1]Hugh Clarke, *Last Stop Nagasaki,* Sydney, Allen and Unwin, Australia
[2]Hank Nelson, *Prisoners of the Japanese,* Sydney, ABC Australia, 1985

limbs broken to avoid work. This camp was dominated by a group of American racketeers and, like everything, limbs smashed by a jackhammer came at a price. Five rations of rice and soup for a broken arm, and eight for a broken leg

In the early months of 1945, Nagasaki was spared the devastating fire bombing endured by other Japanese cities. Their turn was to come. In March, wave after wave of American B-29's levelled miles of Japanese cities, including Kobe, Osaka and Nagoya. On 9 March, 324 B-29s firebombed Tokyo itself, killing nearly 100,000 citizens and injuring many more, in just one night.

Even after the firebombing of Tokyo there was little sign of the Japanese capitulating. For the prisoners, the closeness of freedom was tempered by a heightened level of fear. They were certain that if Japanese troops died defending their homeland against an Allied invasion, the Japanese military would not allow the POWs to live. Both excitement and anxiety increased when American aircraft were seen over Nagasaki itself. So, the prisoners were relieved when the Japanese allowed them to build primitive bomb shelters close to Camp 14b. Having survived the Japanese regime for more than three years, no one wanted to be killed by an American bomb in the final chapter of the war.

In July 1945, in the desert near Almagordo, New Mexico, America tested the atomic bomb. William Laurence, later known as Atomic Bill, was a science writer for the New York Times but also a special consultant to the Manhattan Project. He was a witness that day and understood that he had been present at an epoch-making moment in human history. Twenty years later, he wrote:

In the predawn darkness of Monday July 16ᵗʰ, 1945,
a small group of men, including this writer, stood
in the primaeval desert near Almagordo, N.M. and
watched the birth of a new age. On that morning,
when the first atomic bomb sent up a mountain of
cosmic fire...the world we lived in came to an end,
though few of us realise it even now. The new world
that was born is still in the making, and no one
knows as yet what kind of world it will be.[3]

Just three weeks later, Atomic Bill Laurence was again an eyewitness, this time when the bomb was dropped on Nagasaki.

On 1 August, 1945, Nagasaki was finally hit by its first major bombing raid. At the piercing sound of the warning sirens, POWs ran for their new shelters. Through the entry holes in the clear blue sky overhead they saw scores of planes dropping bombs. They were close enough for Ron Bryer to notice the chalk markings on the bomb casings. The explosions were loud and frequent. 'Already bombs were on their way, black footballs dropping right into our shelter...I felt the crushing blast pressures as the bombs exploded, and the shelter lifted bodily with a crunch like a thousand breaking eggshells. Pieces of the wall stuck out all over the place among dust plastered figures. But we survived.'

The contradiction of a bombing raid by their own side was not lost on the prisoners. On one hand, the attack confirmed that liberation was near; on the other, it was clear that the men were not safe from either the Japanese or the Americans. It was a strange sensation to

[3]*New York Times Book Review,* July 1965

want to cheer the American bombers but to be terrified in the same moment. This time they were alive, but it had been close. The shelter had almost been ripped from the earth. Slabs of concrete and debris were just yards away. Brummie Harrison had blood smeared onto his clothes, and other injured men were thrown upwards on top of piles of the debris.

Ron Bryer was close to the shelter entrance and was one of the first to free himself. 'I climbed from the shelter to see how close to death we had come. For yards in every direction the pulverised ground shook like jelly as we moved. A smell of spent explosives filled the air. In desperation we scrabbled through loose soil until we found a limb. Any limb. And willing hands pulled its owner free. Other hands cleared his mouth of soft earth even as he suffocated. Some were past help, crushed against the roof of their shelter.'

The prisoners then stood and watched wave after wave of American planes unloading their bombs on the dockyard a few miles away as B-29s droned in from the sea. 'They came in singly, one after another, shining silver in the sun...repeated detonations reached our ears like rolls of distant thunder as the industrial life of Nagasaki around the dockyard was destroyed. Installations became a shambles of twisted steel and toppled cranes. Access roads blocked. Factory machines silenced.'[4]

Australian Richard Downie also recalled that raid from his viewpoint in a shelter in Camp 14b. 'It was a beaut. According to my notes, one man killed and six injured in our camp...the ground started to shake

[4]R.E. Bryer, *White Ghosts of Nagasaki*, Settle, Yorkshire, self-published ,1997

as hundreds of bombs spread their pattern along the industrial area. We used to say that those lucky American bastards will be back at their base in a couple of hours, sitting down in their mess eating bloody big steaks and eggs and drinking beer.'

After that bombing, POWs were put to work digging a tunnel in a hillside away from the camp. They reasoned that 'we were digging our own tomb in the event of an invasion; all they would have to do would be to herd us inside and blast the two entrances.'[5] Sidney Lawrence from the RAF was told this was exactly what would happen. He feared slow death by suffocation in the darkness of the blasted-in tunnel. He spoke some Japanese and so he asked a guard that if the prisoners were forced into the tunnel, please could the man shoot him. He agreed that if Lawrence gave him good reason by running away, the guard would shoot Sid Lawrence in a mercy killing.

In Camp 14b, Dr Aidan MacCarthy and other POWs were also forced to dig a pit about six feet deep and twenty feet square. 'Whilst we were digging, civilian carpenters began to erect a long wooden platform about fifteen feet from the edge of the hole. It did not take us long to work out that we were digging our own grave. The platform would be used to mount the machine guns which would carry out our slaughter... we dug on incredulously, our feelings numbed. To dig one's own grave is an extraordinary sensation. I had a fantasy glimpse of my own shot-up corpse lying in the watery mud.'

[5]Hugh Clarke, *Last Stop Nagasaki,* Sydney, Allen and Unwin Australia, 1985

According to the US Strategic Bombing Survey, the attack of 1 August had left 2,300 citizens of Nagasaki dead. The prisoners of war had been lucky. The men had survived fighting in Malaya and Java, incarceration in Singapore and elsewhere, the horror of the Railway of Death, American torpedoes smashing a hellship, and brutal Japanese winters. Malaria, dysentery, beriberi, tropical ulcers or cholera had touched all of them, but magically moved on. Would their luck hold out one last time when the atomic bomb was dropped on Nagasaki? It depended on precisely where the bomb was dropped, and the exact position of the prisoners at that moment.

14

BOCK'S CAR

In the early morning darkness of 9 August 1945, on the tiny Pacific Ocean Island of Tinian, the crew due to fly a specially adapted B-29 bomber carrying an atomic bomb were already hard at work. The aircraft was named *Bock's Car (or Bockscar)* after its regular pilot Captain Frederick Bock, but today the commander was twenty-five-year-old Major Charles 'Chuck' Sweeney, from North Quincy, Massachusetts. In its belly was an atomic bomb more powerful than the uranium bomb that flattened Hiroshima just three days earlier. The 11 foot long plutonium bomb was called *Fat Man*, either to reflect its barrel shape or, as some claim, after Winston Churchill. Its explosive power, the equivalent of 22,000 tons of TNT, was nearly one and a half times that of the Hiroshima bomb.

Flying alongside Sweeney and his crew of twelve men were two observer planes carrying photographic equipment and scientific devices to record the bomb's impact. *The Great Artiste* was piloted by Fred Bock himself and the *Big Stink* by Major James Hopkins Jr. Apart from photographic equipment, the *Big Stink* also carried two representatives of the United Kingdom. They were British scientific adviser William Penny, a mathematician from Imperial College, University of London, and RAF Group Captain Leonard Cheshire who had been personally chosen by the Prime Minister to report back directly to Churchill.

Unlike the smooth preparations for the bombing of Hiroshima, the day was troublesome for *Bock's Car* and its crew from the start. Later it was described as a mission that almost failed. Before take-off, a fuel transfer problem from the auxiliary tank to the main tank was identified. This reduced the amount of fuel available for the long flight by 600 precious gallons. The bomb was already live, and resolving the fuel transfer problem or switching the bomb to another B-29 would take hours. Stormy weather was forecast ahead for the next few days. Waiting on Tinian was not an option. Running out of fuel was a risk but it was decided that the mission should proceed, with the emergency option of refuelling in Okinawa, rather than returning directly to Tinian.

The chaplain on Tinian prayed for the men and their mission. The weather forecast was checked and showed no signs of improvement. In the darkness before dawn, *Bock's Car,* carrying the most powerful bomb ever manufactured, finally thundered down runway A on the tiny island. At the end of the dark runway, where the fat thread of tarmac met the endless ocean, the spotlight had been inexplicably turned off. In the darkness, Chuck Sweeney sensed he was at the very end of the runway, as *Bock's Car* strained and then slowly lifted into the air. Sweeney breathed an inward sigh of relief. This was not a cargo you wanted to be carrying if your B-29 did not become airborne.

However, the difficulties of the mission were only just beginning. On runway C ready to depart, James Hopkins, the commander of the *Big Stink,* discovered that one of his passengers, Dr Robert Serber, an American scientist and photographic expert, had broken safety protocol by forgetting his parachute. Serber might be the only passenger capable of operating such sophisticated camera equipment, but he was still immediately ordered off the plane. He stood, a lonely figure on the dark taxiway, as the *Big Stink* headed off into the distance without its photographic specialist.

On the long flight to Japan the three pilots of *Bock's Car,* Sweeney, 1st Lieutenant Charles Albury, and the co-pilot 2nd Lieutenant Fred Olivi, took turns flying, allowing the others to grab some rest. All was quiet until, during a routine check at 7 a.m., one of the weapons specialists on board, Philip Barnes, spotted a flashing red warning light on the bomb's fuse monitor. Fred Ashworth, the lead weaponeer who was in command of the bomb, was horrified. If the problem was that the timing fuse had been activated there was less than a minute to fix the issue.

Ashworth urgently told the pilot up in the front. Chuck Sweeney had an option to jettison the bomb and hope to escape the blast. That was not an option he wanted to contemplate. They must have been gripped by an unbearable tension as Barnes hurriedly but methodically examined the mess of wires. A circuit malfunction had been caused by two switches having been reversed. Barnes gingerly switched them back and *Bock's Car* continued safely on towards Japan. All Sweeney could say was, 'Oh Lord.'

Aboard *Big Stink,* the crew were trying to overcome a problem the avoidable absence of Dr Robert Serber had created. Flight commander James Hopkins was hurriedly instructed on how to work the special high-speed camera by experts on the ground. All three planes headed towards the target, which was not Nagasaki at all, but the industrial city of Kokura.

* * *

In Nagasaki, the day dawned bright, a blue sky laced with a few white clouds. Around 8.30 a.m. there was an air raid warning, but the locals saw this as routine rather than a warning of the unparalleled horror to come. For nearly 200 POWs left in Camp 14b, the prospects for the day ahead were more promising than usual. The punishing work in the foundry had ceased and most prisoners were detailed for repair work to the damage caused by the heavy bombing raids of 1 August. Ron Bryer was detailed to fix the roof of one of the bomb shelters, which were so small the prisoners called them 'shelters for midgets'. Others were still digging the tunnel in the side of the hill. Tasmanian Peter McGrath-Kerr was repairing a bridge over the Mifune Canal which led to the tunnel.

The night before, some of the men had enjoyed the rare pleasure of eating meat. A horse had died. It was not young or a thoroughbred, but the men had stewed it cheerfully for hours before sharing out their treasure. The prisoners stirred on 9 August and headed out to their jobs.

* * *

As the B-29s thundered towards Japan, an observer on *The Great Artiste,* William Laurence, who was employed by the military but also writing for the *New York Times,* reflected on the historic enormity of what lay ahead. Having seen the bomb tested in the New Mexico desert just three weeks earlier, Laurence knew what to expect. 'In about four hours from now one of [the enemy's] cities, making weapons of war for use against us, will be wiped off the map by the greatest weapon ever made by man. In one tenth of a million of a second, a fraction of time unmeasurable by any clock, a whirlwind from the skies will pulverise thousands of its buildings and tens of thousands of its inhabitants.'[1]

The three American aircrafts planned to rendezvous over a small island off the southern coast before heading off to Kokura, a large industrial city in northern Kyushu, to drop their bomb. The rendezvous never happened. *Bock's Car* and *The Great Artiste* were in place at 30,000 feet at 8.10 a.m. They waited in vain for James 'Hoppy' Hopkins in the *Big Stink* but, unaccountably, Hopkins was up above at 39,000 feet, and flying dog legs of 40 miles looking for the other two planes.

According to Leonard Cheshire, Chuck Sweeney was a very conscientious man and he waited anxiously for nearly forty minutes, wasting precious fuel. Eventually, Sweeney abandoned the fruitless wait, and headed for the primary target of Kokura. On the way they flew over Nagasaki. Down in the city below, both POWs and civilians were starting their daily business. To them everything was normal.

The bombardier was a Texan, Captain Kermit Beahan, aged twenty-seven. Beahan was a skilled bomb-aimer with more than forty successful European missions behind him. He was so good that the accompanying

---

[1]*New York Times*, 9 September 1945. In his report, Laurence wrongly credited The Great Artiste rather than Bock's Car as the B-29 carrying the bomb.

plane, *The Great Artiste,* had reputedly been nicknamed after him. Beahan had strict instructions to only drop the bomb with a visual sighting.

Kokura has always been near the top of possible targets. It was a heavily industrialised city and home to the arsenal that supplied the Imperial Japanese Army. Some Americans called it the Pittsburgh of Japan. When they arrived at Kokura, the military arsenal was shrouded in haze and smoke. This was clearly not just the expected bad weather. It is probable that smoke drifting over from a huge bombing raid the night before on the nearby city of Yawata was responsible.

It was 9.45 a.m. Three times *Bock's Car* swung above the city; bomb bay open, ready to drop its deadly cargo. Three times the smoke was too thick for Kermit Beahan to achieve a visual sighting and to drop *Fat Man* on the vast arsenal below. With each run, flak from the well-defended city intensified. About ten Japanese Zero fighters were also airborne. By now the crew had calculated that the fuel shortage was critical, potentially leaving *Bock's Car* 50 miles short of the safety of Okinawa. Chuck Sweeney was more concerned about the increasing flak than lack of fuel. A fourth run at the target could be fatal. Sweeney ordered the crew to head for its secondary target, Nagasaki. In that second, Kokura lived and Nagasaki died. As journalist William Laurence observed about the target, 'The final choice lies with destiny. The winds over Japan will make the decision...destiny chose Nagasaki as the ultimate target.'

* * *

At 10 a.m., the small group of Australian POWs, including Sergeant Peter McGrath-Kerr, Private Eric

Hooper, and Private Murray Jobling, who had been repairing the bridge over the Mifune Canal, were surprised when their Japanese guard suggested they went back to camp. They had not quite finished the job and, given that it was relatively easy and in the open air, they had hoped to spin it out longer. Despite their protests, their supervisor insisted and about 10.30 a.m. they headed back. It was an extremely lucky change of plan.

Work in the local coal mine had halted, and so just before 11 a.m., Dr Aidan MacCarthy was one of the prisoners clearing the debris from the bombing raid eight days before. He noticed a line of worshippers carrying white umbrellas, snaking their way towards Urakami Cathedral. Then he heard the distinctive engine noise of a US bomber and saw the B-29 over head change direction, as if it was turning back towards Camp 14b. Immediately, the men raced to the bomb shelters. MacCarthy reflected, 'to dig our own graves with a view to being shot by the Japanese was one thing, but to be killed by our Allies was far too galling.'[2]

Ron Bryer was still shoring up the bomb shelter roof with pieces of timber. Arthur Christie was inside sweeping up broken glass. Sid Lawrence was clearing rubble with four Dutch prisoners. Back from his bridge repairs, Peter McGrath-Kerr was sitting on his bunk reading a book. Fellow Aussies Bert Miller and Les Prendergast were having a smoke. Murray Jobling was also laying on his bunk. Eric Hooper and Jack Johnson were on their way back from the latrines.

[2]Aidan MacCarthy, *A Doctor's War*, London, Robson Books, 1979

The shortage of fuel forced Major Chuck Sweeney to fly the most direct 95-mile route from Kokura to Nagasaki even though it risked attack by Japanese fighters. Sweeney turned to co-pilot Don Albury and said, 'Can any other damned thing go wrong?' The crew calculated that they had just enough fuel for a single bomb run over Nagasaki. Instructions had always been to drop the bomb when there was a visual sighting of the target, but Nagasaki, a city of more than 230,000 people, was now obscured by 90 per cent cumulus clouds. Faced with dumping the bomb in the sea because of the terrible visibility, Sweeney and Fred Ashworth, the weaponeer in charge of the bomb, agreed the only option was to drop the bomb by radar.

Sweeney and his crew had no idea that below were two POW camps holding hundreds of Allied prisoners, including Americans. There is evidence that military intelligence knew from captured Japanese troops that prisoners were in Nagasaki and elsewhere. The intelligence noted 'Heard that 2,000 Pw's working at Mitsubishi shipbuilding docks,'; 'saw groups of Allied Pw's along docks' and 'Nagasaki-Working at shipbuilding yards. Well treated and not made to work on Sunday. Unknown nationality but all white.'[3]

Even if the Allies did not know the exact location of prisoner of war camps in Japan, with all the intelligence tools at their disposal it is inconceivable they did not know Allied POWs were captive in Japan. The rescue of so many hellship survivors from the ocean by the *Pampanito* and other submarines gave them direct testimony from hundreds of prisoners headed for forced

[3]*www.mansell.com*

labour. It would not have been difficult to work out that Nagasaki, crammed with shipyards, foundries and a torpedo factory, was a likely destination for this new labour force.

Thirty seconds to go. *Fat Man* was ready to be dropped via radar. Suddenly, Kermit Beahan spotted a hole in the clouds between two arms factories and shouted that he could see the target. In fact, the industrial area was around two miles from the downtown drop point, the Tokiwa Bridge, but making a second run at the designated target in poor visibility was not an option. The giant Mitsubishi steel and ordinance factories were the only possibility now. Kermit Beahan could at last make a visual drop. A few seconds later the Texan shouted, 'Bombs away' and then swiftly corrected himself with, 'Bomb away.' It was 11.01 a.m.

Cradled like a fat explosive baby beneath a parachute, *Fat Man* headed to earth. The bomb door snapped shut. *Bock's Car* banked steeply away to avoid the blast. Forty-seven seconds after Kermit Behan dropped the bomb, *Fat Man* exploded. Chuck Sweeney recalled the moment more than forty years later, 'Time seemed suspended. As the seconds ticked by, I began to wonder if we had dropped a dud. Then suddenly the entire horizon burst into a super brilliant white with an intense flash—more intense than Hiroshima. The light was blinding.'[4] Such was the light that local Japanese called this the sun bomb.

It has been estimated that if *Fat Man* had been dropped just five seconds later, Camp 14b just over a mile away would have been virtually underneath the blast.

[4]Charles Sweeney, *War's End*, New York, Avon Books, 1997

15

FAT MAN

At 11 a.m. on 9 August 1945, Ron Bryer was still
shoring up the roof of one of the bomb-damaged air
raid shelters, which were mainly set below ground level.
Nowhere was safe when the atomic bomb dropped, but
Bryer's good luck placed him in the relative safety of a
shelter. He was out of sight of any guards and decided to
spin out this task for as long as he could. He made the
occasional banging noise to reassure anyone listening
that he was hard at work.

Bryer heard the unmistakeable drone of engines and
peered out through the tiny slit of the entrance. In the
blue sky above, he could see a parachute and wondered
if some unlucky aircrew was baling out. As Ron Bryer
heard a crescendo of engine noise, he instinctively
looked away:

There was this tremendous violet, white flash,
almost liquid in intensity. Not a momentary thing.
It seemed to last for several seconds...there was a
tremendous vibration along with it, not an explosion
at all. And then, as the vibration continued the
wall of the factory came down. I remember bricks
pouring through the hole and thundering on top of
the shelter and the shelter gave way and a weight

*came onto my back. I think I must have been struck
on the head by one of the bricks because when
I came out, I had a mark on my head. Momentarily
everything went black. When I came to there was
nothing to identify with at all. I thought I was dead.*[1]

In a bomb shelter, his fellow prisoner, Geoffrey Sherring
of the Royal Navy, and his Australian mate, Private
Bernard O'Keefe from Warrnambool, Victoria, were
trying to light a cigarette by holding a piece of glass up
to the sun, when Sherring, 'saw the flash from the bomb,
which was exactly like the sort of bluish light that you
get from electrical welding. It was very blue, and it came
in exactly the opposite direction from the sun's rays—it
completely eclipsed them...then we heard the vibration
and shaking, which wasn't a bang by any means. It was
a continuous shaking of the whole air and earth about
it. Then this thundering, rolling, shaking came along
and everywhere went completely dark.'[2]

Arthur Christie from the RAF was inside sweeping up
glass from the windows broken by the earlier bombing.
'Suddenly the sky became a violent shade of blue. The
blue switched to a hideous liver brown. Now the ground
around me was shaking and thudding. A mushroom of
smoke rose. The sun was blotted out. Then came a blast
like a roar of express trains.'[3]

Even five miles away in Camp 2b the prisoners felt the
impact. Edward Anderson from HMS *Exeter* heard 'the
roar of a million Niagras, the roar became enveloped

[1]First Tuesday: *Return to Nagasaki*, Leeds, Yorkshire Television, 4 November 1984
[2]Geoffrey Sherring, London, Imperial War Museum Sound Archive
[3]Arthur Christie, Unpublished notes, September 1981

in an intense brilliance shaded with blue, the sun paled into insignificance, there was a mighty rushing torrent, sickening hot fetid blast laden with blinding debris, and a flaming curtain of red and purple that enveloped me on every side. Whole sides of the machine shop were blown across the road, every pane of glass left its frame in a hail of lethal, screaming splinters. A giant hand pinned me to the road crushing the breath from my body.'[4]

Kermit Beahan, the man who dropped the bomb, recalled many years later, 'I saw a mushroom cloud bubbling and flashing orange and green. It looked like a picture of hell. The ground itself was covered by rolling black smoke. I was told the area would be destroyed but I didn't know the meaning of an atomic bomb.'[5]

Group Captain Leonard Cheshire in the *Big Stink* was about 50 miles behind the other two B-29's when the bomb was released. There had been no contact with the other bombers as they closed in on Nagasaki. 'Although the sun was shining the flash just lit the cockpit. We were aware of the flash. And we all turned round, and there was the bomb. The moment I first saw it, it was like a ball of fire 3000 feet high because it was designed to be detonated 3000 feet above the ground to maximise blast and minimise radiation. It was like a boiling sort of fire, but the fire rapidly died down and became, I don't know what to call it, a cloud, a churning, boiling, bubbling cloud, getting larger and larger and rocketing upwards.' [6]

[4]Edward Anderson, London, Imperial War Museum Sound Archive
[5]*Houston Chronicle*
[6]Leonard Cheshire, London, Imperial War Museum Sound Archive

The Australian and British POWs in Camp 14b were lucky that just before 11 a.m., most of them were relatively protected in a hut or a shelter. The initial danger was from flying steel and bricks. RAF Storeman Arthur Christie was pinned under debris, 'The roof came in and I was buried. I wasn't dead but I thought, this is it, this is how I am going to go. I was really convinced this was the end. At that particular time, I was not too scared or frightened. It was too sudden. Then I started to realise I was alive. I started moving. I started shouting, screaming for help.'[7]

Peter McGrath-Kerr, reading peacefully on his bunk, and his three Australian comrades, heard a change in the engine note of an aircraft overhead and immediately decided to head to the bomb shelters. But it was too late. 'I remember jumping off the bunk and that's it. I jumped into a haze, like a mirage on the road, something shimmering. The haze I think was the heat from the bomb…I don't know whether I was unconscious. One chap said he pulled me out of the wreckage after. I was buried under a lot of timber and steel girders.'[8]

Inside *Bock's Car* itself, the explosion of the bomb was so powerful that some of the crew members were thrown to the floor by the shock waves. They feared that the plane would be broken in pieces by the raw power, or be swallowed in the giant mushroom cloud. 'It was a bright bluish colour. It took about forty-five or fifty seconds to get up to our altitude and then continued up. We could see the bottom of the mushroom stem. It was a boiling

[7]*First Tuesday: Return to Nagasaki*, Leeds, Yorkshire Television, 4 November 1984
[8]Peter McGrath-Kerr, Canberra, Australian War Memorial Sound Archive

cauldron. Salmon pink was the predominant colour. We couldn't see anything down there because it was smoke and fire all over the area where the city was.'[9]

On board *The Great Artiste,* journalist William Laurence was stunned by the bluish-green light and the tremendous blast wave that rocked the aircraft. After forty-five seconds a giant pillar of purple fire had reached the altitude of the B-29:

> *It was no longer smoke or dust, or even a cloud of fire. It was a living thing, a new species of being, born right before our incredulous eyes. At one stage in its evolution, covering millions of years in terms of seconds, the entity assumed the form of a giant square totem pole, with its base about three miles long... its bottom was brown, its centre amber, its top white. But it was a living totem pole, carved with many grotesque masks grimacing at the earth... there came shooting out of the top a mushroom that increased the height of the pillar to a total of 45,000 feet. The mushroom top was even more alive than the pillar, seething and boiling in a white fury of creamy foam.*[10]

Major Charles Sweeney needed to outrun the swelling mushroom cloud. Three days earlier he had flown on the Hiroshima bomb mission, and this cloud appeared to be rising even faster, 'It seemed more intense, more angry. It was a mesmerising sight, at once breath taking and ominous.'[11] He banked the plane hard as the mushroom

[9]Fred Olivi, *Bulletin of Atomic Scientists*, 4 August 2015
[10]*New York Times*, 9 September 1945
[11]Charles Sweeney, *War's End*, New York, Avon Books, 1997

cloud threatened to envelop the B-29. The crew remembered not being sure if the cloud was gaining on them or not. A second dive by Sweeney put them clear. Now they had to reach the safety of Okinawa 457 miles away, but they barely had enough fuel.

Ron Bryer pushed away the bricks blocking his bomb shelter and squeezed his way out into the August air. Blood was coursing down his face which, like the rest of him, was covered in dirt and brick dust. His body felt as it had been scratched all over. Outside the shelter everything was bathed in a strange half-light. Whirls of black smoke curled upwards. He was astonished to see that the huge Mitsubishi factories next door had completely disappeared. The ten-foot tall perimeter fence and the guard hut no longer existed. What little remained of Camp 14b was on fire.

Arthur Christie saw the same devastated landscape. Beyond, the vista was the same. 'There was nothing right away across the hills to the other side, down through the valley. It was just flat. It was as if someone had come through with a broom and swept the whole thing away.'[12]

Big Stink's mission over Nagasaki was to record scientific data and take photographs of the impact. Although their photography expert had not flown on the plane because he forgot his parachute, another crew member had smuggled a personal camera on board. As they made a makeshift photographic record, Group Captain Leonard Cheshire was awestruck by

[12]*First Tuesday: Return to Nagasaki,* Leeds, Yorkshire Television, 4 November 1984

the mushroom cloud. 'It seemed to me to be about 2 miles in diameter. It was still bubbling. It was quite a frightening sight. But what I found the most frightening was its symmetry. Here you had a finely sculpted shape, a mushroom head, a delicate column, reaching through 60,00 feet of space of air...it was completely black. You could actually see particles of dust or soot. And it was impenetrable.'[13]

As Cheshire watched this angry cloud, he thought about the people down below and what had happened to them. The POWs of Camp 14b already had the answer to that question, as Arthur Christie understood. 'We started hearing shouts from badly injured people and began rummaging through what was left of the building, pulling out the injured.'[14]

Although his vantage point was different from Christie's, Dr Aidan MacCarthy was also astonished by the total carnage. 'Bodies lay everywhere, some horribly mutilated by falling walls, girders, and flying glass... those still on their feet ran round in circles, hands pressed to their blinded eyes or holding flesh that hang in tatters from their faces and arms. The brick-built guardroom had collapsed, and the dead guards lay almost naked in a circle round the unlit stove.'[15]

Geoff Sherring and Bernard O'Keefe emerged into a choking brown fog. As the fog was blown away on the breeze, 'We had a shower of the most peculiar rain. It

[13]Leonard Cheshire, London, Imperial War Museum Sound Archive.
[14]*First Tuesday: Return to Nagasaki,* Leeds, Yorkshire Television, 4 November 1984
[15]Aidan MacCarthy, *A Doctor's War,* London, Robson Books, 1979

was in very large droplets, about as big as grapes, and it was entirely mud—just thick blobs of mud falling from the sky.'

Sherring and O'Keefe saw the Japanese guard who was responsible for the storehouse. 'He must have been standing in the doorway, because his skin was completely burnt off him, with a lot of his insides hanging out. I was trying to make him comfortable, but all the skin came off his arms onto my hands, just like thin wet rubber. He, of course, was in great pain, and shouting for a stretcher which I couldn't provide for him, so I left him.'

Ron Bryer peered through the murky half-light, and swirling smoke, 'All around me were members of the prison camp, prisoners and guards alike, many injured, many with their clothes on fire, all moving aimlessly around with the same vacant look on their faces, as if their minds could not accept what their eyes could see.'[16]

RAF Engineer Sid Lawrence, a veteran of the Japanese invasions of both Malaya and Java, was the luckiest of all the POWs. With five others he was unloading rubble from a lorry into a big heap. He looked up when he heard the aircraft overhead and saw the sun reflecting on its wings. Before he could move there was a blinding, vivid flash. He heard the roar of the explosion. The air swirling past him was suddenly hot. Black smoke was followed by a mushroom cloud which rapidly swirled upwards until it blotted out the sun. Sid Lawrence worked his way uncertainly round to the other side of the mound of rubble where the other five men in his

[16]Ron Bryer, Unpublished notes, Settle, Yorkshire 1979

detail had all been working. They were all dead. There was not a scratch on Sid Lawrence. If he had been working on the other side of the huge heap of debris, he would have been killed.[17]

Bombardier Frank Harwood was cleaning a wooden building in the camp with RAF Corporal Ronald Shaw. When they heard the bomber Shaw immediately ran towards the bomb shelter, but Frank Harwood had been ill and was too weak to move. When the building collapsed his teeth were smashed into his lower lip and a piece of roof tile pierced his back, but a large water tank sheltered him from the worst. As the remnants of buildings burned fiercely, with the help of a Japanese guard he found the strength to rescue an Australian trapped under a beam in the rubble. But his work partner, Ronald Shaw, was killed when a wall collapsed on him.[18]

Peter McGrath-Kerr and Murray Jobling had not even made it out of their hut. Jobling was sent flying through the air into what felt like a red-hot furnace. McGrath-Kerr was buried under the debris of the smashed barracks. Luckily, his mates Sergeant Jack Johnson and Private Eric Hooper immediately searched for survivors amid the rubble and noticed a couple of boots sticking out from beneath the ruins. Fire was spreading rapidly. The men hurriedly shifted the debris and dragged the concussed sergeant out before the flimsy timber caught fire and was transformed into a funeral pyre.

[17]Mr Lawrence was mistaken with the number of deaths. Some Dutch POWs did not die until days after the bomb. Only three were killed on 9 August.
[18]Frank Harwood, Unpublished interview, Essex, Jill Turton,1984

Twenty-four-year-old Tasmanian, Private Alan Chick, was working with a Dutch-Indonesian prisoner on the roof of a single-storey building. Chick was blown off the roof by the blast. He was temporarily blinded by the dust and debris but was unharmed. His Dutch companion received burns to one side of his face. Another Australian, Corporal Robert Downie, was buried under rubble but eventually managed to clamber free. The air was hot and thick with dust. His eyes stung. The morning sun had disappeared in the gloom.

Claude 'Boy' Belloni, of the Royal Dutch East Indies Army, was sheltered from the direct blast but some of his Dutch comrades were not as fortunate. 'Almost all the boys who looked at the light were affected by it and suffered horrible burns all over their bodies. The pressure was so great that the whole factory district, which spanned several miles, was completely destroyed, and even houses on the hills were squashed like matchboxes. Except for a few cuts, I was unharmed. I am confused, but my happiness is beyond description. I live!'[19]

The sixteen-year-old postboy, Sumiteru Taniguchi, who was the same distance from the detonation point as Camp 14b, was blown off his bicycle by the tremendous force. As he lay on the ground, he could feel the earth trembling. He spotted his red bicycle laying in a twisted heap several yard away. His letters littered the street. Dust was swirling around him. The skin on his left arm hung down like rags. He felt his back. The skin had been peeled off and hung limply down from his waist.[20]

---

[19]*www.fukuoka14b.org*
[20]Peter Townshend, *The Postman of Nagasaki*, London, Collins, 1984

Arthur Christie was immediately struck by the randomness of survival that day. A few yards away just outside the camp building, he saw his first dead Japanese man. 'A Japanese civilian was laying on the ground, dead. I just stood. I could not believe what I saw. The skin was just peeled from his face and any exposed part of his body was just wiped away as if he had got hold of the skin on his face, and just peeled it off.' Arthur realised he would have shared the same fate if he had not been working indoors.

Ron Bryer was surprised his injuries were not more serious than a cut on his head. He could see men moving like ghosts in the sea of rubble that was once the prison camp, some with their clothes on fire, others apparently blinded. As he stood dumbfounded, Bryer saw Japanese workmen running wildly through the haze, 'Possibly a hundred in number. Leaping and scrambling with desperation over the fallen fences and rubble. None looked either right or left as they passed me on both sides. I heard no sound except the noise of their panting. The desperate noise of animals cornered after the hunt. Deep sobbing gasps of despair from lungs tortured by the demands of a flight from death.'

The Japanese workmen were instinctively heading for the apparent safety of the green hills that segmented the two valleys of Nagasaki and had shielded the city from an even more destructive impact, 'Many wore clothing still on fire. It smouldered and sparked as they ran. But others cared not. Others, almost naked, bore huge blisters as big as party balloons on arms and legs and torn remnants of scorched cloth burned into other body areas exposed to the blast. Blisters collapsed as I watched, and streamers of ragged skin fluttered like wind-torn pennants as the men fled in terror towards the imagined safety of the open countryside.'[21]

Now wearing only pants and a singlet, the Japanese camp sergeant waved vigorously at Bryer to follow this ragged, blistered army of a hundred men towards the hillside. Whether it was to escape the fires of what had once been the industrial heart of Nagasaki, or in case a second deadly bomb was soon to be unleashed from the heavens, he did not really know. Bryer pushed on, scrambling over the debris of houses and factories, past the fires and twisted remains of buildings, towards safety.

From his own shelter, Aidan MacCarthy started running too. He could not find a bridge over the Urakami River. The only option was to swim. Other desperate POWs followed his example. Wet and muddy, they headed for the foothills. 'En route we were physically sickened by the endless stream of burnt, bleeding, flesh-torn stumbling people...the whole atmosphere was permeated with blind terror, and the macabre twilight was illuminated by numerous fires, the crackle of which mixed with the screams of the dying and the injured.'[22]

As they ran towards the hills, MacCarthy and his small band of men occasionally stopped to help, 'But we realised it was useless because one of the chaps pulled a woman and her complete skin came off her face. Another chap tried to help a child and the child's arm came away complete. And the thing was something beyond all understanding, and we kept running.' [23]

[21]R.E. Bryer, *The White Ghosts of Nagasaki*, Settle, Yorkshire, self-published, 1997
[22]Aidan MacCarthy, *A Doctor's War*, London, Robson Books, 1979
[23]*'Away to the War'*, Dublin, RTE Radio, 18 October 1995

Sgt W.F. Heythekker from the Dutch East Indies recalled, 'Out of the debris came the screams for help of thousands of people buried alive under wooden beams. Those of us not heavily wounded set to work to help as much as possible.'

His fellow Dutchman 'Boy' Belloni looked out across the city. 'Little is left of Nagasaki. No flowers, no trees, no more grass. Only boiling concrete and molten iron and steel. Within a minute, thousands of houses were on fire. There were only flames...smoke...and the weeping of the dying.'[24]

British prisoner Frank Harwood described the scene to a German journalist thirty-six years later. 'Everywhere people wandered about, naked, or in charred rags, with fearful burns. There were old people and children amongst them, whose burnt skin hung from their bodies in shreds. They screamed piteously for water.'[25]

On his desperate flight away from the devastation of Camp 14b, the RAF's Sidney Lawrence noticed a strange phenomenon etched in concrete, 'There were shadows in the concrete. No people. Just the shadows... in the concrete was the shadow of a person who had been sitting there and a person standing.'[26]

Java-born 'Boy' Belloni described the same phenomenon in his diary. 'A conflagration of flames, roaring and cracking, all-devouring flames. And then the stench. The pungent stench, in particular, was indescribable, a greasy odour of burnt flesh of thousands

---

[24]*www.fukuoka14b.org*
[25]Winifried Lierenfeld, *Deutsche Volkzeitung*, 23 July 1981
[26]Sidney Lawrence, London, Imperial War Museum Sound Archive

and thousands of people. Many dissolved in nothing. Some of them have only their shadow left, their bodies imprinted on cement or on a wall. People are still in the same position as before the explosion. Only now, charred, thin black dolls.'[27]

Sidney Lawrence was struck not just by the number of bodies, *'a slaughterhouse'*, he called it, but by the strange looks of the dead and injured. Some were badly hurt from head to toe on one side, yet intact on the other, 'I saw a little girl and one side she was burnt and on the other side untouched...she was whimpering, just whimpering.' Lawrence picked up the girl and handed her to a Japanese soldier. He asked the soldier, 'What have we done to you?' The soldier was crying and replied, 'What have we done to each other?' In that moment the years of misery and starvation slipped away, and Lawrence felt at one with the people of Japan.

Leonard Cheshire and the crew of *Big Stink* finished their observation of the mushroom cloud and took their photographs before following the trail of the other B-29s back to safety. Cheshire was awed by the power of what he had seen. 'I thought, this is of an order completely different from anything I had known before. Not just in terms of power, but its nature. The first impression I had was that you cannot fight this weapon. I knew that when I saw it with my own eyes, this has to be the end of the war. I could not believe that any nation could go on fighting that weapon.'[28]

---

[27]*www.fukuoka14b.org*
[28]Leonard Cheshire, London, Imperial War Museum Sound Archive

Arthur Christie also followed the ragged exodus to the hills. He came across a large open space with hundreds of men, women and children lying dead or badly injured. 'The sights were the most dreadful I had ever seen, beyond comprehension almost. The dead were swollen in a grotesque fashion, far beyond their normal size. The injured were so badly burned, the skin hanging from them.'[29] He and another POW carried water bottles and, in the flickering light from the hundreds of fires, they emptied them out into the mouths of the burnt children. But that was all they could do before once again they started running.

On the way, POWs searched destroyed houses for food. Frank Harwood, from Walton-on-the-Naze in Essex, discovered a dead family in their ruined home. In the rubble he was relieved to find a small tin of fish to eat. According to Geoffrey Sherring, one of the more sympathetic Camp guards 'could not find his home. He lost his wife and children and could not even find his house.'[30]

A Dutchman recalled meeting other POWs on the road. 'There were about fifteen of them. Most of them were nude. They had been standing in the open when it happened and then the surging heat wave had swept over them. Their clothes had been scorched off and they had terrible burning wounds all over their bodies.' The prisoners hurriedly helped the injured before continuing their flight, 'Each of us took somebody on his back and went off, with his groaning weight, towards the hills.'[31]

[29]Arthur Christie, Unpublished notes, London, September 1981
[30]Frank Harwood, Unpublished interview, Essex, Jill Turton, 1984
[31]*www.erichooper.org.*

Their fleeing comrades hauled their naked countrymen onto their backs and continued their urgent flight to the hills.

Arthur Christie, Ron Bryer and the other POWs threaded their way up small paths to the hills above the ruined city. On the way, Bryer saw a Japanese woman walking, dazed and alone 'without shoes and clothing, save for a scorched garment hanging from one shoulder. Her face and body appeared as normal, but of a dead white colour...a walking ghost.'

Australian Gunner Murray Jobling was shocked. 'Hundreds had all their exposed skin burnt off their bodies. Hundreds more had blackened skin hanging from them in strips. Others had blisters under the blackened skin. The liquid in the blisters could be measured in pints. I could see it sloshing about as they walked.'[32]

At the foothills of Mount Inasa, the British and Australian POWs stopped running and turned back to look at the devastation they had left behind. As far as their eyes could see, nothing was left that resembled a large industrial city, just debris and rubble lit by the pinpoints of hundreds of fires. One Australian wrote, 'The whole town was one surging mass of flames and the whole sky was blackened by smoke.' He also noted, 'we enjoyed the sight immensely.'[33]

Ron Bryer was also astonished by what he could see below him. 'Climbed the twisting footpaths between the little terraces until, slowed down by the effort, and a return to sanity, we gathered together, and rather

[32]Dennis Warner, *International Herald Tribune*, 9 September 1995
[33]*www.erichoooper.org*

shamefacedly looked down on a destruction the like of which mankind in general can never ever see again and survive.'[34] Fires flickered all over the city, as if it was alive with fireflies. Everything that could be identified as a thriving city full of people had disappeared.

The crew of *Bock's Car* were not convinced they had enough fuel to reach their emergency landing site at Okinawa. They put on their life jackets and prepared to ditch in the sea. Major Chuck Sweeney sent out a May Day alert. As they approached Okinawa all fuel gauges read empty. As Chuck Sweeney put it, 'We were down to fumes.' Sweeney desperately called the control tower in Okinawa but got no response from the busy airfield. Air traffic was still taking off and landing as the B-29 thundered towards the airfield, its 600 gallons of fuel in the unusable reserve tank ready to explode in a fireball if Sweeney did not get his landing right.

As a last resort, Fred Olivi desperately fired every single flare he could find from a porthole. Okinawa finally woke up and ambulances and fire engines were dispatched. As it thumped onto the runway the B-29 bounced 25 feet in the air. The port outboard engine died, and *Bock's Car* jagged to the left towards a parked row of heavily armed bombers. Sweeney slammed on the emergency brakes with every ounce of strength he possessed. Just before the end of the runway the plane finally stopped. They were safe. The B-29 had about 7 gallons of fuel left.

Estimates of the number of people who died differ but the figure of about 70,000 dead immediately, or

[34] Ron Bryer, *Unpublished notes*, Settle, Yorkshire, 1979

within a few days, is the most frequently used. Nagasaki had been protected from even more fatalities by the spur of hills that separated the two valleys of the city. The American authorities lamented the 'waste' of a bomb whose destruction zone include fields and hills. But Nagasaki had still been flattened for about three miles along the Urakami valley, wiping the mighty factories of Mitsubishi away. Only the torpedo factory tunnelled into the hillside survived. If *Fat Man* had hit the intended downtown target the death toll would have been higher. In comparison to the enormous suffering of Japanese civilians, the POWs of Camp 14b were very fortunate. Only eight prisoners died and thirty were injured. If Kermit Beahan had dropped *Fat Man* just a few seconds later, everyone in the camp would have been wiped out.

Within a mile of the epicentre, devastation and death had been total. The POWs in Camp 14b were just on the edge of that radius and many prisoners were protected by being inside at 11.02 a.m. According to one estimate, Japanese in the open were twice as likely to be injured or burnt than those inside. Many locals died further away from the epicentre than Camp 14b. The Manhattan Project report on the bomb estimated that casualties were found in Nagasaki as far away as 2.65 miles from the detonation point. The Nagasaki Prefectural Report on the event claimed, 'Within a radius of one mile from ground zero, everybody died, and within two to four some died while almost all suffered injury. Many who survived the blast later died from radiation sickness, anaemia, leukaemia...'

In December 1945, a detailed study by the US Naval Technical Mission to Japan noted, 'The great majority of casualties resulted from burn, blast, or secondary injury from debris, while many survivors within a radius of four kilometres suffered from radiation effects of varying intensity. Some of these later cases are still dying, some may produce abnormal offspring, and others may be permanently sterile.'

Tasmanian Alan Chick realised his luck when he entered a Chinese barracks not far from Camp 14b. It had been annihilated, 'Fellows were lying there no more two feet apart, lined up on their beds. I touched one on the foot and he crumbled. He was simply ash—they'd been burnt to a cinder.'[35]

[35]*Canberra Times*, 27 July 1995

16

AFTER THE BOMB

From the hillside, the British POWs could see ships ablaze five miles away in Nagasaki Bay. Trees and telegraph poles burned like roman candles. Apart from the occasional girders sticking up at bizarre angles, or the charred remains of a brick wall, there was nothing else to be seen. The industrial heart of Nagasaki might never have existed.

As a doctor, Aidan MacCarthy was pressed into immediate service. Caves in the hillsides above the city were turned into primitive emergency medical centres. The local civilian survivors and the POWs worked together on the difficult task of staying alive, although there was little they could do for the many victims with skin torn from their faces, or molten glass seared into their flesh.

Near the camp, the Australian survivors were astonished to see a horse and cart untouched, as if it was waiting for them like a taxi. Private Eric Hooper, a country boy from a farm in Goomborat, Victoria, was good with horses and took charge of the cart. Nearby was a lorry that still functioned. They loaded up with Red Cross parcels they found in the debris of their camp. The injured Peter McGrath-Kerr was eased onto the back of the cart. His whole body hurt, as the horse and cart rattled through the ruined streets.

A few armed Japanese troops were still patrolling what was left of the roads. One dutiful soldier pointed out to Geoffrey Sherring that survivors on the opposite hillside had no food or blankets. Sherring and three Dutch East Indies soldiers decided to help, and went back into the city looking for supplies. 'The dead were lying everywhere. In the first few days, when we were actually sleeping in the city, my little corner of brickwork was occupied by a Japanese woman whose husband's corpse was with her and she'd covered it over with straw matting, but gradually it became distended and smelly…she would not let them take him away. She had lost everything. That was all she had left in the world. I felt sorry for her.'[1]

Ron Bryer looked round for his friend Brummy Harrison, who had been his constant companion and support in captivity. From his vantage point on the hillside, he could see the blackened, smouldering ruins of Camp 14b. Were there figures moving about amongst the debris? Ron and a mate decided to return to their camp to see who and what they could find. They stumbled back down the hillside as fast as they could, past fleeing survivors, some carrying makeshift stretchers.

Everywhere was blackness, lit up by thousands of fires. The heat was unbearable. Bryer could hear cries of people dying or trapped in the rubble, but they pressed on, past white-faced ghostly survivors and the bodies of the dead. A horse still in its shafts lay lifeless, buried

---

[1]Geoffrey Sherring, Unpublished interview, Jill Turton,1984

beneath a house. At what remained of Camp 14b the men started to search for survivors. Then Bryer had a thought. Could Brummy, ever the opportunist, have used the chaos of the bombing to pilfer food?

The men located the ruins of the Japanese cookhouse. Trapped by his leg beneath the debris they found Brummy. Using a strong piece of wood to lever the rubble up, they eased their friend safely out. Then they headed back through the flattened, black landscape to the foothills, where they left Brummy to rest his injured leg. Then Bryer swiftly headed back down to the camp once more to search for food.

A thick smoke hung over what had once been his camp. Ron Bryer clambered over the smouldering and burning timbers to the cookhouse store. He found a case of corned beef which he quickly grabbed. Then, to his amazement, he saw his rucksack sitting in plain sight, as if it had been waiting for him. Inside were magazines that the POWs had produced in Bandung Camp, Java, as well as his precious boots. He picked up his rucksack. Now the heat and smoke were growing intense. Bryer's hair was singed, and he began to fear the worst. The return had been a dreadful mistake, he thought. He needed both his hands safely to climb back down through the burning timbers. Reluctantly he dropped the case of corned beef, apart from two tins he stuffed inside his shirt.

Bryer saw that Lt Christiaan Alders, the most senior Dutch officer in the camp, was seriously injured. He helped rip a door from the ruins of a building and carry the officer uphill on this makeshift stretcher. Looking at him, Bryer could see that the Dutchman's skull had been almost crushed by a falling beam, and he had been severely burned. He knew he would not survive for long. Frank Harwood also saw Lt Alders. 'He had lost all his face. His face and hands were blackened and had filled up with water underneath. Eventually this burst and the skin hung from him. It was as if he had been burnt with a blow lamp. He was looked after by his brother, Willi, who was with him, and he lived like this for two and a half days.'[2] In fact, Christiaan Alders survived for five days, before succumbing to his injuries and burns on 14 August, aged thirty-two.

Fearing an inferno, the POWs hurried back towards the hillside. On the way they escorted a badly injured Japanese woman and her child to the relative safety of the foothills where their friend Brummy was waiting for them. Injured POWs had to be led by the hand to safety, 'their features swollen to such an extent their eyes could not be seen and the ears appeared several times the normal size.'[3] Ron Bryer recognised a dark-skinned Indonesian prisoner he knew well. The man had been looking up at the sky when the bomb was dropped. He was now white-faced and blind.

Sumiteru Taniguchi somehow managed to stumble agonisingly to the safety of the tunnels where the Mitsubishi torpedo factory was located. A woman employee saw the sixteen-year-old, his skin in shreds, and hurried to fetch him a small cup of water. She gently cut the hanging skin from Taniguchi's arm and back with a pair of scissors, and then did her best to clean up his terrible wounds. A male worker hauled the boy onto

[2]Frank Harwood, Unpublished interview, Essex, Jill Turton, 1984
[3]Ron Bryer, Unpublished notes, Settle, Yorkshire, 1979

his back and carried him for ten minutes up the steep hillside to a patch of flat green grass. The man carefully laid the post boy on his front, a position he would lay in for many months to come. Later that day he lifted his head to see about thirty badly injured people struggling up the hill to join him on the grassy little plateau.

Mount Inasa was only 330 metres high, and for generations the citizens of Nagasaki had climbed to its summit because it gave them unparalleled views of the vibrant city stretching all the way down to the harbour. Now, the picture from here was just empty devastation, a valley of death. As the exhausted men looked down from the crowded hillside, they tried to make sense of what had happened. They knew nothing of Hiroshima, or the atomic bomb.

Several Australians rested in the foothills in a concrete building that had somehow survived the blast. Hundreds of people who could make it no further were huddled there, 'Most of them were nude, their clothes had been burnt away by the blast and they were terribly burnt. The air was filled by cries and groans, and it was a gruesome sight, accentuated by the grey, smoky atmosphere.'[4]

The small band of Australians eased their horse past fallen cables and timber until they could make no further headway. They would have to walk the rest of the way. Peter McGrath-Kerr was gently lowered from the cart, and a wooden stretcher was improvised. The POWs were determined not to touch the precious food parcels on the cart until they could share the food with their fellow Australians. On their way up the hillside, they ate raw vegetables they found in the paddocks.

[4]*www.erichooper.org*

That evening, the exhausted POWs slept in open ground on the hillsides. Food was shared amongst the survivors, but there was a desperate shortage of water. A burst of rain earlier in the day had fallen black and ominous. Ron Bryer lay wearily down and made space for the young Indonesian next to him, his dark skin no longer a pale white but red and scorched; his blindness meaning that day and night appeared both the same, both equally bleak; his face was twisted and distorted. As time passed, the face of the Indonesian turned black as burns seeped through the broken skin. Ron Bryer almost choked on the smell of burnt flesh. The young man did not say a word; his silence only serving to emphasise Ron's aching helplessness. The young Indonesian desperately needed water, but there was none to be found. This was a vision Ron was to carry with him for the rest of his life.

Even if not all the men could see the fires that continued to burn through the night, they could all hear the distant cracking of wood and metal structures, as what little was left of Nagasaki burnt and collapsed in the valley below. One Australian recorded as he looked down on the fiery city, 'The red glow was that strong, that you could have read a book in the dark; but we slept like roses.'[5]

Ron Bryer knew that all around him on the hillside men and women were dying or badly wounded. Yet, there were no human sounds, no cries for help, just the continuous rustling of bamboo, interrupted by the final death throes of a once bustling city. 'All that long

[5]*www.erichooper.org*

night, Nagasaki burned almost from end to end, we heard the houses crashing down the hillside as they burned and fell to pieces, to form yet another heap of wreckage at the bottom. Two gasometers below exploded as fires burned fiercely, making all our hearts skip a beat.'

Camp 2b was further away than Camp 14b from the blast but was not safe from the impact of the world's most powerful bomb. Even five miles from the bomb's epicentre, the dockyard camp was a mass of flying glass, stones, and wood. The roof of the shipyard building was ripped off. Civilian workers and guards ran screaming from the blast in all directions like crazed ants. Almost immediately the POWs were herded into a large shelter that had been hacked into the hillside. The prisoners were pleased to be safe, but the two large steel doors on their shelter made them as anxious as they were relieved. It would be simple, they thought, for vengeful Japanese guards or soldiers to perpetrate a mass killing of POWs in the shelter.

Before they were ordered into the shelter, RAF Corporal Bill Rafter witnessed the aftermath of the explosion from Camp 2b. 'We watched long snakes of children and older students coming towards us from Nagasaki. They appeared to be dressed in ragged and pyjama-like clothing. When they got closer, we could see that some were in rags, but for many it was their skin hanging off their bodies and the designs of their clothing had been burnt into their very flesh. It was quite horrific.'[6]

Although their prison camp had been wiped out, at daybreak the men from Camp 14b were reminded that

[6]*www.far-eastern-heroes.org.uk*

they were still prisoners. Industrial Nagasaki might have been brushed from the face of the earth, but they were still in a war. As they woke up, Japanese troops arrived, presumably from a town inland. The soldiers were uncertain, frightened even, but they took control of the prisoners who were marched solemnly back down the hill. They must have been a sorry sight, as they limped single file along the paths. The blind, hand in hand with their comrades; the injured carried on doors and other makeshift stretchers; all weary, and above all fearful of what was next. They trudged through an intense wall of heat, as fire greedily swallowed up what was left of Nagasaki.

On arrival at what had once been Camp 14b, survivors foraged for broken slabs of corrugated sheeting and wood to build temporary shelters for the severely injured. On the trek downhill the blind boy holding hands with Ron Bryer did not utter a single word of complaint. In the remains of the cookhouse the men found and ate the half-cooked lunch being prepared when the bomb dropped. Miraculously, water and some rice balls arrived from somewhere. There were no medical supplies, and rags were pulled off bodies and boiled for improvised bandages. The 90-degree heat was intense and, under their homemade shelters of tin and wood, the injured lay in silent agony.

Everywhere they looked, POWs could see the bodies of Nagasaki's citizens crumpled in the debris of their own city. British prisoner, Pat Wiltshire, was equally upset by the survivors. 'I saw a nurse from the hospital with her face all burnt away and she was naked from her waist up and it was as if her chest had been ripped open, it was so badly burned. She came towards us with her hands outstretched appealing for help.'[7]

The small band of surviving Australians were not rounded up by Japanese soldiers until a few hours later. The Aussies immediately regretted not having opened the foraged Red Cross parcels because they were immediately confiscated. Eric Hooper recalled, 'We could hear them opening cans etc and eating the contents. We were very hostile. We didn't have a feed ourselves.'[8]

Peter McGrath-Kerr, like the other injured men, was carried on a homemade stretcher down the hillside and placed in one of the improvised shelters. His head and eyes were bloody, and his face was peppered with small burns. His teeth were smashed, and his top lip and tongue badly cut. Five of his ribs were broken plus three bones in his left hand.

By now, the young Indonesian being looked after by Ron Bryer was completely disfigured. 'You couldn't recognise his features at all. His ears had swollen to three or four times their normal size. The suffering he must have been going through must have been indescribable.'[9]

Uninjured survivors were immediately set to work on the grimmest of tasks. For several days the POWs became a temporary cremation party for both their fallen comrades and thousands of Japanese locals. In

[7]Pat Wiltshire, Unpublished interview, Jill Turton, 1984
[8]*www.erichooper.org*
[9]*First Tuesday: Return to Nagasaki*, Leeds, Yorkshire Television, 4 November 1984

the intense heat, the men searched beneath collapsed buildings for bodies. Timber was salvaged to build fires and by the end of the day the prisoners had built twenty ragged wooden pyres with twenty or twenty-five bodies gently placed on each one. At nightfall the pyres were lit, and by morning they had burnt out. The next day the POWs started their unwelcome work in this improvised crematorium once again.

Dr Aidan MacCarthy was deemed more useful by the Japanese secret police burning bodies than tending the injured. He joined the mass cremation squads. 'Parties of women and children carried in loads of wood which were then laid in long piles. After a half-hearted attempt at identification the bodies were laid on the wooden piles, sprayed with oil and set alight. The smell of burning flesh was overpowering; it permeated our bodies and our clothing, and it took several weeks to get rid of that smell from our noses. It remains one of my most horrific memories from those charnel days.'[10]

Geoffrey Sherring was tasked with piling dead Japanese bodies on the pyres of salvaged timber. 'We were left with rows of corpses a hundred yards long. The police chalked the identity of the corpse on the pavement beside the body. Then, as we left in the afternoon, we set fire to the timber, and the following morning the whole thing had burnt out. The calcified skeletons were lying on a row in the road with their names beside them. They were then able to be picked up with chopsticks and put in their little wooden boxes.' Despite this grim task, Sherring showed no sympathy for the local dead. 'The

---

[10]Aidan MacCarthy, *A Doctor's War*, London, Robson Books, 1979

Japanese had scarcely endeared themselves to me. I felt they deserved it.' [11]

There were exceptions to the mass cremations. Robert Shaw from the RAF was the only British POW who was killed by the bomb, along with seven Dutch victims. Arthur Christie and a second POW took personal charge of Shaw's cremation. They wrapped their mate carefully in cloth and placed him gently on the wooden pyre. They lit the fire and stepped back, and then paused for a moment of silence for their dead friend. The two men waited patiently throughout the night until the pyre burnt out. They scooped up the ashes and placed them in a little white box, which they gave to the Japanese authorities for safe keeping.

The death of one British prisoner was deeply personal to the POWs but it was completely overshadowed by the slaughter of thousands of Japanese civilians. Aidan MacCarthy saw the scale of Japanese deaths close-up. He was sent to a Mitsubishi office building. An astonishing and horrific sight greeted him. 'Nearly 500 girls had been working in these offices, and when the building had been hit, they had been catapulted out. They were spread in a human carpet up to a distance of nearly a thousand feet, giving the impression of a nightmare doll factory. The majority lay, unmarked and unburnt, still in their trouser suits, and seeming as if they were waiting to be replaced on a massive shelf.'[12]

Among the Japanese civilian dead were over 1000 doctors, nurses, and patients at different hospitals. The

[11]Geoffrey Sherring, London, Imperial War Museum Sound Archive
[12]Aidan MacCarthy, *A Doctor's War,* London, Robson Books, 1979

Urakami Roman Catholic Cathedral was destroyed and with it two hundred worshippers and twenty priests who had been patiently waiting for confession. One local primary school close to the epicentre lost 1581 pupils and teachers, and in another 1300 died. Less than half a kilometre from the POWs at Camp 14b, about 1000 people were killed in the Mitsubishi Steel Works. Twenty-nine-year-old Dr Tatsuichiro Akizuki was one of the surviving doctors. When he looked out from the ruins of his hospital for the first time, 'There was no sign of any movement, of either man, woman or beast...the town was dead. But where had all its people gone? I believed they also must have all died.'[13]

Dr Akizuki had lost his hospital as well as most of his equipment and medicine, but he immediately did the best he could to tend to his huge number of desperate patients. 'The gaping wounds on their backs seemed to be packed with something like boiled rice, which proved to be maggots. I picked them out individually with a pincette.' His chief nurse lost ten relatives, including her mother, whose 'skin had blackened and only the mucus membrane of her mouth was whiteish. She had hardly any external injuries. Yet her last moments had come. The chief nurse broke down, crying over her old mother.'

On his grassy hillside, Sumiteru Taniguchi faced another day. The sixteen-year-old craned his neck to look round for the thirty injured citizens of Nagasaki

[13]Tatsuichiro Akizuki, edited by Gordon Honeycombe, *Nagasaki 1945*, London, Quartet, 1981

who had joined him on the grass. All of them were dead. He could not think about the corpses surrounding him because his thirst was so overwhelming. He crawled to a persimmon tree a few yards away. With an incredible effort he grabbed a branch and three unripe berries hit the ground. They tasted unpleasant but gave him juice and nourishment.

For three more days the POWs worked in this informal outdoor crematorium. Back in the ruins of Camp 14b the injured and sick still suffered terribly under their makeshift shelters. With food scarce and no medicines there was little that could be done for them in the intense heat. Flies began to swarm around the injured men and their colleagues had to be constantly vigilant for maggots.

The desperate survivors were relieved when they were ordered to leave the smoky remnants of their ruined camp. The men were marched about 8 miles to their new home which was a recently constructed army camp on the outskirts of the city. The injured men, mainly Dutch, were carried on improvised stretchers. British POW Frank Harwood was so weak from lack of food that he climbed the stairs in the new camp on his hands and knees.

This new camp did not free them from the grisly task of burning corpses which continued to be their daily duty. Now the major challenge for POWs and local Japanese alike was food. The men from Camp 14b were delighted to buy an ancient bullock from a local farmer, with a combination of money and a pair of boots. 'Two of the men who had done some butchering carved the bullock up on the floor. You have never seen such a mess in all your life. Then we cooked it. Finally, a magic moment when we ate the first meat any of us had tasted in a long time. It was marvellous.'[14]

Sid Lawrence had been lucky because he had survived while some of his Dutch colleagues working nearby were killed when the bomb dropped. Now he found big cracks between his fingers and toes had suddenly opened, and a vivid green puss was oozing from the fissures. To his surprise, the Japanese found him some ointment which helped mend the cracks.

As the POWs continued their work as a crematorium squad, Sumiteru Taniguchi's grandfather was searching for him. Carefully tracing the postboy's route, he finally found his grandson lying in the shade of a tree. Grandfather was horrified by the condition of the boy but managed to get him to a school that had been transformed into an evacuation centre. The boy was placed gently down on his front and his exhausted grandfather collapsed next to him. Having found Sumiteru, the older man was not going to let him out of his sight now.

A small group of Camp 14b survivors, led by Squadron Leader Aidan MacCarthy, were separated from their colleagues and shipped north to Fukuoka Camp 26 at Keisen. They were spared the grim task of further cremation work in Nagasaki, but now they had to labour in a coal mine owned by the Aso Mining Corporation.

The new Camp 14b just outside Nagasaki was surrounded by paddy fields and a peaceful stream ran nearby. One evening, Ron Bryer was enjoying this

---

[14]Arthur Christie, Unpublished notes, London, September, 1981

tranquil scene as an escape from the daily horrors of burning corpses. Across the stream stood a guard with a rifle, an older man. He stepped across the stream and stood next to Ron. Putting his finger to his lips as a sign of secrecy he said to the Yorkshireman in Japanese, 'The war is over.'

17

SURRENDER

On 15 August, an extraordinary event in Japanese history took place. For the first time, the Japanese people heard the voice of Emperor Hirohito on the radio. In Japan, the emperor was a higher being, akin to a God and he did not speak in public, let alone on the radio. Japan's war cabinet was divided about whether to capitulate or not. So, the momentous final decision was left to Hirohito himself. His decision to end the war was shaped not just by the devastating impact of two atomic bombs[1] and the prospect of Tokyo and other cities being destroyed, but by the declaration of war by Russia and their invasion of Manchuria. A negotiated peace would have preserved Japan's honour, but now she faced the humiliation of surrender.

Young army officers tried to stop the announcement of capitulation. To them, preservation of the emperor and the Imperial system were more important than the vast numbers of civilian dead in Hiroshima and Nagasaki. But their attempted *coup d'état* failed to silence the broadcast, and finally the emperor told his people

---

[1]American War Dept promised a third atomic bomb for delivery by August 17/18th

that the war was over, saying 'the enemy has begun to employ a new and most cruel bomb, the power of which to do damage is, indeed, incalculable, taking the toll of many innocent lives. Should we continue to fight, it would not only lead to the collapse and obliteration of the Japanese nation, but also it would lead to the total extinction of human civilisation.' As the emperor's capitulation message echoed across the airwaves of Japan, his subjects did not hear the shameful word 'surrender', but they understood that the conflict was at an end. When the coup failed, warmonger General Anami committed suicide in the time-honoured way, slitting his stomach with a dagger to commit *hara-kiri*. It took three hours for him to die.

This history-making broadcast was followed by meetings in POW camps all over Japan. In the new Camp 14b, the commandant gathered the prisoners together and told them the war was at an end. Then the guards all marched off down the road never to be seen again. At Nagasaki's Camp 2b, work stopped and their guards also drifted away. This scene was repeated at camps throughout the country. After three and a half years of brutal captivity the POWs from Britain and Australia, the Netherlands and America were free at last.

Prisoners in all corners of Japan cheered and hugged each other. In some camps POWs burst into singing 'God Save the Queen' and 'There'll always be an England.' But with freedom came new dangers; joy was tempered by doubt. There was virtually no rice left to eat, so where would they find food? The health situation had worsened so seriously in recent months, perhaps freedom had come too late?

There was a distinct change of tone and behaviour from their captors. In Announcement 17, in August, the overall commander of the Fukuoka camps sympathised with the 'trouble and agony' of the POWs and noted 'the supreme joy' of returning 'to your dear homeland.' He emphasised how much the guards had done for the POWs but regretted that the conditions in Japan meant that they could not do, 'half of what we wanted to do for you, but I trust in your great understanding on this point.'

This struck a deeply hollow note with POWs who had seen their mates die through neglect and cruelty. Lieutenant Ralph Syred, a surgeon in the Royal Navy, had been lobbying for years for more medicines for Camp 2b. On surrender, he was appalled when he discovered the volume of medicines the Japanese had held back. 'We received thirteen wooden crates with medical materials. In my opinion, failure to provide these medical supplies has caused prisoners to become more seriously ill, and also to death.'[2]

Across Japan the POWs found not just the medical supplies that could have saved the lives of thousands but also clothes, blankets and Red Cross parcels the Japanese had never issued. Australian journalist Rohan Rivett discovered a letter sent by his wife almost three years before, in October 1942, which the Japanese had withheld.

The other major concern for the newly liberated men was security. What if the Japanese plan was still to kill all POWs? After all, the Americans had just wiped out

[2]Ralph Syred, War Crimes Affidavit, Westminster, London, 16 April 1947

two of Japan's great industrial cities, both with a single bomb. Would the guards kill their prisoners in revenge? In one camp this concern took care of itself. 'Then we heard explosions all over the place. Japanese soldiers and Korean privates and corporals were committing *hara-kiri* by blowing themselves to pieces. All the Japs we hated were dead.'[3]

Japan was still extremely unstable and dangerous. Soon after the bomb was dropped on Hiroshima, three American airmen were killed by Japanese in the streets, two beaten to death and one tied to a stake and stoned to death.[4] In this grey zone between captivity and freedom, POWs needed to be their own security guards. At Camp 14b's new barracks on the edge of Nagasaki, the fleeing guards left their guns behind. Now, the POW security patrols could be armed.

On the day after the emperor's broadcast, Sumiteru Taniguchi's grandfather moved him once again because he realised that the postboy needed professional medical help. The flesh on his peeled back was bleeding and the boy was in intense agony. Sumiteru was transferred to a temporary hospital in a nearby town, but not without enduring more terrible pain. Much of the journey was by a solid wooden cart pulled by his grandfather and two volunteers. Every bump on the road was agony.[5]

The uncertainty felt by the Nagasaki prisoners was eased when American aircraft were spotted in the sky. As they circled overhead, the desperate POWs were not

[3]Rohan Rivett, London, Imperial War Museum Sound Archive
[4]Gavan Daws, *Prisoners of the Japanese,* London, Robson Books, 1995
[5]Peter Townsend, *The Postman of Nagasaki,* London, Collins, 1985

sure the American pilots realised there were hundreds of hungry Allied prisoners down below. So, the men from Fukuoka Camp 14b scavenged timber and tore doors from their hinges. They built a giant POW sign that no American pilot could miss. They even added an arrow pointing to their barracks for good measure. An American aircrew dropped a metal container with the welcome words attached, 'The country's yours, boys.'

The men at Camp 2b in Nagasaki harbour also spotted a shiny American plane overhead. The plane was so low the men could see that the Perspex nose was full of cameras for a photographic mission. They waved desperately to the aircraft and then grabbed blankets, and even tore their ragged clothes off, to hastily make a POW sign. With a message scrawled on a field bandage the American crew replied, 'Hang on. We'll be back.' Another American aircraft dropped the message, 'Buddies, the war is over.'

In the following days more planes flew over Camp 2b. Underneath their wings prisoners saw the joyful sign, POW SUPPLIES. Huge oil drums cascaded down from the sky like bombs. Geoffrey Holt, one of the survivors of HMS Exeter, recalled, 'they dropped 45-gallon oil drums on parachutes. Some landed on the hard, rocky surface and burst open...we gorged ourselves on the food. Tins of bacon, chocolates, biscuits. Everything. Our medical officer said, "Take it easy lads, you'll upset your stomachs". But we carried on.'[6] The rescue food came too late for Dutchman Johanne Berg who died of malnutrition on 24 August.

[6]Geoffrey Holt, London, Imperial War Museum Sound Archive

In another Kyushu camp, two drums smashed into a room where Japanese guards were stationed, hitting the concrete floor. 'The contents were tomato puree. Well, you never saw such a bloody mess and you never saw so many red Japs in your life. They ran out of the door absolutely red with tomato puree.'[7]

The American pilots were still learning the skills required for this new manoeuvre. So, the second time they dropped supplies at Camp 2b the prisoners sensibly hid from danger. Having survived the horrors of Japanese imprisonment for nearly four years and finally being so close to freedom, no one wanted to be killed by a drum of food dropped by their own side. Dennis Goodrich, an RAF instrument maker from Wood Green in London, remembered, 'One went straight through the guardroom. A couple of blokes were hurt by flying bits coming out of them, tins of peaches and things like that.'[8]

The POWs in Camp 2b were right to be cautious. A consignment of chewing gum dropped on the new Camp 14b missed Ron Bryer by inches. 'Having survived the atom bomb I don't think it was written that I should be killed by a ton of American chewing gum,' he wryly said. He was lucky. In a sister Fukuoka Camp, an American orderly was decapitated by a container of spam dropped from a plane flown by his fellow Americans.

In his secret diary Les Spence wrote, on the first day food was dropped, 'It was one of the greatest moments

[7]John McNamara, Canberra, Australian War Film Archive, University of NSW, 19 September 2003
[8]Dennis Goodrich, London, Imperial War Museum Sound Archive

of my life. The boys were crying and laughing with joy. I actually saw men with tears streaming down their faces.'[9] At Camp 2b the Americans even dropped a bra with the message, 'sorry we can't fill this for you!!'

In the strange state of semi-freedom at Camp 2b, John Ford from the RAF searched for a young Japanese student who drove a streetcar. Perhaps the young man reminded him of his own work on the trains back in Newfoundland. Ford anxiously made his way to the man's house which was lit only by a candle. Ford thought he could see something sticking to his friend's face and 'realised it was his eyeball stuck on his cheek. He was quivering and close to death. And when I came close to him, he tried to say something and what he said was, "I didn't do anything wrong." After that his quivering stopped.'[10]

Until American troops were on the ground the environment would remain volatile and dangerous. The camp commandant at Keisen was locked up for his own safety. Squadron Leader Aidan MacCarthy was the camp's senior officer. 'A number of the POWs had been all set to hang him immediately. But when the decision was left to me, I decided that it was outside my powers to condemn any man to death. I also felt confident that he would be properly dealt with by the Americans, when they eventually arrived.'[11]

The supply campaign for POWs was codenamed *Operation Blacklist*, and it was touched by tragedy. On

[9]Les Spence, edited by Greg Lewis, *From Java to Nagasaki,* Wales, Magic Rat, 2012

[10]*CBC Canada,* 29 September 2013

[11]Aidan MacCarthy, *A Doctor's War,* London, Robson Books ,1979

3 September, a B-29 nicknamed *Sweet Sixteen* dropped rations for Camp 2b. The aircraft returned the following day for another food drop but *Sweet Sixteen* crashed into a mountainside. Military police and officers from Camp 2b started up the mountain to search for survivors. Eight crew members and all five civilian passengers were dead. On the beach, they found a group of local villagers. With them was a shocked and bruised American called Glen Helm. He was the rear gunner, and the only survivor of the crash.

Despite the tragic accident, supplies continued to be dropped at the two Nagasaki camps, including clothing and toiletries, as well as food. In their fresh US Army outfits the POWs began to feel like new men. They enjoyed the luxury of soap, razors, and toothpaste. The rich food suddenly available to malnourished bodies also brought its own dangers. Not all prisoners listened to the cautionary words of Dr MacCarthy about eating too much sweet or fatty food. Two young Americans gorged themselves almost continuously for fourteen hours, 'Then they went into a coma. Desperately I pumped out their stomachs, but it was no good. Their constitutions were so weak that their gluttony was too much for their enfeebled bodies.'[12]

For the American aircrew, POW food drops were an emotional experience. On 8 September at Nagasaki Harbour, a crew from 99th Squadron flew two very low passes at 500 feet to drop its pallets. Navigator Alex Beichek recalled, 'Between the first and second passes over Fukuoka Camp 2, hundreds of people came out

---

[12] Aidan MacCarthy, *A Doctor's War*, London, Robson Books ,1979

of caves and/or shelters and were waving at us. It was a very emotional moment.' Beichek scrabbled through his case and found a piece of paper. He wrote, 'Gentlemen, we wish you freedom, good health and a return home as soon as possible. Would like to hear from you whenever convenient.' He signed the note and tied it with a piece of string to a food pallet.

After the war he was astonished when a letter arrived at his home in Red Bank, New Jersey. It was from the Dutch Lieutenant, J. J. Budding, an interpreter at Camp 2b. 'When your plane roared as low over our camp as you dared to risk, we stood with tears in our eyes when reading that sympathetic little note, you had dropped... no other words could have gone more direct to our hearts than those few simple sentences. It said what all of us needed so badly — a little cheering up. The first time you came over, most of us stood crying especially when you waved your wings at us. And this time none of us grown men felt ashamed of his tears. And after this those supplies... a rain of the best food we could imagine...million, million thanks.'[13]

About ten days after co-piloting *Bock's Car* and dropping the atom bomb, 1st Lt Donald Albury flew back to Nagasaki. This time his aircraft was not carrying an atomic bomb but doctors and other civilians. In the city he saw the impact of *Fat Man* for the first time. 'Inside the hospital I saw a shadow on the wall—a person had obviously been walking past that wall when the bomb went off. I had never really appreciated until then that this bomb could do something like that. All I could keep

[13]*www.fukuoka2b.org*

thinking was, I hope that there is never, ever another time when we have to use one of those.'

At Camp 14b men continued to die. This was a mystery to the Dutch doctor who had been optimistic the men would recover. On 17 August, twenty-two-year-old Johannes Beer died of burns to his face, chest and back. Five days later Maximiliaan Joseph, also aged twenty-two, succumbed to his burns. Finally, Willem Coumans died on 29 August. The right half of his face, neck, chest and arms had all been badly burned three weeks earlier. Allied doctors were puzzled, as Frank Harwood recalled, 'The doctor was still trying to treat patients, and prisoners helped to care for colleagues. Those who were burnt looked like a beetroot with the skin on. The skin was purple and wrinkled. The Dutch doctor found people dying...and he could not understand why.'[14]

Japanese doctors had also noticed that strange and mysterious deaths were occurring beyond the original carnage found in a circle 500 yards from the epicentre. Now locals were increasingly dying up to a mile or more away. On 2 and 3 September, Nagasaki was hit by what at first seemed to be a second disaster. Torrential rain of a volume and intensity rarely seen in the city washed away the makeshift shelters and flooded the temporary dugouts that families were now living in. Afterwards, doctors and nurses sensed that something had changed, the air felt refreshed and cleaner. Nature had purified the city washing at least some of the radioactivity away.

Nearly a month after the bomb was dropped the outside world had learned nothing about the fate of the

---

[14]Frank Harwood, Unpublished interview, Essex, Jill Turton, 1984

POWs. Journalists were strictly prohibited from entering Nagasaki, or anywhere else on the southern island of Kyushu. However, American war reporter George Weller smuggled himself into Nagasaki in September 1945. The censorship blackout was so total that his vivid reports were not published in 1945 or for decades after, apart from a few bland articles about American heroes returning home. Almost all Weller's writings were destroyed, and they only resurfaced in 2003, nearly sixty years later, when carbon copies were discovered.

In 1967 he did contribute to an anthology of reporters' memoirs:

> *Whenever I see the word 'Nagasaki', a vision arises of the city when I entered it on September 6th, 1945, as the first free westerner to do so after the end of the war. No other correspondent had yet evaded the authorities to reach either Hiroshima or Nagasaki. The effects of the atomic bombs were unknown except for the massive fact that they had terminated the war with two blows in three days. The world wanted to know what the bomb's work looked like from below.*

Weller somehow escaped the surveillance of both General MacArthur's censors, and the American military police. In one of his banned articles, he described his first sight of Nagasaki. 'When I walked out of Nagasaki's roofless railroad station, I saw a city frizzled like a baked apple, crusted black at the open core where the searing sun born at Alamogordo[15] had split open the blue sky of midday. I saw the long, crumpled skeleton of the Mitsubishi electrical motor and ship fitting plant, a

[15]USA Nuclear Weapons Testing Site, New Mexico

framework blasted clean of its flesh by the lazy-falling missile floating under a parachute.'[16]

In his first banned report of 6 September, Weller was surprised that the city's population had not been completely wiped out. 'Nagasaki cannot be described as a city of the dead. The unquenchable Japanese will to live has asserted itself. Though the smashed streets are as barren of production or commerce as Pompeii's, yet a living stream of humanity pours along them.'

Not far from Camp 2b, Weller spotted a ship still on fire a month after the bomb. 'In the harbour, I remember, there still burned the last altar kindled by the fireball. A small freighter, crisped like dry bacon down to the waterline, still smoked, glowed and puffed.'

Later in the same report, which was buried by the military censors, Weller wrote, 'Dropping the atomic bomb on Nagasaki, after Hiroshima's bomb, was like hitting Pittsburgh after Detroit. The puff of death quickly scurried up the valleys of hilly Nagasaki. Whereas Hiroshima was a plain, these small hills tossed the blast from crest to crest like a basketball.'

It had been more than a month since *Fat Man* had been dropped on the people of Nagasaki. The prisoners finally had sufficient food but there was still no sign of American forces on the ground. When would they be rescued? The men just wanted to go home. Ron Bryer, Brummy Harrison, Arthur Christie, Pat Wiltshire and two other newly liberated British POWs decided that they would not wait for the Americans. It was time for them to leave.

---

[16]George Weller, *First into Nagasaki*, New York, Three Rivers Press, 2006

The six British POWs packed a small bag each and headed for the railway station. They were surprised when their way was immediately blocked by four Dutch-Indonesian prisoners who were now acting as the camp police force. The British prisoners were unambiguously instructed to go back to Camp 14b, but Harrison clubbed the biggest of them to the ground with a stick, and the six escapees headed towards the station.

Rail was the only way to get people and supplies into the ruined city. In the four weeks since the explosion of *Fat Man*, repairing the railway line had been a priority for the Japanese authorities. Even so, at first sight the possibility of an escape by rail seemed unlikely. Debris was piled so close to the line that Ron Bryer was not sure a train could even get through. 'Nagasaki Railway Station was just a platform littered with debris at the end of a single line. Over it hung the nauseating smell of death and decay.'[17] They had no real idea where they were going, but an American journalist, presumably George Weller, had mentioned Kanoya, where he himself had arrived in Japan.

To their immense relief a train finally arrived and made its slow, weary way along a track lined with the skeletons of the buildings that had once stood. The men jumped into the first carriage. Efforts from the conductor to get the POWs to pay were met with laughter and suggestions that Mitsubishi would foot the bill. Arthur Christie recalled, 'The last view we had was a very, very sad sight, to see a city flattened and so many dead.'[18]

[17] R.E. Bryer, *The White Ghosts of Nagasaki*, Settle, Yorkshire, self-published, 1997
[18] *First Tuesday: Return to Nagasaki*, Leeds, Yorkshire Television, 4 November 1984

In camps all over Kyushu, POWs waited patiently for the Americans to arrive, but at Camp 17 about 40 kilometres from Nagasaki, the first American they saw was not a soldier but a journalist. George Weller arrived at Camp 17 unescorted just a few days after arriving in Nagasaki. This was a miserable place where hungry prisoners slaved for hours every day down a dilapidated and dangerous coal mine. He filed more stories from here, and from nearby Camp 25, but they too were banned by the military censors.

Eventually, Americans troops arrived. Alistair Urquhart was working in the hospital of Camp 17. 'As I stepped out, I caught my first glimpse of US marines. They had driven into the camp in seven or eight lorries with white markings. For a stunned moment I gazed at them. It was so long since I had seen a white man who did not resemble a skeleton...smiling and strapping Yanks dispensed cigarettes by the fistful, hugging rag-and-bone strangers. Men were shouting and screaming, throwing things in the air, weeping, and kissing the earth, lost in the emotion.'[19]

The six British escaping POWs on the train to Kanoya faced a long journey ahead of them. Ron Bryer sold Pat Wiltshire's battered boots for food for them all. A sympathetic station master gave them shelter and something to eat in his station waiting room before they boarded a second train. After a second long day they eventually pulled into the last stop on that line at 10 p.m. Ron Bryer and Arthur Christie finally understood that their war was over. Two American soldiers stood on the

[19]Alistair Urquhart, *The Forgotten Highlander*, London, Little Brown, 2010

platform, both wearing battledress and steel helmets. 'Welcome back pals, it's the end of the line.' One of the Americans casually said, '"Climb on the truck for supper." In the G.I cookhouse we sat and ate cheese and macaroni pie, washed down with strong black coffee. No one believed we came from Nagasaki.'[20]

The twenty-four Australians imprisoned at Camp 14b had also grown impatient for the Americans to arrive, and they too headed to the ruins of Nagasaki Railway Station. They were intercepted by a British Brigadier who, according to Eric Hooper, ordered them 'in a Pommie accent that all POWs must return to their respective camps. Our reply would not be fit to put on paper.' The Aussies clambered onto the crowded train and headed south. With them the Australians carried the ashes of their eleven colleagues who had died in Camp 14b. Like the British, they too were scooped up by American Military Police at the end of the line and driven into Kanoya. Instead of mac and cheese, the Australians were fed hamburgers.

As groups of POWs from Camp 14b were liberating themselves, Sumiteru Taniguchi was on the move too. His grandfather realised that he needed to be treated in a major medical centre, not an emergency clinic. Once again, the postboy was placed on a wooden cart and was pulled by his grandfather and two other relatives. A fourth man shielded the boy from the fierce sun by holding an umbrella. They pulled the cart for nearly nine weary miles. Every bump on the uneven surface was agony for the postboy but eventually they arrived at a hospital.

---

[20]R.E. Bryer, *The White Ghosts of Nagasaki*, Settle, Yorkshire, self-published, 1997

By now medical supplies from the Red Cross and the US Army had arrived in Nagasaki. Taniguchi was given blood transfusions and penicillin injections before moving to the Omura Naval Hospital where the most serious bomb cases were treated. It was clear that he was suffering from the effects of radiation. His blood cell count and platelets were well below normal. Sumiteru remained at Omura for eighteen more long, agonising months. The whole time he lay on his front.

A second group of Australian POWs, who had been moved out of Camp 2b to work in the mines and then in oilfields to the north, were spared the long railway journey. They had been free for more than a month but there was no sign of Allied rescue until one day an American pilot in a small plane arrived to test the runway. The amiable pilot offered to take a dozen men, the most his plane could carry, down to Kanoya.

Hugh Clarke was one of the lucky ones, and when the pilot flew low over Nagasaki the men could scarcely recognise the city where they had imprisoned for so long. 'I stared down in horror. The entire city once surrounded by beautiful green hills had gone. What remained was blackened desolation with a few scattered buildings and twisted girders protruding like obscene tombstones. I could not imagine what evil holocaust could have wrought such a catastrophe.'[21]

An early escape was not an option for Dr Aidan MacCarthy because he carried the responsibility of leadership in his new camp, Fukuoka 26 at Keisen.

[21]Hugh Clarke, *Last Stop Nagasaki*, Sydney, Allen and Unwin Australia, 1985

On one of his regular forays for food, MacCarthy was astonished to find two Chinese forced labour camps nearby. The filthy conditions in those camps were worse than anything Allied POWs had endured.

After three agitated Chinese entered Camp 26 and confessed to MacCarthy that they had killed four Japanese guards, he accompanied a group of armed POWs to one of these camps.. 'When I arrived, I found the camp overcrowded and very dirty. In the centre of the camp, kneeling on the ground were four unrecognisable corpses. Their heads were mere pulp and every imaginable kind of insect buzzed and crawled over the carcasses.'[22]

The Irish doctor was horrified. The Japanese guards had been beaten to death by every single man of the seven hundred and fifty in the camp. That way no individual could be blamed. MacCarthy realised that the Chinese feared Japanese reprisals for the murders and had come to him for protection. He ordered the corpses to be buried, and told the Chinese that, although he understood, he would never have committed such an act himself. He left a small armed guard in the camp and found some food for the workers.

The Chinese were not the only prisoners who committed crimes in the first weeks of freedom. Stoker Robert Hartley, a survivor of both the sinking of the *Prince of Wales* and the Railway of Death, was still working on the railway in Thailand when the war ended. He reported that two POWs grabbed a local native girl and raped her. The rapists' colleagues meted

[22]Aidan MacCarthy, *A Doctor's War,* London, Robson Books, 1979

out summary jungle justice. 'Of course, they never made it back home. I believe they were suffocated, which was wrong of course, but we didn't go through all that for them to let us all down at the end. I suppose their families were told they did not survive.'[23]

Sergeant Len Baynes, one of the Fen Tigers, was also still in Thailand when the war ended. He caught sight of cattle trucks full of sick and injured Japanese troops when it stopped at a station. 'Those poor chaps must have been shut in without water or food for several days. Nearly every truck contained several dead; many had terrible wounds, undressed and covered in flies.'[24] The British POWs, remembering their own horrific experience crammed into cattle trucks on their way to Thailand, walked along the wretched train offering the desperate men water.

George Weller witnessed the eventual liberation of Fukuoka Camp 17. On 14 September he reported, in yet another banned article, 'Headed by flag-draped American, Dutch, Australian and British coffins, the first columns of released prisoners marched singing this morning to a train and to freedom from Kyushu's largest and most notorious prisoner of war camp.'

Weller observed that each of the four coffins contained several rows of wooden boxes containing the ashes of a total of about 120 prisoners who had died from malnutrition, disease or mine accidents. He also noted that some of the men alive, 'were emaciated to the point that they resembled inmates of Nazi prison

[23]BBC WW2 People's War, *www.bbc.co.uk* 15 October 2014
[24]BBC WW2 People's War, *www.bbc.co.uk* 15 October 2014

camps.'[25] Fukuoka 17 was a particularly hostile place to be imprisoned. American doctor Thomas Hewlett kept meticulous notes of the death toll. They numbered 126 in all, a significant majority due to pneumonia and deficiency diseases. Hewlett noted five deaths by execution, including a prisoner bayonetted seventy-five times for learning to read Japanese.

Stephen Alexander, in his book *Sweet Kwai, Run Softly*, summed up the random lottery of both death and survival. 'Death came sometimes like a bolt from the blue, sometimes like a thief in the night, and sometimes—as for me—it passed inexplicably by at the last moment. Survival, perhaps all victories, demanded a judicious balance between contempt for death and respect for it, between courage and circumspection...'

RAF Aircraft Engineer Fred Neale, a silversmith from Birmingham, described his condition on liberation from Camp 2b. 'I did not weigh six stone and was all bones, gums all receded and teeth all rotten at the roots. We had no hair...amazingly, we suffered no radiation from the bomb; Jesus must have been blowing the wind the other way that day.'[26]

As Fred Neale observed, survival was down to luck. Some POWs sailed safely to Japan; others had the bad luck to be crammed into hellships that were torpedoed. The conditions in different camps, the work they undertook, the quality of the Allied officers and medical staff, and the personality of the Japanese camp commandant, were all factors in whether a prisoner lived or died. The lucky ones avoided mortars and

[25]George Weller, *First Into Nagasaki*, New York, Three Rivers Books ,2006
[26]*www.fukuoka2b.org*

firing squads in Malaya and Singapore, cholera on the River Kwai, or beriberi in Java or Changi. No prisoner avoided hunger and malnutrition, and most suffered from malaria multiple times. For those in Nagasaki, the final slice of good fortune was their precise location in the camp when the bomb was dropped.

If luck played its capricious part, it was not the only reason why a man lived or died. The basic will to live, the determination to pull through, was essential. Once a POW in a jungle camp lost his desire to survive, he was lost. Some men were driven by a determination to see their families again. Others felt they lived for the opposite reason. They did not have a wife and family back home, so could live more easily in the moment, not in the past or future.

Some prisoners had already been hardened in the Great Depression of the 1930s. Paul Stein of the Lost Battalion, the 131st Field Artillery, had been raised in abject poverty in a small Oklahoma town. 'I dare say I was tough. I knew how to suffer; I knew how to go hungry; I knew that I didn't have any money.'[27] His comrade Clyde Shelton had joined up aged sixteen just to help put food into the mouth of his family. Yet, he thought that his fellow prisoners in Camp 2b from Britain had suffered greater hardship during the Depression.

Concert parties, religion, keeping a secret diary or drawings, even a hatred of the Japanese, gave lives a purpose. St Trinian's author Ronald Searle called his

[27]Paul Stein/Dr Ronald Marcello, Denton, Texas, University of North Texas Oral History Collection, November 1998

jungle art, 'a mental life-belt…the graffiti of a condemned man, intending to leave rough witness of his passing through, but who found himself — to his surprise and delight — among the reprieved.'[28] For another superb war artist, Gunner Jack Chalker, his vivid drawings of the Thai-Burma Railway helped keep him alive. 'It was a great godsend…there seemed to be some reason, a very important reason for doing it. And this was a blessing, part of the survival kit.'

Prisoners had little or no control over their own lives and so camps were not for dreamers, but for living each day as it happened. Patience and calmness were valuable attributes. POWs who were good at 'keeping their head down' avoided being beaten as frequently as those who challenged their Japanese masters. Some prisoners called this invisibility 'going grey.' Practical men survived because the shipyard or foundry work, although back-breaking, came naturally to them. They also possessed the mechanical skills to create handmade radios, or medical equipment, or eating utensils, out of bits and pieces scavenged in the foundries and factories where they worked.

Len Baynes of the Cambridgeshire Regiment was a classic survivor. A county rugby player aged twenty-three, he was fit and strong. Before the war he had been a builder, and he put all his practical skills to good use. From the start he accumulated pieces of scrap that could be turned into useful tools. On the Railway of Death he turned discarded Japanese food tins into mugs

---

[28]Introduction by Stephen Walton, Meg Parkes, Geoff Gill, Jenny Wood, *Captive Artists*, Lancaster, Palatine Press, 2019

with handles and sold them for a few cents. He became adept at building huts, fashioning tools, digging graves, butchering beasts and trading with the locals.

Not all the survivors had learnt the rough living skills of survival in the fields of East Anglia or the outback of Western Australia. 'Blood' Bancroft was a bank clerk. Ray Wheeler and Rohan Rivett worked as journalists. There were doctors and padres, university lecturers and teachers amongst the survivors. Many had one experience in common. They been toughened by the depression of the 1930s, 'an apprenticeship in survival' one POW called it.

The mutual support offered by friendship, or mateship as the Australians called it, was essential to almost all survivors. In Nagasaki Camp 2b, when their mate Bandy Donaldson was seriously ill with dysentery, two other Australian prisoners risked a serious punishment by stealing seven tins of food to revive Donaldson.

Even in death, mateship offered emotional nourishment. Australian Stan Arneil compared the clinical nature of death in a sterile hospital bed at home, to dying as a POW on the Railway of Death. 'When a man died, he died in an aura of love and brotherhood which is not available now possibly anywhere in the world. You died with your head in the lap of a man, with somebody holding your hand, with somebody with their hand on your forehead, saying a little prayer and people actually sorry to see you die.'[29]

Mateship was not confined to the Australians. British POW Len Gibson was sustained by a group of close

[29]Stan Arneil / Hank Nelson, *Prisoners of the Japanese*, Sydney, (ABC Australia), 1985

friends from Sunderland, some even attended the same school — West Park. They laughed and sung together, and always knew that there was a mate looking out for them. Humour was also an important survival tool. Jack Chalker reflected, 'If you couldn't laugh, you'd die. You just had to laugh at anything. If someone broke wind, you'd laugh. It was an event. It was absolutely, bloody marvellous. Anything that was funny meant a great deal.'[30]

Twenty-five years after the war, Padre Eric Cordingly was still inspired by the resilience and spirit of the survivors. 'The truly remarkable thing was the way the human spirit rose to magnificent heights. After months of sheer degradation, gradually the spirit to care for each other revived, incredible kindness and self-sacrifice as in evidence.'[31]

Common humanity helped survival, but not every survivor was noble. Most became adept at thieving because that was essential to supplement their feeble diet. But there were some who stole not just from the Japanese but also from their own comrades. Forty miles from Nagasaki, Fukuoka Camp 17 was dominated by a group of American racketeers, a camp 'mafia' who made sure they were well fed and cared for. So, selfishness was also a road map for survival. Some men grabbed every opportunity to avoid work, and not do their fair share of anything. These men were in a small minority, but they existed.

[30]*Secret History: Miracle on the River Kwai*, London, Channel 4 Available Light, 1998
[31]Eric Cordingly/Louise Reynolds, *Down to Bedrock*, Norwich, Art Angel, 2013

As a member of an Intelligence Section, Sergeant John Stewart Ullman possessed a sharp eye for wrongdoing. 'Crime took many shapes. Certain senior NCOs kept men off working parties in exchange for bribes; a sick man would then have to take the place of a fitter and healthier companion.'[32]

Officers were mainly camp-based, and their role carried a different risk. They were the interface with the Japanese and standing up to the captors was dangerous with a risk of beatings or execution. Some officers were superb leaders but, as the poor hygiene at some British camps on the Thai-Burma Railway show, that was not universal. The Australians felt that some British officers were stuck in an out-of-date hierarchical structure. 'Young Pommy lieutenants. Blokes who had come out of officers' training a year or two before. They didn't have a clue how to handle men or anything. They were just so arrogant.'[33] American POWs like Frank Fujita were equally dismissive of the 'well fed, pompous, stuffed shirts'[34] he encountered in Changi in 1942.

Some British prisoners agreed. Dennis Goodrich encountered poor leadership early on at his camp in Java. 'The C.O. in charge was hopeless. He couldn't talk to the Japanese. He was sort of inept...he was no good at all.'[35]

Australian officers were seen as more approachable and less hierarchical. Australian sailor Arthur Bancroft

[32]John Stewart, *To The River Kwai,* London, Bloomsbury, 1988
[33]John McNamara, Canberra, Australian War Film Archive, University of NSW
[34]Frank Fujita, *Foo,* Texas, University of North Texas Press, 1993
[35]Dennis Goodrich, London, Imperial War Museum Sound Archive

noted that 'our officers were good blokes and looked out for us.' Benjamin Manning summed it up. 'The social distance between British officers and other ranks was so great that it was almost as if the British officers and other ranks were different nationalities...one of the most startling things about reading the diaries of British officers is how rarely they mention other ranks. Whereas the British insisted on blind obedience from their social inferiors, the Australian officers had to gain co-operation from their social equals.'[36]

The Bridge on the River Kwai has shaped public perception of all officers imprisoned in the Far East. Generalisation is dangerous. There were brilliant British officers, and some not up to the job. Not all Australian officers were perfect models of leadership. The senior officer in Singapore, Major General Gordon Bennett, was rightly criticised for escaping to Sumatra on the day of surrender, and then home to Australia, leaving his men and fellow officers to face years of misery in Japanese hands.

Whatever luck or skills led to their survival, Ron Bryer and the other POWs enjoyed their hamburgers and mac and cheese in the US cookhouse in Kanoya before they travelled to Okinawa to begin the long journey home to their families. The POWs who had stayed in their camps waiting for the American rescue were delighted to be given showers on the dockside in Nagasaki before they too headed home. Their ragged, filthy loin cloths were burned, and the men were given fresh clothing.

[36]Benjamin Manning, *Embedded Behind Barbed Wire*, Sydney, Dissertation, University of NSW, 2011

The prisoners were deloused, and Geiger counters were run over their bodies searching for radioactivity. Jack Ford relished his new cleanliness. 'We soaped up and they sprayed water on us, and at the time it was the best feeling in the world...Nagasaki was a horrible sight. A stench covered the city from the burnt bodies still lying on the streets. We wanted to get out of there as fast as possible.'[37]

Behind them, the liberated POWs left thousands of dead colleagues. Over 3,500 POWs perished in camps on the Japanese mainland, a death rate of ten per cent. To that should be added 12,600 Allied prisoners who died on the Railway of Death, around twenty per cent of the total. Thousands more died on the hellships to Japan, mainly from attacks by their own side. For an Australian imprisoned by the Japanese the chances of surviving the war were about one in three, a total of around 8,000 men. Examining these statistics at a unit level is revealing. The 5th Suffolks from the 18th Division lost thirty-four men in action in the Far East, but 271 later died in Japanese captivity. The Cambridgeshire Regiments, the Fen Tigers, lost 784 men. Some sources claim that over thirty per cent of the ill-fated 18th Division died.

The survivors of Camp 2b and Camp 14b who were now safely on their way to Okinawa, also left something strange behind in Nagasaki, a phenomenon they could never have known or understood at the time. It was what the civilian hospitals in the city came

---

[37]Jack Fitzgerald, *The Jack Ford Story*, Newfoundland, Canada, Creative Publishing, 2007

to call Disease X. Men, women and children with absolutely no signs of injury were mysteriously dying every day, having apparently been left unharmed by the bomb.

18

Homecomings

The POWs who survived the Nagasaki bomb and years of Japanese ill-treatment now focused their minds on meeting their families back home. Many were married or had sweethearts they had not seen for nearly four years. Contact had been almost non-existent. Now they started to wonder what a return would be like. Had their wives changed? Or found another man? Will my children remember me? Will my parents or siblings be alive? Will they ever understand what hell I have been through?

At their homes in Perth or Portsmouth, Rotterdam or Rhode Island, wives and families were equally anxious. Had the men changed by being brutalised by so long in captivity? How was their physical health? Will they still love me? And, most basic of all, is he still alive? Some families, like Fred Neale's in Birmingham, had not heard from their son since the Fall of Singapore in February 1942 when he had been posted 'Missing believed killed.' They were astonished to discover three and a half years later, in September 1945, that he was not only alive, but on his way home.

News of the men captured in Java had scarcely filtered through to their waiting families. John Baxter was expecting change. 'We had no contact at all with the Red Cross, or the facility of writing home. Consequently, the majority of those in Java were reported as missing believed killed, which had rather dire results when our people arrived home, to find in many cases that chaps' wives, girlfriends had married again, houses sold, businesses disposed of. It was a terrible situation. I was engaged at the time and, after six months without any news, my fiancée married a chap who was a great friend of mine.'[1]

In the haste to depart the men left precious possessions behind. In Thailand, Lance Bombardier Len Gibson was told no heavy objects were allowed on the plane flying him to Burma on the first leg of his journey back to Sunderland. On the tarmac he hurriedly handed his much loved homemade guitar to a young Thai man who was standing and admiring the American aircraft. Thinking that Thai money would be of no value in Burma, Len had stuffed the guitar with banknotes from the sale of silk he had liberated after the Japanese surrender. When he landed, Len saw rows of currency exchange huts. Clearly, Thai cash was not worthless in Burma after all. The young Thai man must have been amazed when he looked inside the battered guitar and realised that Len Gibson had given away a fortune.

Dr Bill Frankland also had an excess of local currency. On his final morning, there was no toilet paper so he wiped himself with a 100-dollar Malayan bill, which he thought was worth nothing. Next day he saw a sign offering to exchange Malay dollars for British pounds,

[1] Meg Parkes, Liverpool School of Tropical Medicine, February 2008

at a handsome rate: 'Was it worth it? That morning I think it was,'[2] he later laughed.

In the twelve days from 12 September, American forces in Nagasaki evacuated around 10,000 newly liberated prisoners. Jack Ford and many other POWs boarded the *US Chenango* at Nagasaki for Okinawa, then flew by military plane to Manila. Liberated prisoners on one rescue ship cried when they heard the chimes of Big Ben echoing over the tannoy, followed by the rich tones of Alvar Liddell reading the BBC News. The men basked in their new-found freedom. The doctors had told them not to indulge, but it was hard not to relish the food and the beer. Almost as important was a comfortable lice-free billet and the freedom to talk about anything to anyone.

Bandsman Dennis Morley sailed on an American hospital ship, the *Admiral Hughes,* 'It was fantastic. They used to have the Glenn Miller orchestra on the tannoy. This night I was on deck when that came on and there was a big moon. There were fluorescents from the waves and Moonlight Serenade was being played and I saw people who were tough, crying. We all cried.'[3]

It was everyday sights and experiences that made the men appreciate their freedom. In Okinawa, Tasmanian Peter McGrath-Kerr noticed, 'The first European woman I'd seen for several years was a girl in a pie stall on the way to the aerodrome, with doughnuts and Coca Cola.'[4]

[2]'The Reunion', London, BBC Radio 26 April 2015
[3]Meg Parkes, Liverpool School of Tropical Medicine, 22 July 2007
[4]Peter McGrath-Kerr, Canberra, Australian War Memorial Sound Archive

John Fletcher-Cooke met an American doctor in Okinawa who was 'the first white woman I had seen for over three years. She was not very pretty, but she was warm and sympathetic, and she was a woman. She threw her arms around me and kissed me repeatedly on the mouth, my emaciated cheeks, and my shaven head. I burst into uncontrollable tears.' [5]

Medical orderly, Ken Adams, was transformed by a smart, tropical uniform. 'I was a human being again. I wasn't an animal wearing rags. Wearing decent clothes gave me a huge psychological lift. Using a knife and fork was the single most thrilling and important trapping of civilisation for me.'[6]

Lance Bombardier Len Gibson shared those feelings. 'We met European ladies for the first time. We ate with a knife and fork for the first time. We sat on chairs for the first time. We saw food that he hadn't seen for many years, and I don't think we could eat it properly for crying.'[7]

In Okinawa, Squadron Leader Aidan MacCarthy found himself drinking with an American stranger in the Navy Club. He was called Richard O'Kane. He had commanded the submarine USS Tang which had torpedoed the Tamahoku Maru, killing 560 of the 772 POWs on board. MacCarthy had been a lucky survivor of that attack. O'Kane himself had also become a POW in October 1944, when the Tang itself sank due to a

[5]John Fletcher-Cooke, *The Emperor's Guest,* Barnsley, Pen and Sword, 1971
[6]Ken Adams, edited by Mike Adams, *Healing in Hell,* Barnsley, Pen and Sword, 2011
[7]Len Gibson, Royal British Legion/Martyn Cox/Mike Thompson

faulty torpedo. Now MacCarthy was sharing a drink with the man whose torpedoes had killed so many of his friends and colleagues. No doubt it was an uncomfortable conversation and ended with O'Kane getting very drunk.

Thoughts turned to the women they had left behind. Many men wanted to make up for lost time. Before leaving for Australia, hellship survivor Arthur Bancroft wrote to his girlfriend, 'Dear Mirla, I'm a free man, just been rescued by a submarine, blah, blah, have you married a Yank yet?' Mercifully, although an American had come calling, Mirla was still unattached.

Lt Gillon Griffith, from Melbourne, wrote to his wife in his secret diary, 'How I am longing to see you again, sweet, in the past there has scarcely been a single night passed that I have not gone home in thought to you, and wished you goodnight, and now just to think that I'll soon be seeing and holding you, and telling you some of the many things I've felt over these three and a half years. They have been terrible, darling, just as they have for you, but I have planned such a wonderful time from now on.'[8]

At war's end, Ron Bryer was a seven stone skeleton, nearly half his pre-war weight. He enjoyed his few weeks in Okinawa, building his body up. He recalled the nightly pleasure of open air cinema and the limitless American food including massive steaks and chops that he could only have dreamt about for nearly four years.

Bryer and the other liberated British prisoners from Nagasaki sailed from Okinawa to San Francisco. Bands

[8]*www.pows-of-japan.net*

played, crowds cheered and drum majorettes marched in a warm welcome. As they sailed under the Golden Gate Bridge, scores of boats came out to meet them. In Vancouver they received an equally rapturous reception. They were showered with fruit and other gifts by hundreds of cheering locals.

From Vancouver, Nagasaki veterans Ron Bryer, Arthur Christie and Jack Ford crossed Canada by train to Halifax, Nova Scotia, to board the ship home for the final leg of their journey. This was the *Queen Elizabeth*, a luxury liner converted into a troop ship earlier in the war. Seeing a British ship on the dockside finally brought home to the POWs the closeness of home.

For Jack Ford, spotting the *Queen Elizabeth* sparked the opposite reaction. Ford was in the RAF, but his family lived in Portes aux Basques, Newfoundland. The *Queen Elizabeth* would take him to Southampton, thousands of miles in the wrong direction. He had not seen his family for nearly six years, over three of those in Japanese prison camps. As the men queued up to board the *Queen Elizabeth*, Jack Ford, the only Canadian in the line, feared that, 'after five years in the Pacific I would only get to see Newfoundland as the ship passed the island.'

Squadron Leader Aidan MacCarthy also took a train from Vancouver across Canada. He was still trying to come to terms with the family news he heard in Manila. In a chance meeting with navy officer from his hometown of Castletownbere, MacCarthy discovered that his brother Barry was dead, killed by the last German bomb to fall on London.

Dr MacCarthy sailed home with a thousand other men on another luxury liner converted into a troop ship, the *Queen Mary*. He was struck by how little the crew understood what the men had been through, but how could they? They lived in a place of plenty, so how could they know that a tiny piece of dried fish or a ragged loin cloth had recently meant everything to these men? The British officer commanding the troops on board issued a string of orders, including fatigue parades. The former POWs responded mutinously and refused the officious instructions. Eventually, their own officers took control and good sense was restored, although civilians still complained about ex-POWs daring to use their deck.

Les Spence was also on the *Queen Mary*. As they left New York, his private diary must have echoed the thoughts of many of his fellow passengers. 'I received five letters today. Very good. Pleased to see that Babs is still waiting. I hope she will accept my proposal. Lovely day, beautiful sunshine.'[9]

The *Queen Elizabeth* finally docked at Southampton in November 1945. Even the driving winter rain could not dampen the spirits of Ron Bryer and the other returnees. At the bottom of the gangway from the ship he spotted two women from the Salvation Army, 'Standing one on each side in the chilling downpour. No one else was there. They smiled and clapped gently as I came ashore. I followed the sign to H.M. Customs shed. Pushed open the door. "Anything to declare", said the man.'

If there was an official national welcome, few Far East POWs were aware of it. Tom Jackson did spot a banner,

---

[9]Les Spence, edited by Greg Lewis, *From Java to Nagasaki*, Wales, Magic Rat, 2012

but it was not what he expected. 'It was a miserable winter's day, wet, miserable, dank, dark, cloudy, foggy, the lot...you could see the shore, bits of gloom and lights and everything. As you got closer to the quayside you could see a great big banner...as we got closer, it read "Goodbye to our American friends".'[10]

Coming from the sunshine and colours of the tropics, the drabness of post-war Britain was a shock. Gunner Jack Chalker landed at Liverpool. 'We went into some old, sort of Nissen hut, running with water on the ground...everything was tired and dirty and there was no sun, and people squabbling over half a pound of tomatoes; it was a sad, tired England that had gone through an awful time.'[11]

When Bandsman Dennis Morley arrived home in Brighton, he took a taxi from the station. The taxi driver would not take any fare money. 'That was the first act of kindness we had in England because...we were treated worse in England than the bloody Japs treated us...the attitude, we couldn't care less about you mate. Get on with it. I have never forgiven the government.'[12]

The returnees were vastly different from the naive young men who had left five years before. One returning prisoner was so thin and unrecognisable that his family walked past him on the railway station platform. The survivors might be carrying emotional and physical scars inflicted by the Japanese, but they were home.

[10]Meg Parkes, Liverpool School of Tropical Medicine, 21 November 2007
[11]Geoff Gill, Liverpool School of Tropical Medicine, 27 July 2010
[12]Meg Parkes, Liverpool School of Tropical Medicine, 22 July 2007

For the children who had not seen their dad for four or even five years, it was a strange experience when a gaunt looking man calling himself father turned up. But they were swept up in the joy of dad's homecoming, as Mike Nellis recalled at Scarborough Station. 'It was a dank sort of night and the train came into the station with all the steam and hissing and what have you, and we looked down the platform and the doors opened and this figure came out and my mother stiffened up a little bit and my sister grabbed her hand...then this figure with his cap dropped his kitbag on the platform and they just rushed into each other's arms...and my father huddled up to me—and that's the last time he ever cuddled me. I can remember it like yesterday! He was shaking and there were tears in his eyes.'[13]

For some prisoners, a noise or an image could trigger a horrific memory, sparking off an outburst of temper. Some had been away from children so long they had no idea how to relate to them. Mike Nellis respected his POW father but was also afraid of him, especially at mealtimes if he did not eat his food. 'He would start to glower, and he'd grind his teeth together and we all knew he was getting mad and the left corner of his lip would turn up and he had dark brown eyes and they were like liquid pools and they'd take on a look of pure malevolence.'

For the first Australians returning home in Autumn 1944, the men lucky enough to be rescued from the sea by the USS *Pampanito* and other submarines, reintegration was an unsettling experience. After the long journey,

---

[13]Louise Cordingly, *Echoes of Captivity,* London, High Winds Publishing, 2020

POWs serving in the Australian Army were shipped in windowless vans to a large former convent perched above Brisbane called Stuartholme. They were well fed and looked after, examined thoroughly by doctors and dentists, and carefully questioned by military personnel. They were shown movies and played tennis and badminton. Yet, for all this reassuring support, the Australians continued to be prisoners. The building was surrounded by high walls.

The Australian government did not want to reveal the horrors of POW life to the public because there were still thousands of Allied prisoners in Japanese hands. How would Japanese guards react to stories of brutality from the survivors now safely home in Brisbane? The returning prisoners became a state secret. Some were happy at Stuartholme and pleased to have the chance to recuperate. Others were resentful that they could not meet their families because the Australian Army banned direct contact.

Memories differ as to how long it was before family reunions finally took place, but it probably took weeks rather than days. What is clear is that it was a month before the Australian government told its citizens about the remarkable rescue at sea by the *Pampanito* and other US submarines, and the repatriation of eighty-six Australians. Eventually, the people of Australia were told about the appalling conditions in Japanese camps. A handful of POWs were allowed to be interviewed by the press, but only under strict conditions.

The 'prisoners' at Stuartholme were serving in the army. The Royal Australian Navy were equally tight-lipped, but they allowed their sailors a more immediate and joyous return home. On landing at the airport in

Perth, Blood Bancroft raced across the tarmac into the arms of his parents. 'I pulled them tight, all three of us hugging and kissing; my mother howling with joy...I had survived for this moment. All so I could come home. The bastard Japs hadn't got me. Instead, Mrs Bancroft had got her baby boy back.'[14] Six days later Arthur Bancroft proposed to his girlfriend Mirla, after over three years as a POW. They were happily married for the rest of their lives.

Bancroft was soon bombarded with letters from relatives of men who had been on the Railway of Death or in a Japanese Camp. Over 100 letters alone were sent by families of men lost on the *Perth*. Replying to every single letter, invariably with bad news, was one of the most distressing responsibilities of the return.

Even when prisoners were released from captivity in their own country, they still felt unwelcome. The work they were given by the authorities was menial, demeaning for a soldier and war veteran. Arthur Bancroft, having survived the horrors of building the Thai-Burma Railway, was even given a job ballasting a railway track. After seven months of frustration, ex-POW Bill McKittrick summed it up. 'Other than relatives I never met anyone who knew about or cared about the POWs in Japan. In fact, it seemed the authorities were ashamed, and were trying to cover it up.'[15] The men felt they were no longer soldiers or sailors, but a national nuisance, an embarrassment.

[14]Arthur Bancroft with John Harman, *Arthur 's War*, Sydney, Viking Australia, 2010
[15]Aldona Sendzikas, *Lucky 73*, Gainesville, Florida, University of Florida Press, 2010

Alan Chick from St Helens, Tasmania, was one of the few Australians who did not leave the forces. Most of the men were happy to have finally escaped Japan, but Chick returned to the country of his imprisonment as a member of the occupying forces. When he finally returned home in 1953, he brought a Japanese wife back with him to Tasmania.

The men of the Lost Battalion returned home to Texas. At the bus station in Abilene, Sergeant Frank Fujita did not recognise his mother and sister and walked straight past them. Then his mother 'let out a whoop that could be heard for a few blocks and grabbed me from the rear. It still took me a few seconds to realise this was my mom. I still didn't know my little sister at all. We hugged and cried and kissed…it seemed that everyone in the bus station had joined in on the homecoming. It was a happy moment, and it was sure good to be back home.'[16]

In Halifax, Nova Scotia, the British boarding officials on the *Queen Elizabeth* finally realised that although Jack Ford was serving in the RAF, he was Canadian. He was given leave to go home to Newfoundland. The small community of Portes aux Basques welcomed him back as a hero. His family were in tears as they hugged him again. The only person missing was Jack's father. He had died in May 1945, still convinced his son was alive.

But Ford was not even allowed the pleasure of his first Christmas at home since he had enlisted in the RAF six years before. He was back with his family for just ten days when he was ordered to Nova Scotia to catch a ship to England. After three purposeless months, Jack

---

[16]Frank Fujita, *Foo*, Texas, University of North Texas Press, 1993

Ford resigned from the RAF. He returned to Canada, and his old job on the Newfoundland Railway.

Aidan MacCarthy finally made it back to Ireland. He had an emotional meeting with his family in Dublin, but his mother was too ill to travel. The death of one son from a German bomb in March 1945, and the uncertainties over Aidan's long incarceration, had taken their toll. On Christmas Eve 1945, she died.

Sapper Lionel Morris had been away for seven years and had been posted as 'missing-presumed dead'. He finally returned to his home in Cheshire:

> *My heart beat like a hammer. I rang the bell a third time…a window opened above my head and my father's voice enquired, 'Who is it?' I answered, 'It is Lionel.' He, somewhat bewildered, asked, 'Lionel who?' 'It is Lionel your son, who else should it be?' He came down the stairs two at a time; the door flung open, and he stood gaping, unbelieving. I thought he was going to fall but at last he got the message. 'I'm all right,' I said, 'I've come home.'[17]*

---

[17]Brian MacArthur, *Surviving the Sword*, London, Time Warner, 2005

19

Aftermath

The tearful homecomings did not signal the end of struggles for the returning POWs. They had survived Nagasaki, prison camps, the River Kwai Railway and hellships. They would still need courage and resilience to manage the rest of their lives. How does a man settle into normal, peacetime life when all they have experienced for nearly four years is disease, brutality, and death? How could friends or family understand what prisoners had suffered, without living through it themselves?

Their average incarceration was three years, much longer than POWs in Europe, and in significantly worse conditions. Some former prisoners had left home in 1940 and had not seen their families for over five years. Many Far East POWs stayed silent; others confronted their experiences. Some were told not to talk; others just could not talk. Britain did not feel familiar, but a strange, alien place. So much had happened while the men had been locked up by the Japanese. The former POWs had changed, but so had the nation they had served.

When he arrived in Southampton and stepped on British soil for the first time in nearly four years, Captain Bill Frankland, a prison camp doctor, made a resolution.

'I decided there and then that I would never mention being a prisoner of war.' He kept that promise to himself until the age of ninety-nine, when he finally relented and talked about his experiences.[1]

Whatever path men chose, the remarkable spirit and determination of these survivors marks them out as war heroes. Unlike the pilots and soldiers of the Battle of Britain and D-Day, these men were forgotten and not feted. Was there a sense of failure, shame perhaps, in being captured? The liberated men were veterans of Dunkirk and the Middle East, Malaya and Java, but were now defined not by their military service but solely by their captivity. As one ex-POW put it when he landed at Southampton, the authorities did not think 'we warranted even the most cursory medical examination. We felt we were an embarrassment to them, to be rid of as quickly as possible.'

Captain Henry McCreath echoed that sentiment. 'While everyone else had been involved in a war of tanks and machine guns, we had been engaged in one of disease and malnutrition. Nobody was very interested in us, so we formed our own FEPOW (Far East Prisoners of War) associations to look after one another.'[2]

There was no excuse for government indifference, but lack of interest from the wider public was less surprising. To families up and down the land the glorious celebrations of VE Day in May signalled the end of the war. In the five or six months that had passed since the victory in Europe, men and women concentrated

[1]'The Reunion' BBC Radio 26 April 2015
[2]John Crace, London, *The Independent*, 1995

on bringing normality back to their lives. Marriages happened, babies were born and careers were restarted. Japan was an afterthought, a postscript. This desire for a fresh chapter in British life was signalled by the painful general election defeat in July 1945 for Winston Churchill, the man who had led Britain to a war victory.

For years, some survivors still battled tropical illnesses. Malaria did not disappear with freedom. Many former prisoners suffered recurrences, enduring twenty or more bouts of malaria during captivity and after. One man had malaria more than fifty times. A study of FEPOW by the Liverpool School of Tropical Medicine reported increased mortality amongst these men in the first ten years after liberation, mainly from tuberculosis, hepatitis B, and suicide. Australian research showed that the mortality rate of ex-POWs was higher than the general population for fourteen years, before levelling out.

In 1980, Dr Geoff Gill and Dr Dion Bell at the Liverpool School of Tropical Medicine reported that, in a study of 602 former Japanese POWs, twenty per cent still suffered from Strongyloides worm infections. Len Gibson was sixty before he was successfully treated in Liverpool, and suffered for more than thirty-five years from these, 'little creatures who entered through the soles on my feet when I was barefoot in the jungle, and then had Christmas parties in my stomach.'[3] Another ex-POW in the Liverpool study still had ten rib fractures thirty-six years after being beaten by the Japanese.

That only eight of the 700 men in the two Nagasaki camps died in the explosion or immediately afterwards

[3]Author Interview, West Herrington, Co Durham, 2021

was miraculous. Whether, like the citizens of Nagasaki, they suffered a disproportionate number of cancers or other radiation-linked illnesses we will never know. There has never been a research project in the UK of the cohort of men imprisoned in Nagasaki when the atomic bomb was dropped.

In Australia, the Cancer Institute in Melbourne published a study in August 1976[4] of 'chromosome aberrations in the peripheral lymphocytes' of seventeen prisoners in Camp 14b Nagasaki, thirty years after the bomb was dropped. The study concluded that only three men displayed discernible evidence of radiation damage to the chromosomes of their lymphocytes. However, it did note two other Camp 14b POWs had died prematurely from cancer twenty years after the bomb was dropped, and a third five years later. One ex-POW also died from an aortic aneurysm. These men would have been in their forties. At first glance, this seems a high percentage of premature deaths, but we should be cautious about drawing conclusions from such a small number of survivors, especially as the link to the atomic bomb is not clear cut. There is even less scientific evidence to support the theory of some Nagasaki POWs that the iodine-rich seaweed soup in their regular diet may have offered some protection against radiation-linked cancers.

Sumiteru Taniguchi spent a year more in the Omura Naval Hospital lying on his front. This led to terrible bedsores. Penicillin no longer worked for the boy, and

[4]Chee and Ilbery, Cytogenic Findings 30 Years after Low Level Exposure to the Nagasaki Bomb, Melbourne, Cancer Institute,16 August 1976

he slowly slid downhill. In summer, it was impossible to stop flies laying their eggs in his raw wounds leaving his back a carpet of maggots and pus. His family, and the postboy himself, thought that he could not possibly survive. Then, in October 1946, a new doctor arrived with a different treatment. By early 1947 a thin layer of skin began to grow over his back. That Spring he eased himself out of bed for the very first time in one year and nine months, and grabbed a pair of crutches. Those watching him, including the grandfather who had done so much to save him, burst into a round of applause. Sumiteru Taniguchi had survived.[5]

Mental scars were often more difficult to heal than the physical. The horror of their experiences had changed the men. Ernest Benford served alongside his father, who died in the Far East. Benford was frank about his problems, 'I suffered a personality change which was obvious to those dearest to me, yet too complex for them to understand or to talk about. I felt an outsider...I had seen my father and so many others die and had become practised at keeping my distance. My spirit was hardened...left alone with my mixed-up feelings I found solace in drink.'[6]

Others found comfort in the church or work, rather than the pub. Dr Harry Silman used humour as his coping mechanism. In his first letter home at the end of the war he wrote, 'As you probably know, in spite of the strict censorship at the time, I was nabbed by the Nips in Feb 1942 and have been resting here all the time except

---

[5] Peter Townsend, *The Postman of Nagasaki,* London, Collins,1984
[6] E.S. Benford, *The Rising Sun On My Back*, England, Lane Publishers, 1997

for a short trip up country to Thailand and Burma lasting nine months, during which we constructed a model railway.'[7]

In Australia, Arthur Bancroft, whose resilience and ingenuity had saved his colleagues after their hellship was torpedoed, returned to work in a bank. He embarked on a pub crawl after his return because he was missing the intensity of the unique friendships that could only exist in the camps. 'It was a strange feeling because I felt lonely. Sounds strange, I wasn't lonely because I had a wife not to be lonely with, but I was lonely because of my mates. I didn't have any.'

When Ken Adams finally arrived back in Harrogate, homecoming was not the romanticised experience he had dreamed of on the Railway of Death. His wife, Marion, had not been told her husband was alive until after the war with Japan had ended. 'It felt like a reunion of strangers, as indeed it was. I'd effectively disappeared with the fall of Singapore...we had both gone through an intense period of personal growth and development. We were different people.'[8]

The marriage of Bombardier Frank Harwood, a Camp 14b Nagasaki survivor, collapsed less than a year after his return. 'My wife eventually left home because the sex was no good for 9-10 months afterwards. I then married a nurse 14 years younger, and I have been very happy.'[9] When Harwood was interviewed by German

[7]Harry Silman and Jaqueline Passman, *Harry's War,* Leeds, Tambar Arts,2020
[8]Ken Adams, edited by Mike Adams, *Healing in Hell,* Barnsley, Pen and Sword, 2011
[9]Unpublished interview, Essex, Jill Turton, 1984

journalist Winifried Lierenfeld in 1981 he was clearly still deeply troubled by his experiences decades earlier. 'His description of the bodies which he had to burn in Nagasaki cannot be easily given. Harwood often breaks off his story, and sometimes he weeps. His wife has to put her arm round his shoulders and comfort him. Minutes pass before he can speak again. I am deeply shaken. I can scarcely ask questions.'[10]

For many, nightmares were common. Gerry Ford never escaped the memory of a fellow POW. 'He put his hand out of the bed, and said, "Hold my hand will you." Shortly after, he died. He was only a kid. He couldn't have been more than twenty. It had a terrible effect on me. I've carried it with me all my life. The nightmares were so vivid that when I came out, I sometimes didn't know where I was. I thought I was in a prison camp'[11]

Ken Adams waited a long time to explore his experiences. He was ninety-one when *Healing In Hell*, edited by his son, Mike, was written. On his return he found it difficult to suppress his anger. 'Suppressed feelings of anger and frustration rose to the surface and were directed at full force at those I considered were trying to oppress me. I just couldn't just flick off a switch and move on. I had a lot of the POW left in me. I tried to expunge it but something as simple as the smell of fish conjured up memories of washing ulcer patients' dressings, started my heart racing and made me sweat and want to retch.'

[10]Winifried Lierenfeld, Deutsche Volkszeitung, 23 July 1981
[11]'Not Forgotten', London, BBC Open Space, 1984

The survivors were never going to slip back easily into family life or working life. Their experiences as a prisoner had been so extreme, how could their peacetime lives be like everyone else's? 'I'd broadened my experience beyond anything I could have anticipated a few years earlier. But what had that experience taught me; it had taught how to survive as a slave worker among mates who provided mutual support. It hadn't taught how to fit more comfortably into 'normal' society or how to establish a normal and comfortable relationship within the family. That side of me hadn't matured at all. If anything, it had just been snapped frozen while society at large and the family had changed and evolved.'

Eric Hooper, from Goorombat, Victoria, had survived fighting in Java, the sinking of the hellship *Tamahoku Maru*, and the detonation of the atomic bomb just over a mile from his camp in Nagasaki. Before the war his sisters remembered a likeable brother. His fiancée, Marion, had been engaged to a man who was a 'bundle of joy, often laughing.' On his return, says his son Kevin, 'he never really embraced people as a good friend. He did not engage well with other people. His only close friends were his mates from the army.'

Return was complicated because, like many others captured in Java, he had been listed as 'missing believed killed'. For three years his family and his fiancée had presumed he was dead. In the meantime, Marion had met another man at the factory where she worked. Eric's return was an enormous surprise, but she decided to stick to her promise and the two were married. It was painful. Eric was a good father to his son and daughters, 'but he was critical of mother, short tempered. He gave both her and my younger brother, who was adopted, hell.'

As he grew older, Eric became even more agitated and unhappy. The marriage deteriorated further. As a result, there would be occasional separations or long bouts of drinking. Eric Hooper had survived the war but, in some way, he had lost the peace. He owned a farm in Victoria, married his fiancée, and had four children; idyllic circumstances he must have dreamt about in his Japanese prison camps. But the extreme nature of his war experiences had changed him. He suffered nightmares right up until his death and, overall, 'Dad was rarely happy. He didn't enjoy life a lot. He had a tormented life.'[12]

The changes in the returning prisoners were not entirely for the worse. Life as a prisoner was a very painful but a valuable lesson in human nature. Surviving the horrors of Japanese imprisonment made many stronger. They learned more about their own resilience than they had ever wanted to. If POWs could endure more than three years of malnutrition, disease and brutality, they could manage anything life threw at them. Some believed that captivity had made them better men. The sharing, the friendships, the common humanity had shaped them positively, despite the physical and emotional legacy of imprisonment.

As Harry Smith, a hospital orderly at camps on the Railway of Death put it, 'I know I would have been a worse person if I hadn't been through that experience. There would have been a quality missing. It taught me a lot.'[13] Others, like Jack Chalker, focused on the positive

[12]Kevin Hooper, Interview with Author, 2021
[13]*Secret History: Miracle on the River Kwai*, Channel4/Available Light,1999

aspects of his gruelling captivity. 'Always remember the positive times, the times that were to do with survival, with good humour, with kindness towards other people.'

Tom Jackson also knew that his POW experience had altered his trajectory in life, 'Without a shadow of a doubt it was the making of me, no question about it... if it hadn't happened, I would have been a different sort of person...I am not bothered where I go and do things, I will stand up and be counted. I still can't spell. I can't spell diarrhoea for the life of me. Yes, I picked up a good education in life if nothing else.'[14]

Padre Eric Cordingly summed up the end of the war as 'The most wonderful time of my life, in spite of the grim and hungry times...for once, and for three and a half years, the thin veneer of civilisation, or reticence, had been stripped from men. We were all down to bedrock. One saw people as they really were.'[15]

John Stewart Ullman, working in intelligence for the 18th Division, shared that perspective after his time on the Railway of Death. 'With its societal skin flayed, human nature became visible as never before. Greed, cowardice and vanity; perseverance, altruism and generosity, in brief the wide panoply of virtue and vice were there to be observed in the open, without pretence, with no place to hide.'[16]

After the war, geography split mates apart, but they never forgot. Australian Ken Gray, from F Force, lost touch with Jim Birse, a Gordon Highlander

[14]Meg Parkes, Liverpool School of Tropical Medicine, November 21 2007
[15]Eric Cordingly/Louise Reynolds, *Down to Bedrock*, Norwich, Art Angels, 2013
[16]John Stewart, *To The River Kwai*, London, Bloomsbury, 1988

from Inverurie, near Aberdeen. In the hospital hut at Songkurai on the Railway of Death, when Gray suffered from tropical ulcers and dysentery, 'Jim would wash me and clean me when I fouled myself. He emptied my bedpan. He was the greatest mate I could ever wish for. Without a mate, you died.'

The two men agreed they would meet after the war and share two bottles of whisky but were dispatched to different camps when the railway was finished. Over thirty years later, in 1978, Ken Gray finally tracked Jim Birse down and knocked on his door in Inverurie unannounced. He was carrying two bottles of whisky, 'He just surged forward and grabbed me...we stood thus for what must have been a full minute—an unforgettable emotional minute—both with tears in our eyes. The greatest reunion I have ever known.'[17]

For many years Frank Farmer, one of the first Australians rescued by the *Pampanito*, rang one of the submariners, Robert Bennett, at his home in Iowa to say 'Thank you for another year of my life.' Other survivors attended a reunion with the *Pampanito* crew in San Francisco to mark the 50th anniversary of the rescue.

The most common thread of post-war survival was the role of women in pulling men through. They made the ravaged bodies and damaged minds whole again. They were as heroic as their husbands and boyfriends. Women had waited patiently, never knowing if their partner was dead or alive. Some brought up children alone, not knowing if the kids would ever see their father again. When their husbands finally returned,

[17]*www.pows-of-japan.net*, Western Australia, Peter Winstanley

women had to cope with significant changes in the men they had kissed goodbye several years before.

Even physical touch was strange. Returning to his home near Sevenoaks, Gus Anckorn was finally reunited with his fiancée. 'Just touching hands was the most incredible experience you could imagine. I had known only harsh, sun-parched and calloused skin for so long and now, suddenly, the softness and wholesomeness of Lucille was like an electric shock, awakening me.'[18]

Betty Gwillim learned to manage her much-changed husband. 'When he came home, he was a rattle of bones, and very, very nervous. He couldn't even stand the children when we had our family. The children had to be kept quiet.' In many cases the anxiety grew with time, as Gladys Reid recalled, 'As they've got older it's got worse. Living with them is like living on a knife-edge. It takes us wives years to understand it.'[19]

Readjusting was difficult for both parents and children, as Gerry Ford noted. 'My parents, my wife, probably expected things to return to what they were before. But we couldn't do that. We were not the same people anymore. My daughter, bless her heart, it took her time to accept that this man who had suddenly come into her life was really her father. That was the beginning of a difficult time of adjustment.'

Arthur Turbutt just could not face marrying his fiancée Lola, and on return to Friern Barnet in London, plucked up the courage to tell Lola's father, 'And I went back home and sobbed my heart out...but I knew in my

---

[18]Peter Fyans, *Conjuror on the Kwai*, Barnsley, Pen and Sword, 2016
[19]*Forgotten Heroes*, London, BBC Open Space, 1984

heart of hearts that I'd done the right thing, I couldn't have gone through. Then began a long period when, I was terribly in love with Lola, deeply in love with her, but I just couldn't take the step of being married.'[20] They finally married two painful years later, after Lola insisted that her fiancée sought professional help.

Pte Wally Holding returned to Western Australia and praised 'the unsung heroines' among the ranks of wives and girlfriends. 'They were the ones who lived a life of uncertainty, dreading the knock on the door by a representative of the Government to tell them the worst...it is wives who have borne the brunt of their husband's erratic behaviour. The inability to express their feelings to their wives was perhaps the most damaging part of post-war years.'[21]

As Ernest Benford put it in his self-published memoir, 'Ena still wanted to marry although I know she saw a marked change in me...our marriage was punctuated by outbursts of fury. As time passed, the frequency of my outbursts decreased due to my beloved wife whose sense of truth and right was my strongest incentive.'

Footballer Johnny Sherwood was another who fought off nightmares. 'I can get very moody and depressed, but the worst thing is the nightmares nearly every night of my life, ever since I came home from war...these invisible scars were just another legacy of my three and a half years of hell and murder, as a guest of the mighty Japanese empire...Christine was always marvellous with me, and never once complained about her broken sleep.

[20]Meg Parkes, Liverpool School of Tropical Medicine, 30 April 2009
[21]Wally Holding, *www.pows-of-japan.net*

Whenever I was woken by one of those nightmares she sat up and stroked my forehead to calm me.'[22]

Time did not necessarily reduce the anguish. In several cases it was years later, once the reassuring structure of family and career was over, that former POWs began to unravel. More than sixty years after his imprisonment by the Japanese, Arthur Turbutt started to have episodes two or three times a year. 'I get a sudden rigour. It strikes like lighting. I get absolutely no warning at all...I start shivering and eventually, within a few minutes, I'm shaking, my knees give way, and I can do nothing more than to fall into bed. And I'm shaking. I can't speak because my teeth are chattering so much. I'm bitterly cold.'[23]

On return, the POWs of Japan were not offered help or counselling, as Gerry Fox found out. 'My mind became almost totally occupied with what happened all those years ago. You can think of nothing else. It's all-consuming, and I was desperate about it.' Decades after his return, Fox finally sought help. 'It was like coming out of a black hole, having the door opened and coming out into the light. All those years, I had desperately wanted to talk to somebody, and I couldn't.'[24]

POWs were on their own. Their only support were family and former comrades. Some ex-prisoners never wanted to attend reunions but, for many, mates from Japanese camps were the only men who fully understood. Friendship, mateship, had helped POWs

---

[22]Johnny Sherwood with Michael Doe, *Lucky Johnny*, London, Hodder, 2014
[23]Meg Parkes, Liverpool School of Tropical Medicine, April 30 2009
[24]*Forgotten Heroes*, London, BBC Open Space, 1984

endure the war and, in many cases, it also helped them through the peace. As entertainment at reunions, POWs would dress up as St Trinian's girls in homage to fellow FEPOW Ronald Searle. Anything for the comfort of laughter. The Far East Prisoners of War Association (FEPOW) was set up in 1947 as an early self-help group for the returning POWs. The very active Java 1942 Club, COFEPOW for the children of former prisoners of Japan, and regimental and battalion reunions have all played, and continue to play, an important part in ensuring that the POWs are not forgotten, but also in bringing them together in mutual support.

Barbara Wearne, wife of Padre Edwin Wearne, saw this bond first-hand at the reunions. 'The men were always together...they were back again as they had been in prison camp and they were buddies again...that's one of the things they must have missed terribly when they came back...it had been a very special fellowship...I am sure it kept a lot of them alive, that they survived on that.'[25]

A study of Far East POWs was undertaken at Liverpool School of Tropical Medicine by the well-respected consultant psychiatrist Dr Kamal Khan. Khan concluded that patients suffered from what today would be called Post-Traumatic Stress Disorder. By comparing them to other Far East veterans, Khan concluded that this was a unique type of depression, 'which affected nearly one-half of survivors, over 30 years after release.' His case studies included a sixty-eight-year-old who stopped speaking to his son after he bought a Japanese stereo,

[25]Meg Parkes, Liverpool School of Tropical Medicine, March 2008

and a sixty-four-year-old who 'had frequent nightmares and would often wake up screaming. Once his wife awoke to find he had his hands round her throat.'[26]

Some survivors displayed remarkable resilience. Despite the appalling deprivations of building the Thai-Burma Railway and then the Mergui Road, Len Gibson never reported nightmares or other mental health issues. Gibson suffered from continuing physical problems, but he remained resolutely cheerful, comforted by his music and a loving family.

Ron Bryer was another who appeared to take his long imprisonment in his stride. Throughout his life he was a practical, down-to-earth person. He built pigeon lofts, repaired machinery, laid concrete paths. The physical toughness that had helped him survive Nagasaki remained. When a crank handle flew into his face while he was mixing concrete, the idea of going to hospital like most people did not enter his head, despite smashing several teeth and splitting his lip open wide. As his son Chris observed, 'Some people are crushed by the experiences, others, like my dad, just seem to come through them.'

Nonetheless, his Japanese experience remained unfinished business for Ron Bryer. As his children set out on their own paths in life, Bryer grew more interested in Japan. In the late 1960s he wrote to Mitsubishi asking about the shipyard where he had worked and what it was like now. Mr Hirose, a retired senior employee, wrote back and sent photographs. An enduring correspondence between the two men followed.

---

[26]Meg Parkes/Geoff Gill, *Captive Memories*, Lancaster, Liverpool School of Tropical Medicine/Palatine Books, 2015

Whatever the interpretations of historians or journalists, only those who lived through Japanese imprisonment can sum up what it meant. Ken Adams, a hospital orderly, called his thoughts on the POW experience 'reflections of an old man':

> *I lived in very close proximity to a wide cross-section of people, knowing them under stressful conditions that stripped away social graces and revealed true character. The standout impression for me is that people are both very fragile and very resilient. Lives can be snuffed out so easily but, for the most part, blokes hung on tenaciously to life without any pretence of bravery. What could be endured month after month, year after year, was amazing: battered and shrunken men struggled on with little food, occasional repairs from doctor and support from mates. This triumph, both for those who survived, and those who had the bad luck ultimately to succumb, deserve the highest respect, and, for me, is the principal reason for perpetuating the memory of Far Eastern Prisoners of War.*[27]

[27]Ken Adams, edited by Mike Adams, *Healing in Hell*, Barnsley, Pen and Sword, 2011

20

RETURN TO NAGASAKI

On 9 August each year, around twenty thousand people mark the anniversary of the dropping of the atomic bomb on Nagasaki. The Peace Park where the ceremony is held sits directly beneath the point where *Fat Man* detonated back in 1945. On the eve of the anniversary, thousands of homemade candles are inscribed with messages of hope and peace and then lit in memory of those who died.

In 1984, Ron Bryer, Arthur Christie and their wives were invited to the anniversary event. Although their lives had been entwined in Java, on a hellship, and in their Nagasaki camp, this was their first meeting for thirty-nine years. They sat silently in the heat, as a list of victims who had died in the previous year was solemnly read out. The visitors felt intensely moved as the thousands present came together in a minute's silence. For Ron and Arthur, it was a moment to remember the many friends and colleagues they had lost in Japanese prison camps.

At 11.02 a.m., the reflections of Ron and Arthur were interrupted by the loud tolling of church bells and the wailing of air raid sirens. Finally, scores of peace doves were released, and the former POWs watched as the birds circled above the huge peace statue up into the blue summer sky above Nagasaki. The two men from the RAF were not the only survivors to attend the peace ceremony. In other years Jack Ford, Hugh Clarke, Peter McGrath-Kerr and many other nuclear survivors joined the anniversary event.

It was their way of trying to reconcile the irreconcilable. How could the kind and gentle Japanese they met on their return be the same race as the brutal guards they were subjected to in the war? How could good come from the evil of incinerating so many civilians with one huge bomb? Why had they survived, when so many who had stood alongside them had perished unnecessarily? For some former POWs the Japanese would always be hated, and they would never even think about owning a Japanese television set or car, especially anything made by Mitsubishi, the owners of the foundry and shipyard where so many of the POWs worked. For others, like Ron and Arthur, they had reached the point in their lives when returning to Nagasaki was the next, even final, stage of a healing process.

Ron Bryer found it hard to sleep in Nagasaki. He was a tough Yorkshireman who had buried his feelings about the horrors of Camp 14b deep inside. He had not hesitated to return to Nagasaki when the invitation came but now the 'ghosts', as he called them, had surfaced. The sticky heat of an August night reminded him of so many humid nights in captivity, nights he thought he had cleared from his mind. Early one morning he woke restlessly and stood on the balcony of his hotel overlooking the town that had been wiped out nearly forty years earlier.

As he watched the first fingers of morning light he glimpsed a marker for the epicentre of the atomic bomb.

'I thought I'd got over this business. It hasn't worried me since the war. As I stood on my hotel balcony about 5 o'clock this morning I suddenly filled right up, something I thought would never happen. But you see, you drag all the memories to the front again and remember how it was. It upset me very much. I never thought I could be as upset as that.'[1]

In the early morning peace, Bryer was gripped by an overwhelming sadness as he recalled those who had died and the scenes of complete devastation and human carnage after the bomb dropped. For a moment he thought that his tears were an unwelcome and rare sign of weakness, then he realised that they were part of the coming to terms with the events of August 1945.

It was the first time, too, that Rob Bryer and Arthur Christie had fully comprehended the long-term impact of the bomb on the local population. After the war, Allied governments censored reports and supressed stories about the powerful initial impact of *Fat Man*, and then its long-term consequences. On 9 September 1945, journalist George Weller filed a story about multiple deaths in Nagasaki from a mysterious illness local doctors called Disease X. Weller reported that, 'Men, women and children are dying daily in hospitals, some having walked around for three or four weeks thinking they had escaped...they are dead from the atomic bomb, and no one knows why.'

Like so much of his Nagasaki journalism, Weller's report was never printed. The same fate befell the work of the first filmmaker to enter Nagasaki after the bomb

---

[1] *First Tuesday: Return to Nagasaki*, Leeds, Yorkshire Television, 4 November 1984

dropped. Herbert Sussan was in the US Army and was assigned the task of recording the impact of the bombs on Nagasaki and Hiroshima in colour. His powerful footage remained secret for thirty-seven years.

Appalled by the human tragedy he saw unfold, Sussan disobeyed his strict instructions to film only the devastated buildings. He also recorded the suffering of the people who had lived in those buildings. The most disturbing images were of Sumiteru Taniguchi, the 16-year-old postboy who was delivering mail close to Camp 14b when the bomb was dropped.

Herbert Sussan filmed Taniguchi in hospital and, when Sussan returned to Nagasaki decades later, he was astonished to find that the young postboy was still alive. 'I thought it was the most terrible thing I had ever seen. I couldn't believe that this man, a boy at this point, would ever live. I merely thought we were photographing a medical record. It is the most amazing story of courage and somehow Man's inner strength to survive.'[2] It was only after a campaign lasting nearly four decades that the American military allowed Herbert Sussan's Nagasaki footage of Taniguchi and other victims to be made public.

In a detailed study, the American Naval Technical Mission to Nagasaki, December 1945, reported widespread hair loss, bloody diarrhoea and low cell counts due to radiation. They reported the 'Disastrous effects of atomic bomb on pregnancy' with no normal births within 2 km of the detonation point. In the four months since the bomb was dropped, half of the young

---

[2] *First Tuesday: Return to Nagasaki*, Leeds, Yorkshire Television, 4 November 1984

girls had stopped menstruating. The numbers of long-term deaths and illnesses in Japan from the bomb are elusive. In the decades after the bomb was dropped, cancers commonly associated with radiation including thyroid, breast cancer and leukaemia were all reported as several times higher than normal. Cataracts and birth defects were also often seen in survivors. On their return to Nagasaki, Arthur Christie met one of these long-term victims, Zinichi Hashimoto. 'That was a very emotional time. There was one lad there who was still in his mother's womb when the bomb exploded. He's been laying there for forty years and will do so until the day he dies.'[3]

Arthur and Ron also met Sunyo Katuoka who was twenty-four when the bomb was dropped. Her face was bulging from the huge keloid scars which made it look as if she had two lower lips. 'I had so many dreams for the future, but the atomic bomb snatched them all away. It was torture to go out with my monster face...I hated war and cursed the bomb.'

Of course, the survivors they met made them question their own future health prospects, but these meetings also began to see the bomb in a different way. They had to live with the unsettling thought that the weapon that had liberated them from forced labour and certain death had not only killed around 70,000 innocent people almost instantly, but thousands more had died slowly and painfully from cancers.

Their return to Nagasaki enabled the two men a chance to meet Jidayu Tajima, a guard at Camp 14b. He

[3]Arthur Christie, London, Imperial War Museum Sound Archive

was the soldier who met the POWs in Moji when their hellship docked. That day, he had insisted on finding food and water for the sick. He had written to Ron Bryer recalling the day 'where your painful life in the concentration camp really began.' He goes on, 'From the bottom of my heart I want to apologise to you for I was one of the soldiers.' [4]

The effects of the atomic bomb had caught up with him. Now Tajima was very frail and blind, and looking much older than his sixty-four years. Tajima had stayed behind at Camp 14b after the bomb dropped to help rescue survivors, including Allied POWs. Ron Bryer and Arthur Christie were clearly touched to meet him again. Tajima simply said, 'Very happy today to join with you for the repose of the souls of those prisoners who died.'

For Ron's wife, Pat, the journey to Nagasaki was an important pilgrimage. She knew that her husband's experience under the Japanese was a major part of his life and had shaped him into the man he had become. Pat wanted to understand. It was only when she met long-term casualties of radiation, and then visited the Peace Museum in Nagasaki, that she fully appreciated what her husband had survived. Pat was visibly upset by the photographs of women and children in the Peace Museum and those emotions stayed with her when she returned home to the Yorkshire Dales.

Nagasaki has been rebuilt as a thrusting, modern city, still dominated by Mitsubishi. In the old industrial district, Camp 14b is now a bus depot. Out on Koyagi Island, the site of Camp 2b is a high school. The mines

[4]Jidayu Tajima, Letter, Nagasaki, 29 August 1978

40 miles away where POWs worked at Omuta are now a UNESCO World Heritage Site. Jack Ford returned to Camp 2b in Nagasaki with a Canadian television crew. 'As I stood on the soil that was once the camp, and prayed silently, thoughts passed through my mind of the anguish suffered there. I could see the faces of those who had died at the hands of the Japanese, and those who went home to suffer a life of tormented memories. I hope the world is a better place thanks to the sacrifices so many made in that war.'[5] In 2015, a memorial was unveiled on the site of Camp 2b, commemorating the seventy-three POWs who died there.

Other former POWs have returned to Thailand and to the railway they so painfully constructed. River Kwai tourism grew rapidly following the success of the film, bringing with it with train rides and T-shirt stalls. But the museum and memorial at Kanchanaburi and the peaceful cemetery at Chungkai remain quiet places of pilgrimage. John Stewart Ullman, by now a successful photographer, returned to the Kwai in 1979 and visited Kanchanaburi. 'Away from the river a large cemetery is laid out and maintained. Flamboyants and hibiscus spread over the gravestones. I read the names of the farm boys who enlisted in the 18th Division's East Anglian Units...it's Sunday, and Thai families, with their children and picnic baskets, have come to spend the day in the cemetery, the cleanest and neatest, perhaps the only park of Kanchanaburi.'[6]

[5]Jack Fitzgerald, *The Jack Ford Story*, Newfoundland, Canada, Creative Publishing, 2007
[6]John Stewart, *To The River Kwai, London*, Bloomsbury, 1988

Aged ninety, David Arkush visited the same cemetery and stood by the graves of several Jewish boys he had buried. At the first, his son Jonathan saw his father 'snapping a smart military salute that I'd never seen him give before and then he said the Kaddish and broke down. And that was repeated seven or eight times.'

In her book, *Echoes of Captivity*, Louise Cordingly, whose father was a Padre on the Thai-Burma Railway, charts the impact Japanese captivity had on the children of POWs like Jonathan Arkush. Some never knew their father. Cuthbert Stanley was trained at St Thomas's Hospital in London and joined the medical service in Malaya before the Japanese invasion. His son Nigel, also a doctor, described his father's torture by the *Kempeitai* (Japan's secret police) in 1943 because he was suspected of operating a radio device. 'He wasn't just beaten and put through the water torture with a hosepipe in his mouth. He was also given electric shocks to you know where, fingernail evulsion, suspension and you name it.' After more than three weeks of torture Cuthbert Stanley died. Nightmares were common amongst survivors of Japanese cruelty, but his father's brutal death also weighed heavily on his son. Since the age of twenty-two, when he first read about his father's torture, Nigel Stanley has suffered from nightmares and daytime flashbacks two or three times a week. He is now aged eighty-three. He cannot forgive the secret policemen who tortured and murdered his father. To him, forgiving and forgetting are intertwined, and he never wants to forget.

Private John Tidey, 1st Battalion, Cambridgeshire Regiment, was another who could not find full forgiveness. 'The Japanese, funny people: they will hit you and strike you for no reason at all. Another time they'd come and give you a cigarette...there's some you like and some you had to dislike. No, no, the Japanese I'm sure will do the same thing again given the opportunity. It's their way of life. They're an evil people...I could never forgive them.'[7]

Geoffrey Sherring's views remained undimmed by the years. From his vantage point in his Nagasaki camp, he had no regrets for the deaths of the innocent Japanese. 'I did not feel sorry for them. There were 74,000 Japanese corpses, and I didn't mind a bit. I would drop an atomic bomb on any enemy. You can't negotiate with these people.'

Time gradually distanced the survivors from their grim experiences, and many differentiated between the ordinary Japanese and their war time military leaders. Dr Frank Murray from Belfast took that view. 'I know it's fashionable to talk about reconciliation and forgiveness, but I don't think he ever forgave the Japanese, not for what happened to him, but for the way the prisoners were treated. However, he distinguished between the Japanese military and the Japanese people.'[8]

Even years later, a chance event could bring anger flooding back. Arthur Turbutt was visiting Canterbury when he saw Japanese men in kimonos. His wife Lola recalled that 'He stopped and the look of hatred in his eyes as he saw those men, I'd never seen anything like it...he's a mild-mannered lovely man and to see hatred coming from his eyes, it was quite scary, it really was.

[7]Meg Parkes, Liverpool School of Tropical Medicine, January 2008
[8]Carl Murray, BBC News Northern Ireland, 14 August 2020

I had to tap him on the shoulder to bring him back to the present day.'[9]

Dr Bill Frankland took a more philosophical attitude. 'I don't hate the Japanese. It doesn't do them any harm for me to hate them, but it does me harm, psychologically. I think hate is a horrible word.'[10]

Ron Bryer was another who had no hatred for the Japanese people. He enjoyed cordial post-war relationships with non-military Japanese, including employees of Mitsubishi. Bryer understood that the Japanese civilians in Nagasaki had as little to eat as the prisoners, and those who worked alongside the POWs in the foundry or shipyard were also subject to regular beatings. They lived, he said, 'close to the ground', meaning that their existence was very basic. Coming from a large and poor family in Yorkshire himself, Ron had some empathy and understanding for the people of Nagasaki. His son Chris says, 'I never ever heard him utter any grievance against the Japanese people.'

On 7 November 2000, the Labour government under Tony Blair announced an ex-gratia payment of £10,000 for each Far East Prisoner of War. It had taken fully fifty-five years and intense lobbying by the British Legion and Far East POW groups for a government to finally recognise the unique and enduring pain suffered by prisoners of Japan. Many had already died but this payment was extended to their widows. Back in the 1950s, these former POWs had received a maximum payment of £76.10. Peter Dunstan, who had laboured

[9]Meg Parkes, Liverpool School of Tropical Medicine, 10 April 2009
[10]*www.singaporeevacuation1942.blogspot.com*,1 September 2016

on the Thai-Burma Railway commented,[11] 'For years both our government and the Japanese have been stalling, telling us that the £76 we received in the Fifties was all we were entitled to. It has been a dark blot on this country's history which needs removing.'

The Japanese government has apologised several times for its wartime actions, but former POWs remained unconvinced by the sincerity of their statements. Failure to include apologies to the Chinese for the massacre at Nanking, and to Korean women forced into prostitution for the Japanese troops, has not helped this perception. Glaswegian Jack Caplan, from the Royal Corps of Signals (18th Division), one of the thousands who built the River Kwai Railway, fought for over fifty years for the government of Japan to apologise and offer compensation to POWs. His protests included publicly burning the Japanese flag on The Mall when Japanese Emperor Akihito was welcomed on a state visit to London in May 1998.

Some POWs also reserved a special bitterness for the giant Japanese corporations like Mitsui, Mitsubishi and Kawasaki, who profited from the 'slave' labour of the POWs. In 2015, Mitsubishi finally said sorry when a senior executive apologised to ninety-four-year-old James Murphy and relatives of survivors at a ceremony in Los Angeles. The following year, the first POW from Camp 14b in Nagasaki was compensated by the Japanese government, having filed a lawsuit for the suffering. Dutchman Willy Buchel was aged ninety-five. He received £6910.

<hr>

[11]*The Independent*, 6 November 2000

Ever since the bombing of Hiroshima and Nagasaki there has been intense debate about the morality of the atomic bomb. Was it morally right to drop bombs of such devastating power and long-term impact on an innocent civilian population? The bomb may have helped end the war, but did it speed up the Cold War and the nuclear arms race? Was the Nagasaki bomb necessary so soon after Hiroshima? Would the Russian declaration of war have ended the conflict anyway? Would, as some scientists believed, a public demonstration of the bomb's power in a desert, or other remote place, been sufficient to stop the war?

For the prisoners in Nagasaki, fortunate not to be killed by the atomic bomb themselves, there was wide agreement. They were appalled by the horrors they saw after the explosion, but very few of them regretted the dropping of the bomb. In their eyes, despite all the thousands of innocent lives lost, it enabled the POWs to live. Having seen the barbarity the enemy were capable of, few were in any doubt that if the Americans had invaded, or the war been prolonged, they would have died, either from disease or murder. More than that, hundreds of thousands of American and Japanese troops would have lost their lives in any invasion attempt.

Milton Fairclough from Perth summed up the feelings of many. 'I think how lucky we were that the atom bomb was dropped, because that stopped the invasion of Japan. Had there been an invasion there wouldn't have been any POWs, the whole lot of us would have been annihilated.'[12]

[12]Milton Fairclough, Perth, ABC Radio, 3 October 2016

American Lester Tenney echoed these thoughts. 'The bombs inflicted indiscriminate, total devastation... ruined two cities, brought suffering and death to many tens of thousands of people. We POWs — men who were starved and tortured, who suffocated in the holds of hellships, who were beaten at will, who died for lack of medical care and who saw friends worked to death — have no doubt that the atomic bombs ended the war.'[13]

American President Harry Truman took the same view. 'I have no qualms about it whatever...the Japanese in their conduct of the war had been vicious and cruel savages and I came to the conclusion that if two hundred and fifty thousand young Americans could be saved from slaughter the bomb should be dropped, and it was.'[14]

Warning leaflets had been dropped on Japanese cities earlier in December, but Group Captain Leonard Cheshire, who had seen the astonishing power of the bomb from the window of an American bomber, questioned whether Japanese civilians had been warned clearly enough. To Cheshire, the massive bombing raids on Germany were fair because the British had suffered civilian casualties too, 'But Nagasaki did not seem fair. Not in the sense that it shouldn't have been done. I maintain to the end that it had to be done because of what the alternative was. But on a personal level I didn't like it...the people of Nagasaki had been warned that an attack was coming upon them, but that was standard

[13] *Wall Street Journal*, 7 August 2015
[14] Harry Truman, Letter to Roman Bohnen, Washington DC, 12 December 1946

procedure. So, at that level I didn't like it, and felt uneasy.'[15]

Ron Bryer shared some of the same ambivalence. In its pure sense he believed that dropping a nuclear bomb was morally indefensible. On a practical level, he knew that if Americans had invaded many more innocent people would have died than at Nagasaki, and that the prisoners of war, including him, would have been killed by their captors. It was a difficult moral wrestling match in his mind that he never fully resolved.

Arthur Christie, heavily influenced by visiting the long-term victims of the atomic bomb forty years after the war, shared the moral repugnance of his fellow Nagasaki prisoner. 'I think the sacrifice was too great...I personally don't think they should have been dropped.'[16] However, he also pointed out that the bombs may have preserved the peace because they acted as a warning of the terrible consequences, particularly as modern nuclear bombs are so much more powerful. Yet even this thought did not dissuade him from opposing the bomb.

The most passionate opponent of nuclear weapons among the survivors in Nagasaki was Sumiteru Taniguchi, the postboy. In the decades after the bomb was dropped, his frequent operations and hospitalisations were a permanent reminder of the damage that nuclear weapons could bring. His body was a laboratory for the after-effects of radiation. When he was not in hospital, he devoted himself to the Peace Movement and became a prominent anti-nuclear campaigner.

[15]Leonard Cheshire, London, Imperial War Museum Sound Archive
[16]Arthur Christie, London, Imperial War Museum Sound Archive

The lucky ones who had been picked up from their ordeal in the sea by the USS *Pampanito* in 1944 escaped the slave labour of the mines and shipyards of Japan, as well as the dropping of the atomic bomb. Their post-war pilgrimages were more joyful. Some visited San Francisco Harbour, where *Pampanito* is docked as a museum. As he paid his museum entrance fee, Australian Bill McKittrick could not help joking that the last time he had been on the *Pampanito* entrance had been free.

It was not until May 2021, seventy-six years after the bomb was dropped, that a memorial to the men of Camp 14b was unveiled in Nagasaki. The moving force behind the memorial was a small group of Dutch men and women whose fathers had been imprisoned in the camp. Rob and Lies Schouten, Ruud van Kraaij and others worked with a handful of determined Japanese people, and together raised the money, found the site and designed the memorial. Due to the worldwide Covid-19 pandemic, the unveiling was a virtual ceremony but there are plans for a bigger, more formal face-to-face event in 2022.

Japan's treatment of their prisoners was a war crime. It was not just the massacre of Australian nurses on Banka Island, or the wounded soldiers executed after surrender in Malaya at Parit Sulong. Nor was it even the most grotesque of all Japan's extreme brutality — the human medical experiments on eight captured American airmen at Kyushu University in May 1945. What made these experiments so horrific was that the airmen were still alive when lungs were removed, and skulls drilled.

The true horror was not in the extreme but in the day to day; the malnutrition, much of it avoidable; the untreated sickness even though medicine was available;

the daily casual beating and ill-treatment; and the total indifference for the lives of their captives by cramming them into the holds of hellships without sufficient food or water. Beginning in Tokyo in 1946 there were several War Crime Tribunals. The number of death sentences across the many nations, including China and Russia, was over 900. But they certainly were not complete. Prisoners did not even know the names of most of the guards who had killed or beaten their comrades, except for their nicknames like *Gorilla* or *Scarface*. A handful of senior politicians and military leaders were executed. The leader of the massacre at Alexandra Hospital in Singapore escaped justice, but the officer responsible for the killing of four escaped prisoners at Changi Beach a few days later was executed for his crime. As Columbia University historian, Sarah Kovner, wrote recently, 'Like the treatment of POWs, the treatment of war criminals was haphazard, and highly variable.'[17]

Nigel Stanley, whose father was tortured and murdered by the Japanese secret police, has made a study of war crimes. Apart from a handful of senior leaders, many of those convicted were low in the hierarchy and, overall, 'The Japanese have been let off the hook.' He believes, 'The Japanese didn't confront their own criminality and the idea was allowed to germinate that they were victims themselves, largely because of the use of the atomic bomb.'[18]

---

[17]Sarah Kovner, Prisoners of the Empire, Cambridge, Mass, Harvard University Press, 2020
[18]Author Interview, Topsham, Devon, 2021

The average time in a POW camp in Germany was a year. Under the Japanese, the average was three years. At the Tokyo War Crimes Tribunal in 1946, it was stated that the death rate of POWs under the Japanese was 27.1 per cent, seven times higher than POWs in German and Italian camps. The Japanese did not have a monopoly on war crimes, as many other conflicts have shown. Nor was their regime comparable to the planned and systematic holocaust the Nazis were responsible for, but Japanese indifference and cruelty to those in their care, including the Chinese and native Tamil labourers, ran the Nazi concentration camps a plausible second.

Given the severe malnutrition and sickness they suffered from over years, it is surprising how many former Far East POWs lived into their eighties, nineties and beyond. There are no statistics comparing their death rate to the general population, but the anecdotal evidence is striking. It may be that the Far East prisoners were what experts call 'a survivor population'. These men could do nothing if they were unlucky enough to be on a torpedoed hellship, but otherwise many had the physical and mental strength to endure. They may have been hard-wired to live a long life, whether they had been imprisoned by the Japanese or not.

Just before his rescue by the American submarine *Queenfish* after almost six days adrift on the ocean, Arthur 'Blood' Bancroft was so feeble he thought that death was inevitable. He went on to live to the age of ninety-one. His fellow Australian, Dr Rowley Richards, was rescued by the Japanese after the sinking of his hell ship the *Rayoku Maru* in which 1149 of his comrades died. Dr Richards lived until he was ninety-eight. The last Australian survivor of Camp 14b was Alan Chick who died in 2014 in his mid-nineties.

The most remarkable survivor was Sumiteru Taniguchi. The postboy in and out of hospitals for the rest of his life undergoing countless operations, several for tumours. He was an anti-nuclear weapons activist all his adult life. He married, and his wife Eiko gave birth to a daughter and a son. Sumiteru was eighty-eight years of age when he finally died of the cancer that had been trying to kill him since he was sixteen.

It took a worldwide pandemic to reduce the final handful of survivors still further. Having endured the horrors of the Japanese camps, several long-lived Far East POWs fell to Covid-19. Eddie Hunn, the last surviving FEPOW in Great Yarmouth in Norfolk, the county that had delivered so many men to the ill-fated 18th Division, died of Covid-19 in 2021 aged 100. A month earlier, Dennis Morley, who had survived the sinking by torpedo of the first hellship *Lisbon Maru*, also succumbed to Covid -19 in Gloucestershire. Dennis was aged 101.

Bill Frankland, who had survived the horrors of the Thai-Burma, returned to St Mary's Hospital in London, where he had trained. He became director of the busiest allergy clinic in the country and was hailed as the grandfather of British allergy medicine. He died of Covid-19 in 2020 at the age of 108.

As I write this in mid-2021, a few Far East POWs are still alive, although no one quite knows how many. Bert Warne from Southampton celebrated his 100th birthday in late 2020. Wearsider Len Gibson, who had entertained so many in the camps with his homemade guitar, returned to Sunderland and, fittingly, became a music teacher. He celebrated his 101st birthday in January 2021.

And what of the men from Camp 14b in Nagasaki, the prisoners at the centre of this story? Dr Aidan MacCarthy stayed in the RAF, was awarded an MBE, and rose to become an Air Commodore. A new RAF Medical Centre at RAF Honington, where his rescue of a crew from a burning plane in 1940 had earned him a George Cross, was named after him. He died aged eighty-two. Ron Bryer, resourceful, intelligent and determined, settled for a quiet life in North Yorkshire. He eventually became chief engineer for two large dairies in the Dales and died aged eighty-four.

In June 2021, I was privileged to meet one of the few survivors of the war with the Japanese. Sitting in the front room of Len Gibson's bungalow in the small village of West Herrington outside Sunderland, it was curiously difficult to reconcile the horrors of Japanese cruelty and neglect with the man sitting opposite me. Len was 101 — the twinkle in his eyes, his keen sense of humour, marked him out as a survivor. He was a neat, trim man who did not drink, and ate in moderation. He was supported by his West Herrington community as well as his family, and in return had devoted his time to a local cancer support charity, *Daft As A Brush*. His 101st birthday was marked by a Spitfire flypast and a serenade from a choir of 129 schoolchildren.

Six young men from the local choir, including Len, were sent to fight the Japanese just before the fall of Singapore. Only three of them returned home. Music as well as friendship was what enabled Len to endure. Len Gibson had played his makeshift guitar with officers and encountered the full range of human behaviour, good and bad. Although he continued to be plagued by tropical illnesses in peacetime, Gibson had returned a more confident and capable young man. Before the war he worked in a factory, but on return he became a music teacher and Deputy Headmaster at Hastings Hill School.

He was helped that on his first hospitalisation with malaria soon after his return home he met his future wife, Ruby. As Len was fond of saying, other returning POWs searched everywhere for the right woman, but he just woke up in hospital and found her, the nurse who was to be the love of his life.

As our conversation wound down, Len Gibson, aged 101, could still remember the ditty he wrote in a Japanese prison camp. He explained that gippo was what POWs called boiled water with anything edible in it. Then Len burst into song. He could have been sitting around a campfire on the River Kwai, and so I will leave the last words to him.

For dinner there's rice, tea and gippo,
For supper there's rice, gippo and tea,
And unless a miracle happens, I know what my
breakfast will be,
Last night as I lay on my pillow,
I dreamt of a gooseberry tart,
To follow Roast Sirloin and Yorkshire
But I woke up before I could start.

Then he reflected that on his first night home when he had lain back in his own bed and stared at the ceiling and simply said to himself. 'You lucky fellow.'

A few weeks later, I received a message from Len's friend and neighbour, Clinton Leeks. Len had caught Covid-19. He was out of hospital but was 'going downhill very fast. He is unrecognisable from the person you met a few weeks ago.' As his body finally failed him, Len passed away peacefully soon after, dying with Covid rather than as a direct result of catching it. He was a man of unquenchable spirit and determination. At our lunch just a few weeks before he had been lively, vibrant and fun. Like so many of the survivors, Len Gibson had lived a remarkable life lasting over a century and more than seventy years later would still have described himself as 'a lucky fellow'.

ACKNOWLEDGMENTS

My greatest debt of gratitude sits with the remarkable men who lived through years of Japanese captivity and survived malnutrition and tropical diseases, brutal labour conditions and the sinking of the hellships they were forced to sail on. If that was not enough, in August 1945 the forgotten prisoners in Nagasaki also survived the most powerful bomb ever released by man.

Some prisoners of war had the courage and ingenuity to write down their experiences at the time. Others told their stories years later to their children or to archivists and historians. Together they weave an invaluable oral tapestry, their words and deeds available for generations to come. I was privileged to spend time in Nagasaki with two of those men, Ron Bryer and Arthur Christie. To see that city through the eyes of two survivors of the atomic bomb was a vivid and direct experience.

My deep thanks to Ron's son, Chris Bryer. Not only did we work together on the original *Return to Nagasaki* documentary for Yorkshire Television, but Chris has been hugely supportive of this book, answering my requests with care and patience. I thank the original YTV team, led by John Fairley, for all their support back in 1984, especially Jill Turton whose diligent research was a helpful original source for this book.

Decades later it was an honour to meet the late Len Gibson who had worked on the Thai-Burma Railway.

His sense of humour and resilience gave me a sharp insight into survival. My thanks to Clinton Leeks for his help with that interview. I owe thanks to many other men and women who spared me time or offered advice. They include Ty and Kevin Hooper and Andrew Carter in Australia, Rob and Lies Schouten in the Netherlands, and Sears Eldredge in America.

In the UK, special thanks to Meg Parkes and Louise Reynolds for their enormous encouragement. Not only did they capture the POW stories of their own fathers and others, but they graciously gave of their time and expertise for me to tell my version of this story. I also owe gratitude to Geoff Gill, Kamal Khan, Martyn Cox, Michael Thompson, Greg Lewis, Jaqueline Passman, Craig Murray, Keith Andrews and Nigel Stanley, amongst many others. Thanks to Nicola MacCarthy in Ireland for her support, and permission to quote from her father's book.

When compared to other theatres of the Second World War, the experiences of Japanese incarceration are too often neglected or forgotten. So, I have been lucky that the Australian War Memorial and the Imperial War Museum have diligently collected interviews with many men who were prisoners of the Japanese. More focused archives such as the University of North Texas Oral History Collection, which contain interviews with the Lost Battalion, were also invaluable. Unfortunately, the pandemic prevented me from visiting the Thai-Burma Railway Museum and others in Thailand and Singapore.

Luckily, a small number of individuals, many the children of FEPOWs, in different corners of the globe have kept the fires of memory burning bright with remarkable passion and determination. I owe them all a debt of gratitude. The website started in America by the late Roger Mansell and continued by Wes Inerd is a phenomenal resource. In Australia, Peter Winstanley has built a treasure trove of memories on his website, as has Ron Taylor on a string of websites in the UK.

Several other organisations and websites are active in the field. They include Researching FEPOW History Group, Malayan Volunteer Group (MVG), National FEPOW Fellowship Welfare Reunion Association (NFFWRA) and www.captivememories.org.uk from the Liverpool School of Tropical Medicine. There are lively websites and Facebook pages for both Fukuoka 14b and Fukuoka 2b Camps. The work of the POW Research Network of Japan illustrates the capacity of the Japanese people to remember the impact of the bomb on other nationalities.

I must also mention Lesley Clark and Margaret Martin of the JAVA FEPOW 1942 club. Not only have they captured important memories in their newsletters and book but are very active in their practical support for survivors and their families. Many thanks to them.

Although there is only one English-language mainstream memoir that puts the POW experience of Camp Nagasaki 14b centre stage, there are many excellent books by historians, journalists, and former prisoners about other aspects of the conflict with the Japanese from 1942-45. They have been duly credited on the relevant pages but so many years after the event any writer on this subject inevitably stands on the shoulders of others.

Thanks to Richard Charkin at Mensch for his enthusiasm for this book from the moment I told him the story. Miranda Vaughan Jones has again done a meticulous and sympathetic job on the copy editing and thanks to Phillip Beresford for another memorable cover.

Finally, thanks to friends and family for their support. My children, Tom and Beth, have done everything they can in terms of support, and Janet has not only put up with my obsession but has, as always, exercised her brilliant judgement on all aspects of the book.

Also by John Willis
Johnny Go Home (with Michael Deakin), London, Futura Publications and Quartet Books, 1976
Churchill's Few, London, Mensch, 2020
Secret Letters: A Battle of Britain Love Story, London, Mensch, 2020

A NOTE ON THE TYPE

The text of this book is set in Linotype Sabon, a typeface named after the type founder, Jacques Sabon. It was designed by Jan Tschichold and jointly developed by Linotype, Monotype and Stempel in response to a need for a typeface to be available in identical form for mechanical hot metal composition and hand composition using foundry type.

Tschichold based his design for Sabon roman on a font engraved by Garamond, and Sabon italic on a font by Granjon. It was fi rst used in 1966 and has proved an enduring modern classic.